Brevity

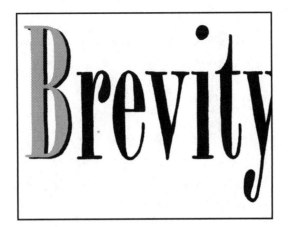

Brevity

A COLLECTION OF COMICS BY guy & rOdd

Andrews McMeel
Publishing, LLC

Kansas City

06 07 08 09 10 BBG 10 9 8 7 6 5 4 3 2 1

ISBN-13: 978-0-7407-6042-6
ISBN-10: 0-7407-6042-4

Library of Congress Control Number: 2006925045

www.andrewsmcmeel.com

—— **ATTENTION: SCHOOLS AND BUSINESSES** ——

Andrews McMeel books are available at quantity discounts with bulk purchase for educational, business, or sales promotional use. For information, please write to: Special Sales Department, Andrews McMeel Publishing, LLC, 4520 Main Street, Kansas City, Missouri 64111.

Introduction

A couple years ago, Guy started drawing comics, but no one liked them.

This is why:

oh no, loose lips!
guy

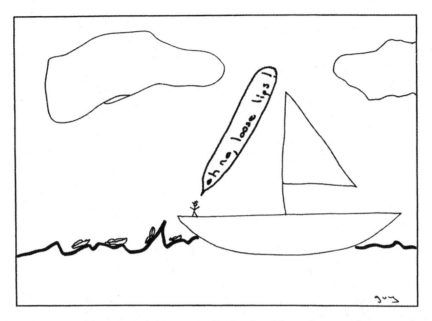

Then Rodd came along. In addition to being a tall drink of handsome, he can draw like the wind.

Many of the comics in this book appeared on the Internet for free before we discovered that newspapers would pay good money for them. And by "good," we mean "not a lot."

Guy would like to thank Gary Larson and *The Simpsons* writers. Everything he knows about humor he stole from them.

Rodd would like to thank Radio Paradise, his companion in the night, for playing a great mix of songs by which to draw comics.

Guy and Rodd would both like to thank Jake Morrissey, because every other syndicate editor sent a form rejection letter.

guy & rOdd

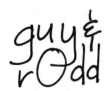

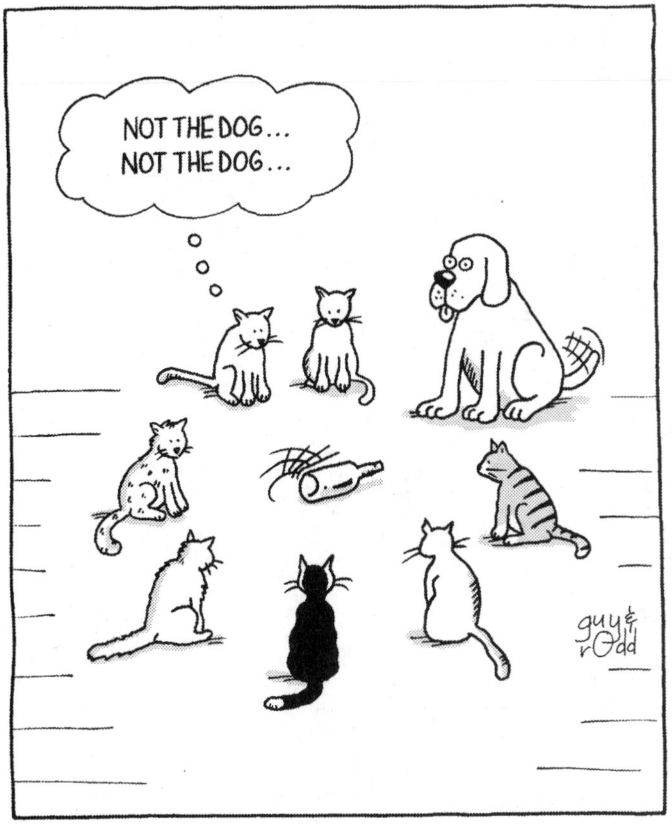
NOT THE DOG...
NOT THE DOG...
guy & rodd

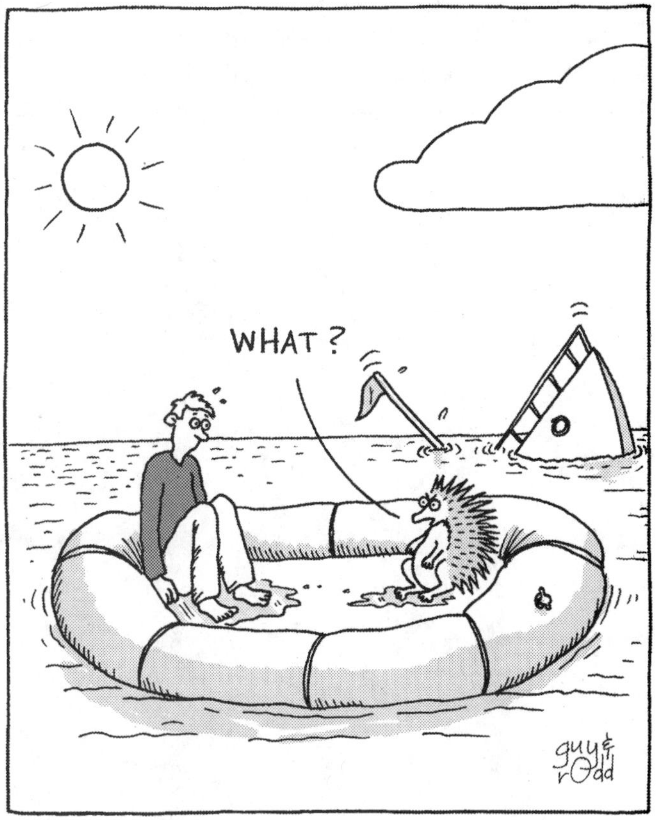
WHAT?
guy & rodd

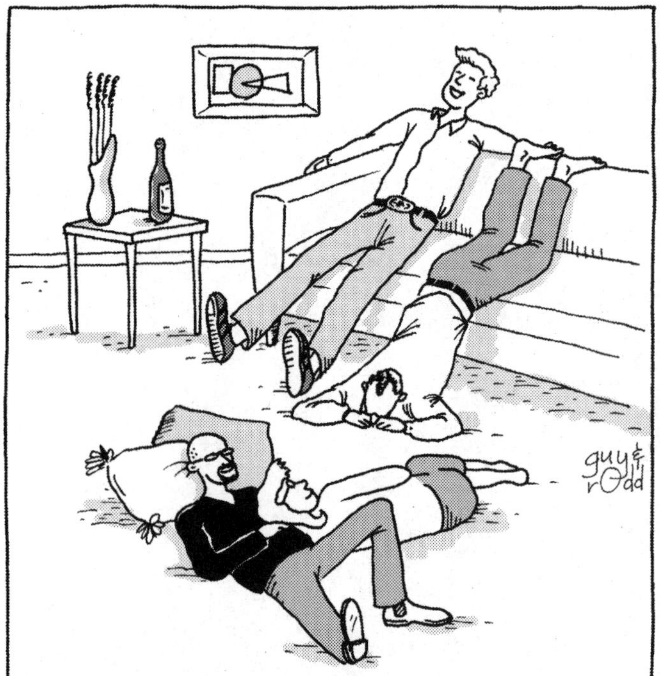

THEY STAYED UP ALL NIGHT, LISTENING TO NATIONAL PUBLIC RADIO AND DRINKING A SHOT EACH TIME THEY HEARD THE WORD "UNILATERAL".

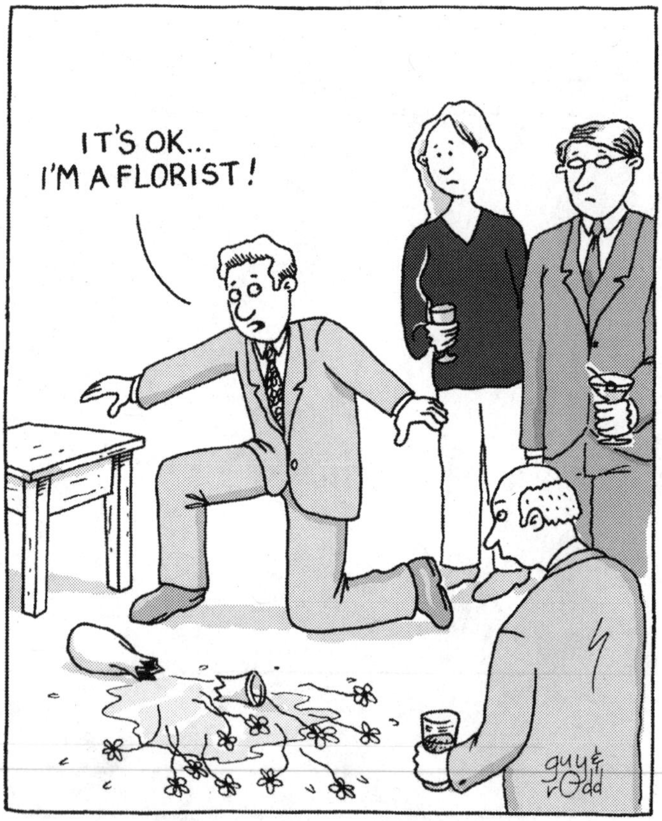
IT'S OK...
I'M A FLORIST!

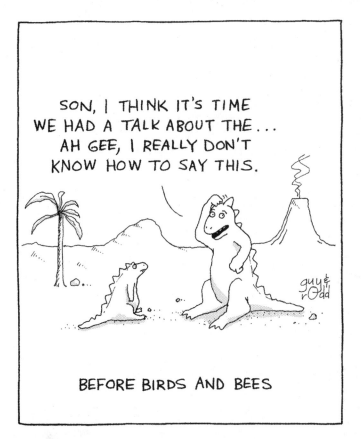

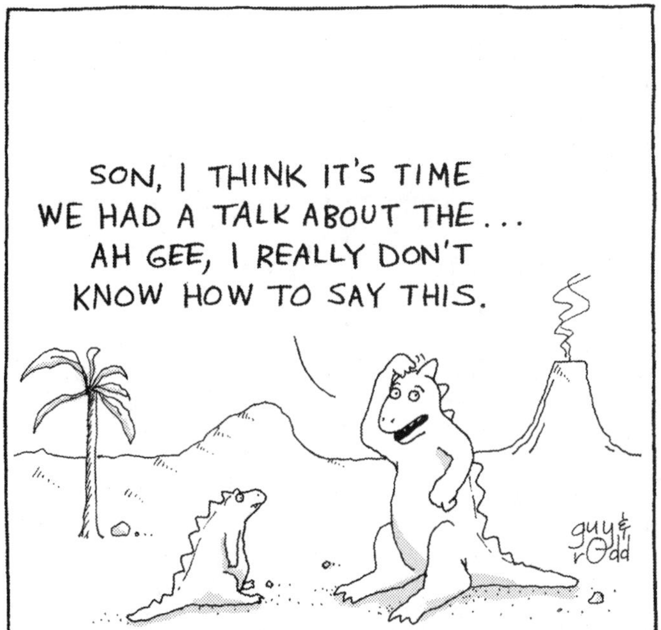
SON, I THINK IT'S TIME WE HAD A TALK ABOUT THE... AH GEE, I REALLY DON'T KNOW HOW TO SAY THIS.

BEFORE BIRDS AND BEES

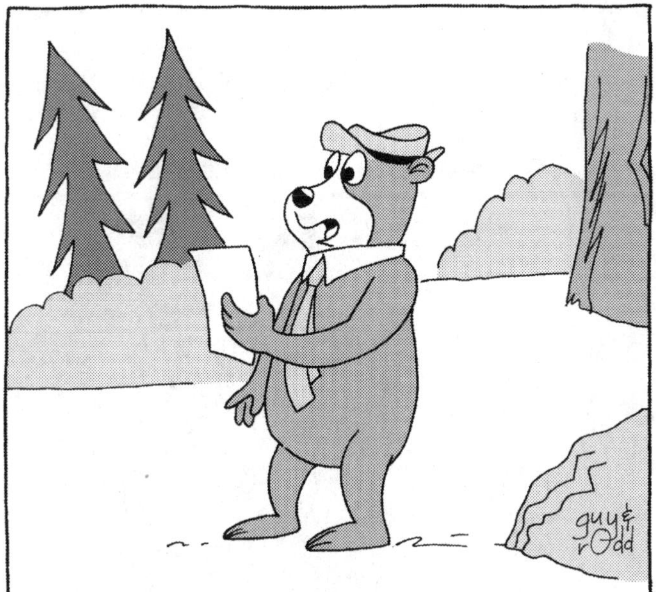

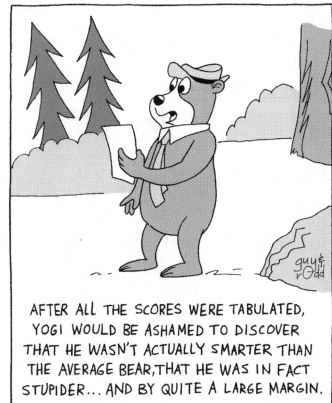

AFTER ALL THE SCORES WERE TABULATED, YOGI WOULD BE ASHAMED TO DISCOVER THAT HE WASN'T ACTUALLY SMARTER THAN THE AVERAGE BEAR, THAT HE WAS IN FACT STUPIDER... AND BY QUITE A LARGE MARGIN.

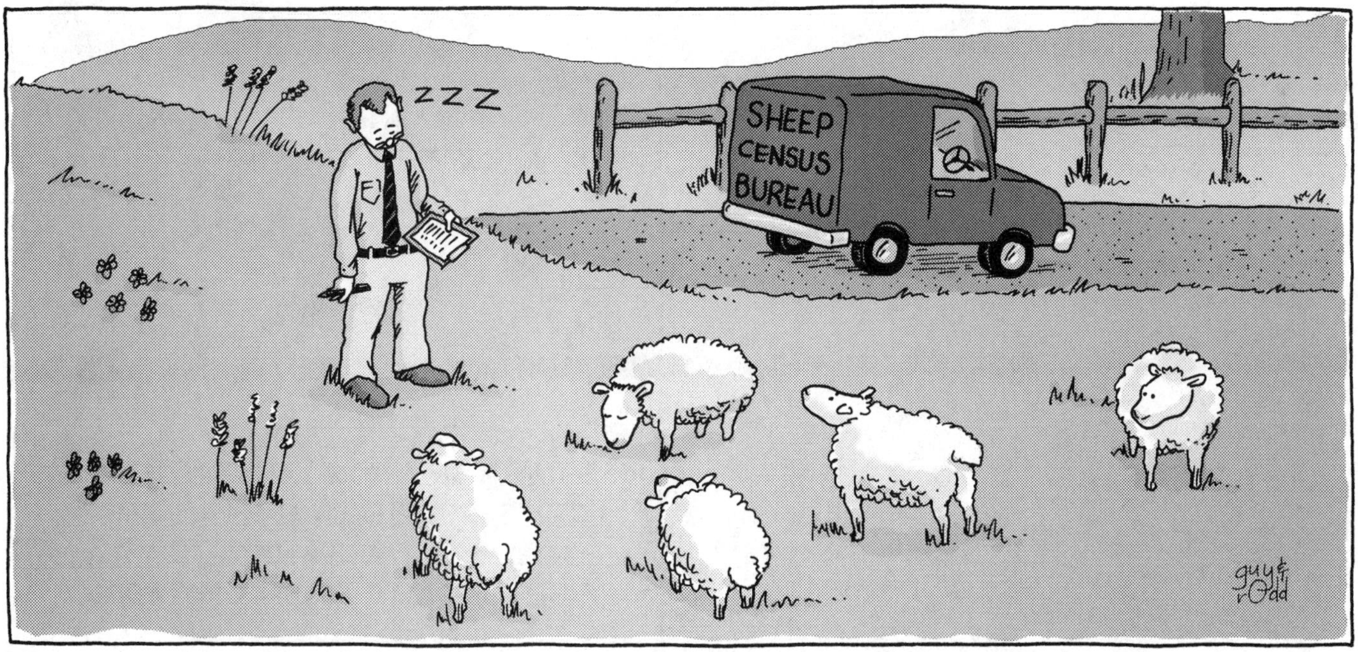
ZZZ
SHEEP CENSUS BUREAU

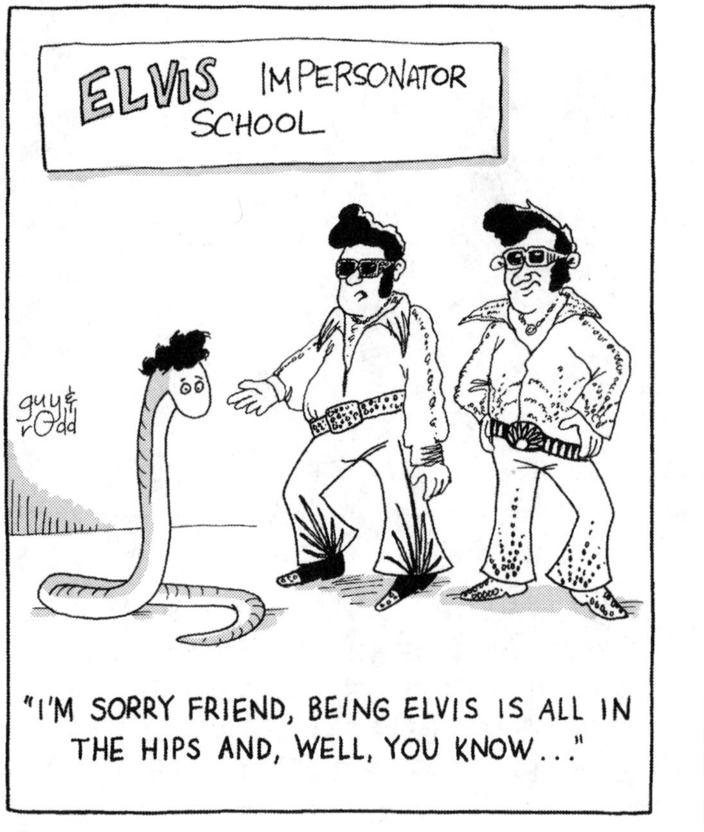
ELVIS IMPERSONATOR SCHOOL
guy & rOdd

"I'M SORRY FRIEND, BEING ELVIS IS ALL IN THE HIPS AND, WELL, YOU KNOW..."

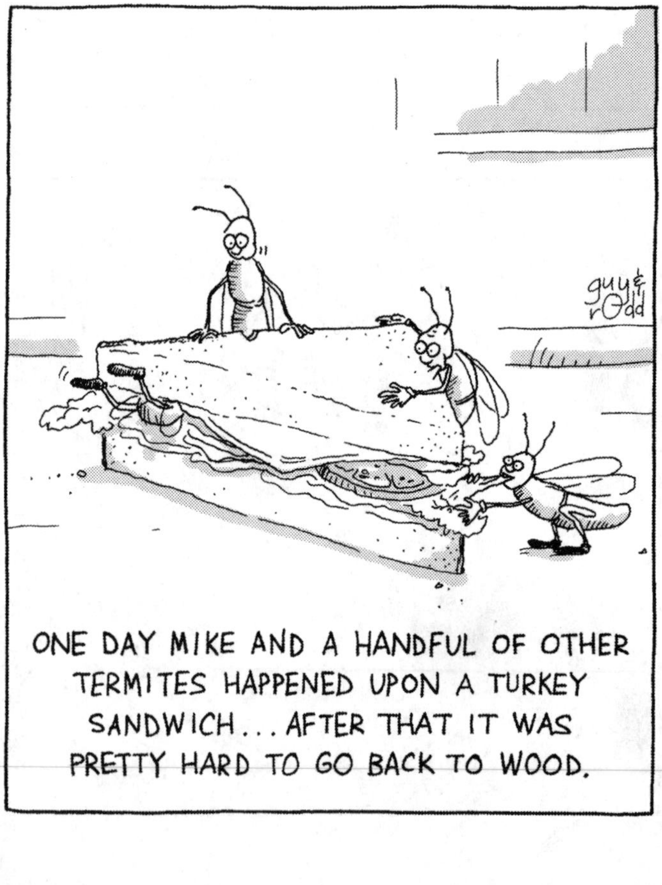
guy & rOdd

ONE DAY MIKE AND A HANDFUL OF OTHER TERMITES HAPPENED UPON A TURKEY SANDWICH... AFTER THAT IT WAS PRETTY HARD TO GO BACK TO WOOD.

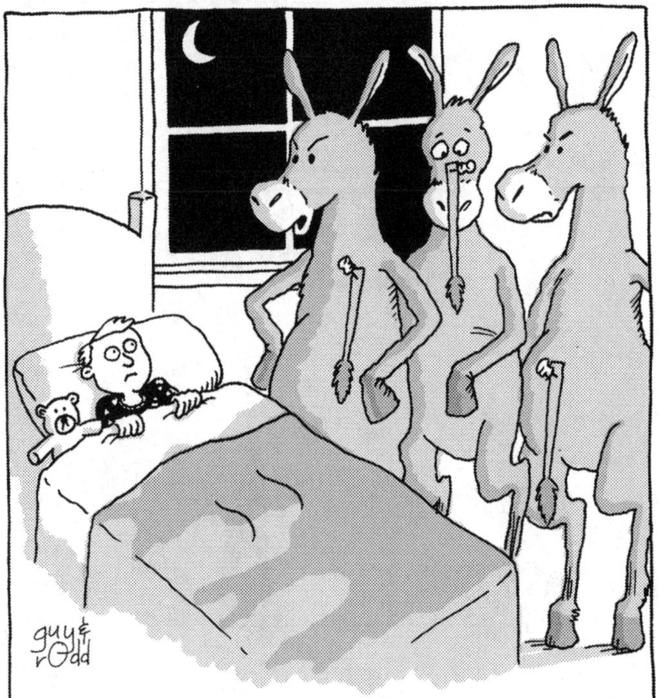

" WAKE UP, KID. WE'VE GOT SOME PARTY GAMES OF OUR OWN WE'D LIKE TO PLAY."

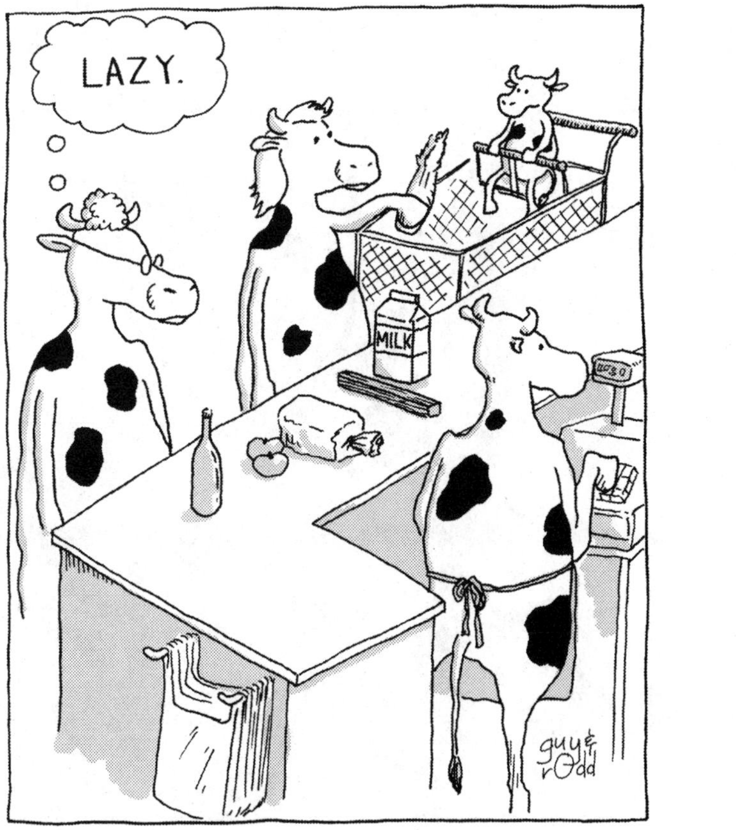
LAZY.
MILK

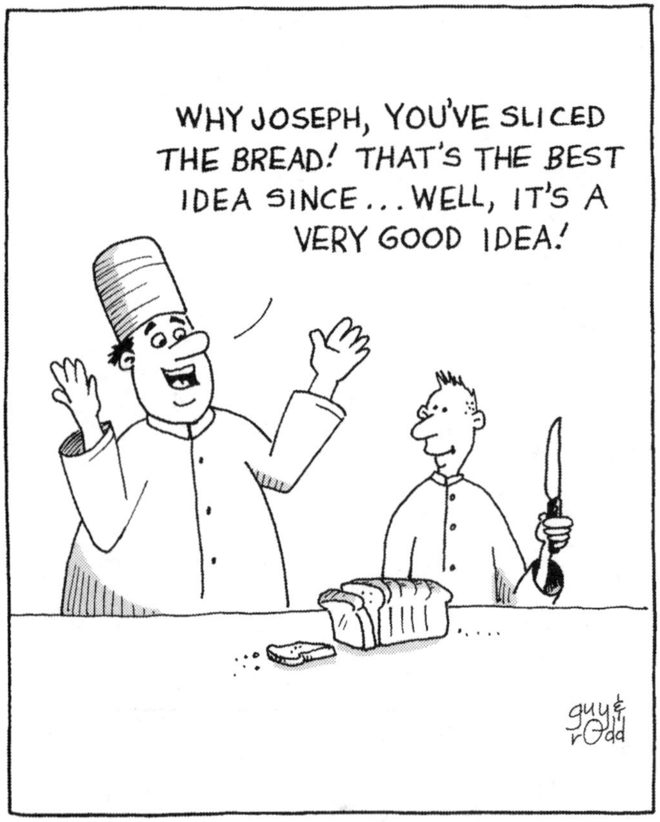
WHY JOSEPH, YOU'VE SLICED THE BREAD! THAT'S THE BEST IDEA SINCE...WELL, IT'S A VERY GOOD IDEA!
guy & rOdd

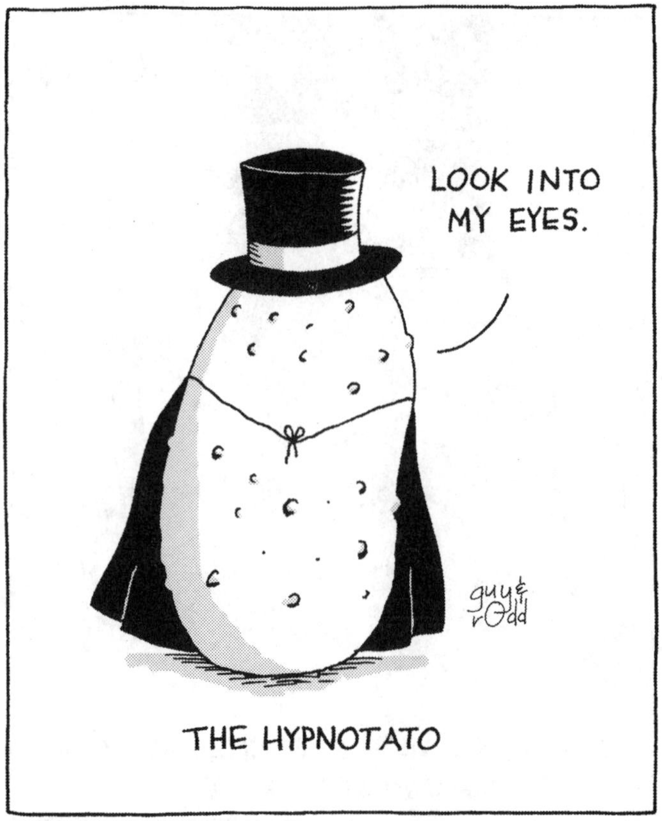
LOOK INTO MY EYES.
guy & rOdd
THE HYPNOTATO

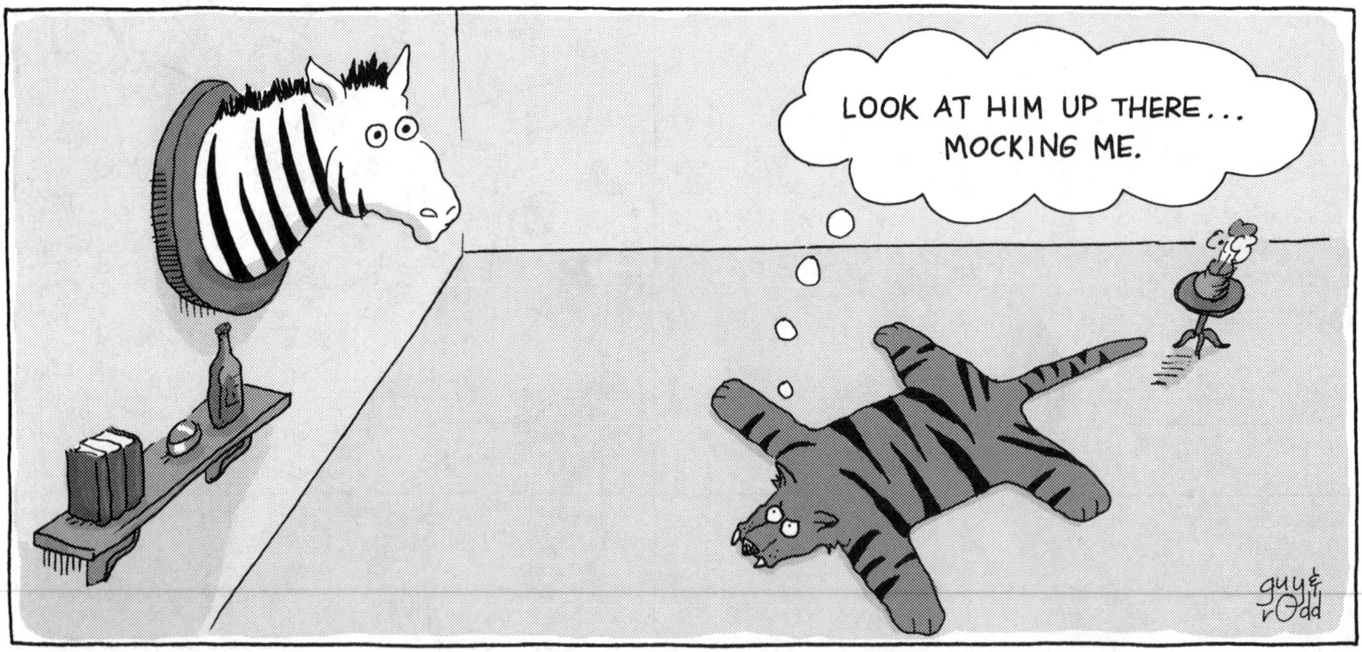
LOOK AT HIM UP THERE... MOCKING ME.
guy & rOdd

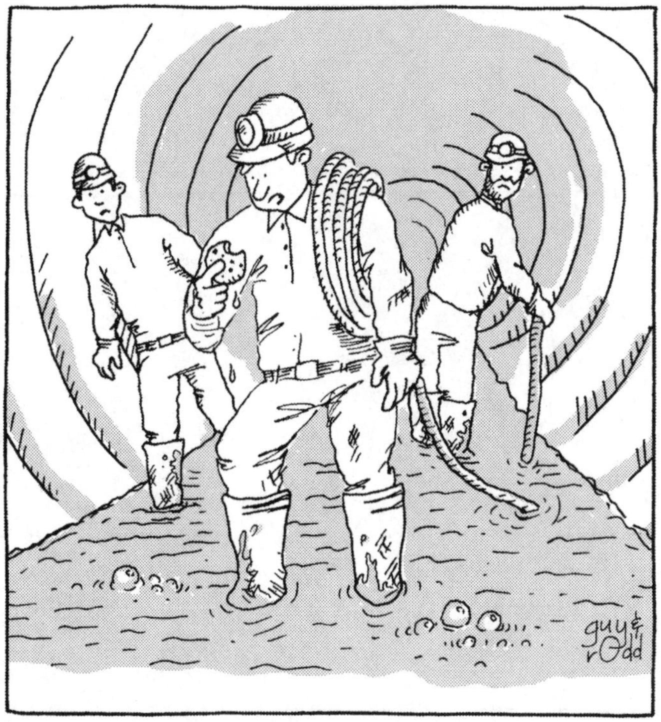
guy & rOdd

NOBODY TOLD JAMES THAT THE FIVE SECOND RULE DIDN'T APPLY IN THEIR LINE OF WORK.

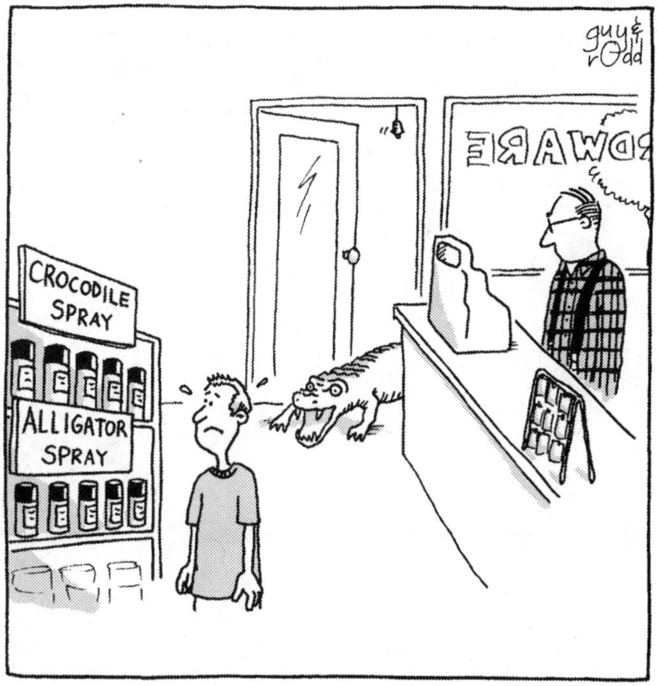
guy & rOdd
CROCODILE SPRAY
ALLIGATOR SPRAY

HE ONLY HAD ENOUGH MONEY FOR ONE, AND FOR THE LIFE OF HIM HE COULDN'T REMEMBER THE DIFFERENCE.

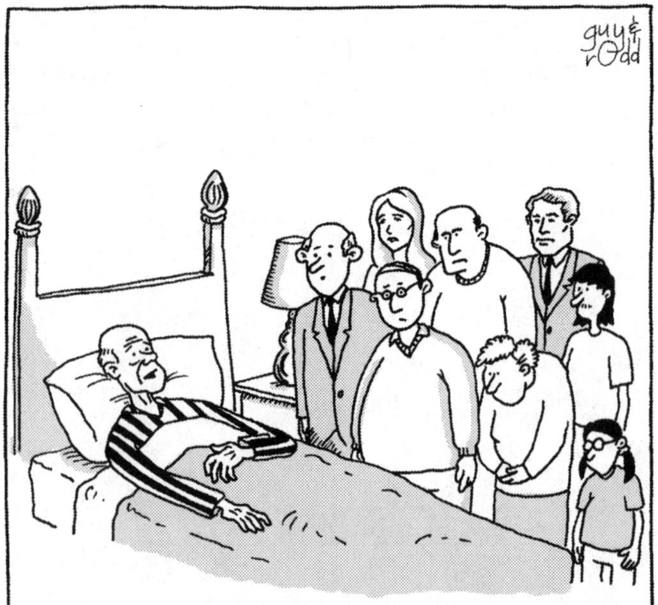
guy & rOdd

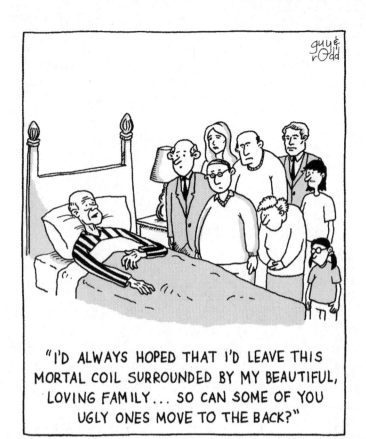

"I'D ALWAYS HOPED THAT I'D LEAVE THIS MORTAL COIL SURROUNDED BY MY BEAUTIFUL, LOVING FAMILY... SO CAN SOME OF YOU UGLY ONES MOVE TO THE BACK?"

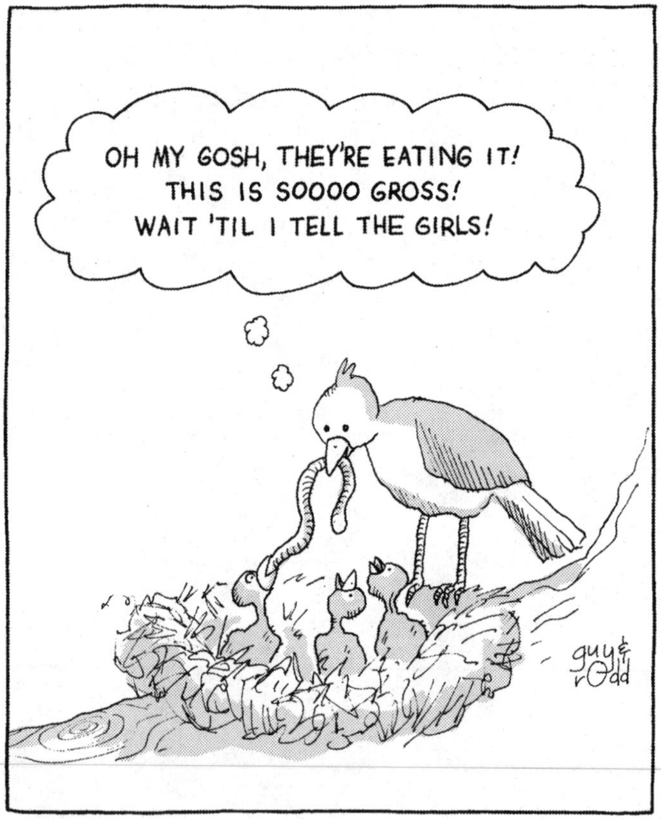
OH MY GOSH, THEY'RE EATING IT!
THIS IS SOOOO GROSS!
WAIT 'TIL I TELL THE GIRLS!
guy & rOdd

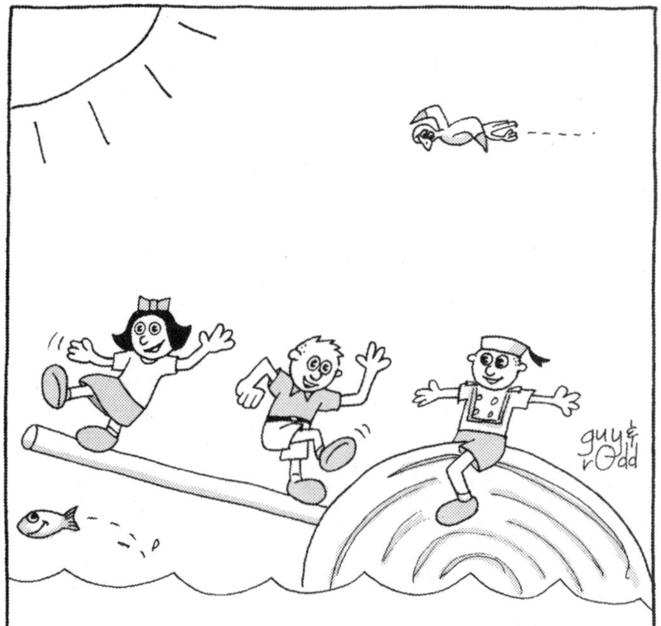
guy & rOdd

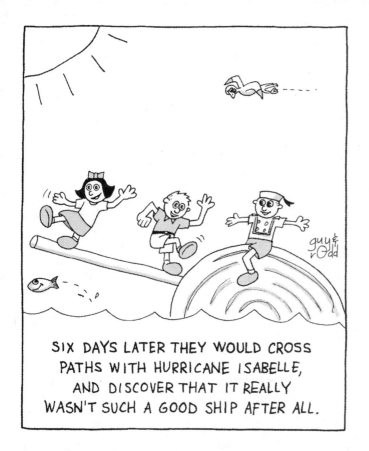

SIX DAYS LATER THEY WOULD CROSS PATHS WITH HURRICANE ISABELLE, AND DISCOVER THAT IT REALLY WASN'T SUCH A GOOD SHIP AFTER ALL.

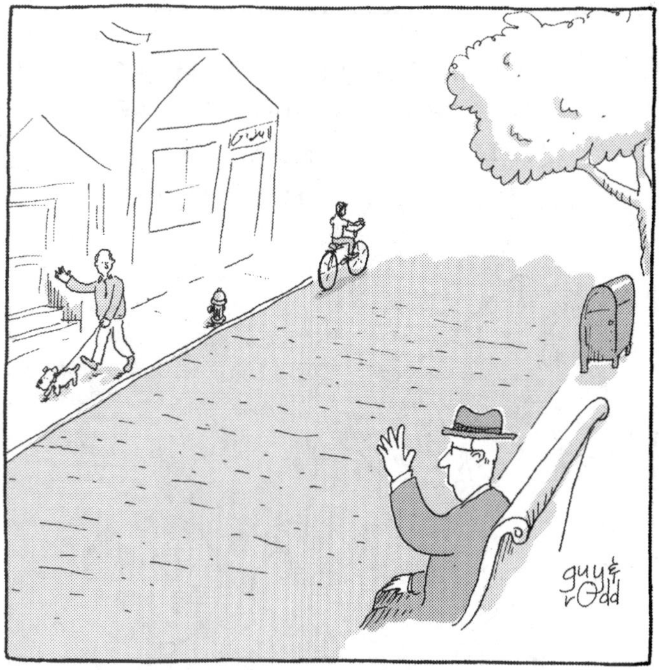
guy & rOdd

THE TOWN OF IRONY, PENNSYLVANIA HAS LONG BEEN KNOWN FOR BEING VERY LITERAL.

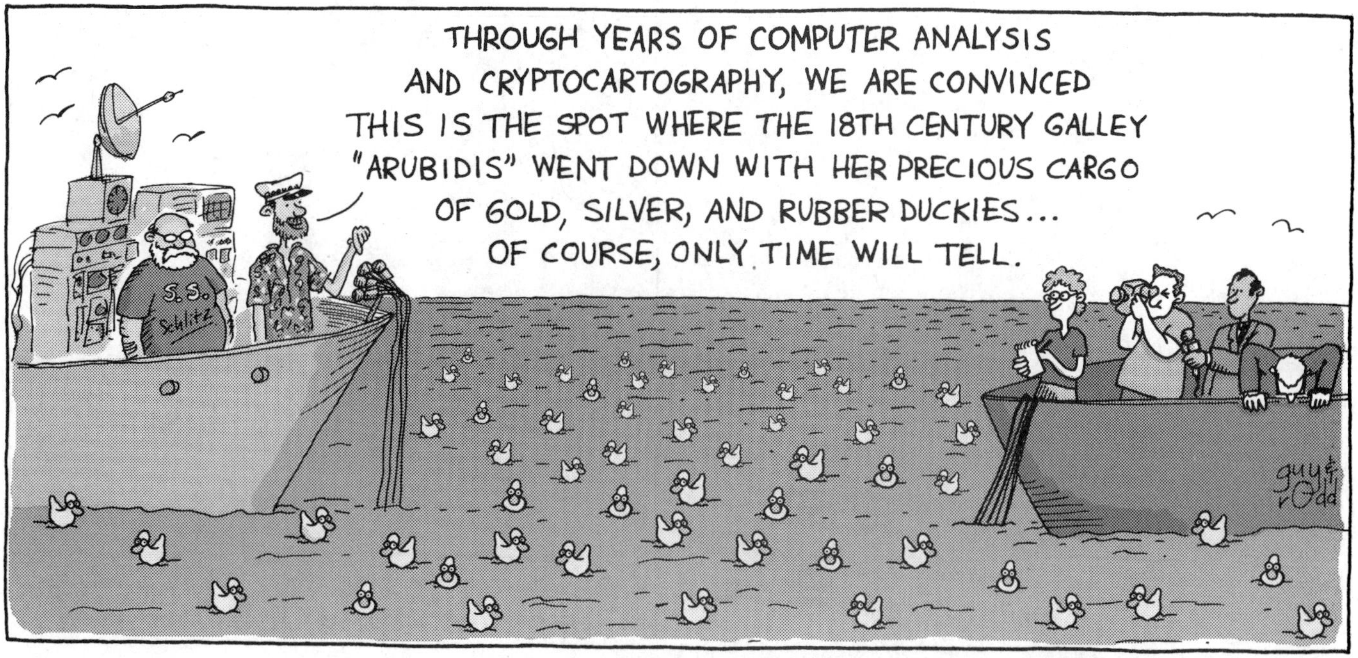
THROUGH YEARS OF COMPUTER ANALYSIS AND CRYPTOCARTOGRAPHY, WE ARE CONVINCED THIS IS THE SPOT WHERE THE 18TH CENTURY GALLEY "ARUBIDIS" WENT DOWN WITH HER PRECIOUS CARGO OF GOLD, SILVER, AND RUBBER DUCKIES... OF COURSE, ONLY TIME WILL TELL.
S.S. Schlitz
guy & rOdd

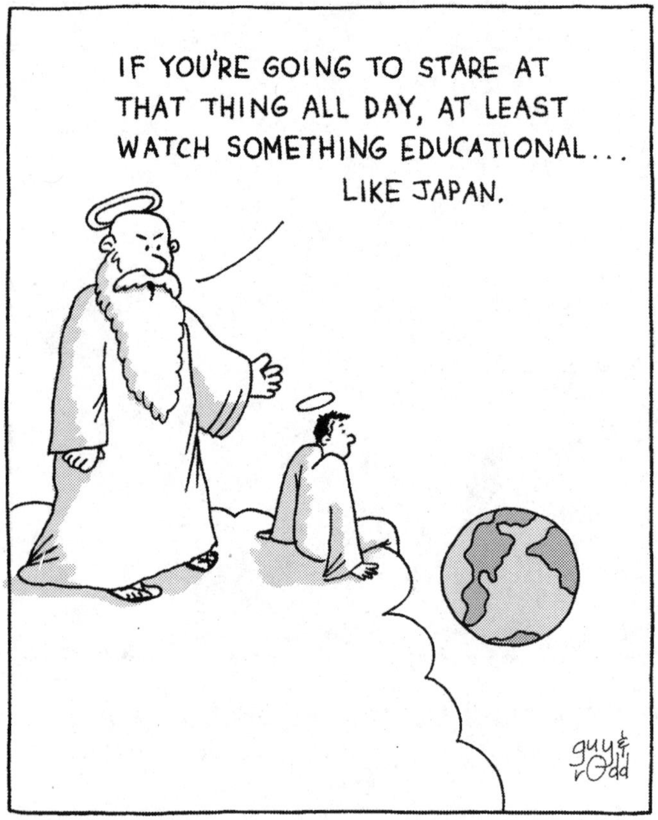
IF YOU'RE GOING TO STARE AT THAT THING ALL DAY, AT LEAST WATCH SOMETHING EDUCATIONAL... LIKE JAPAN.
guy & rOdd

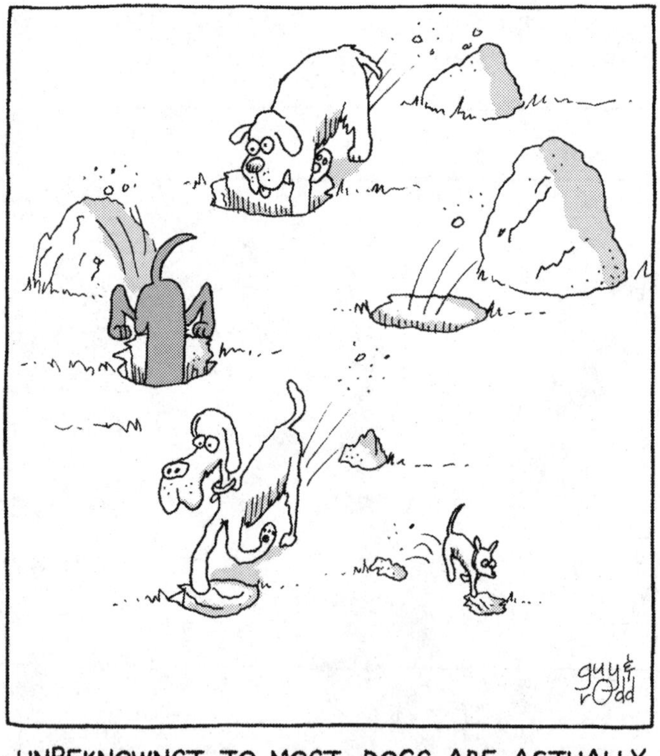
guy & rOdd

UNBEKNOWNST TO MOST, DOGS ARE ACTUALLY GREEDY BASTARDS SEARCHING FOR GOLD.

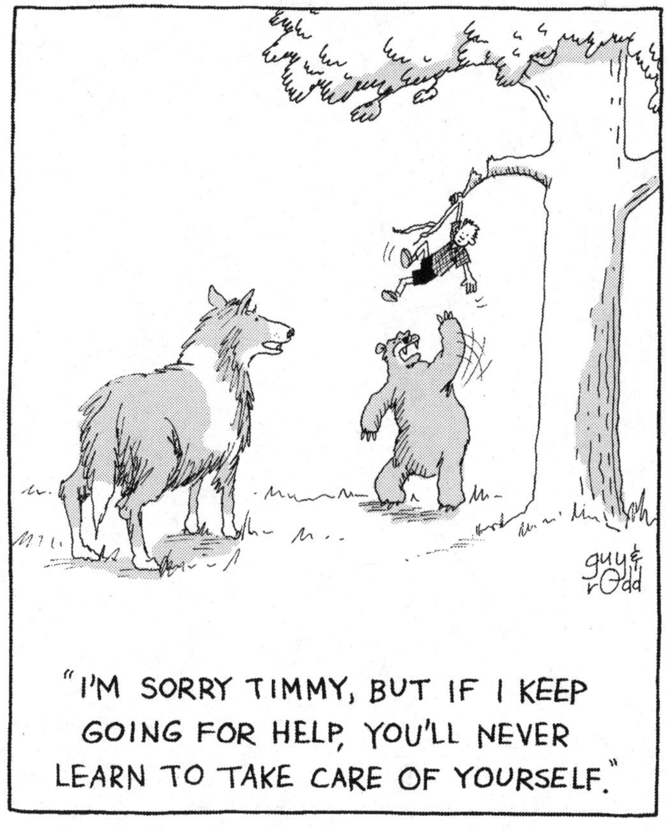
guy & rodd

"I'M SORRY TIMMY, BUT IF I KEEP GOING FOR HELP, YOU'LL NEVER LEARN TO TAKE CARE OF YOURSELF."

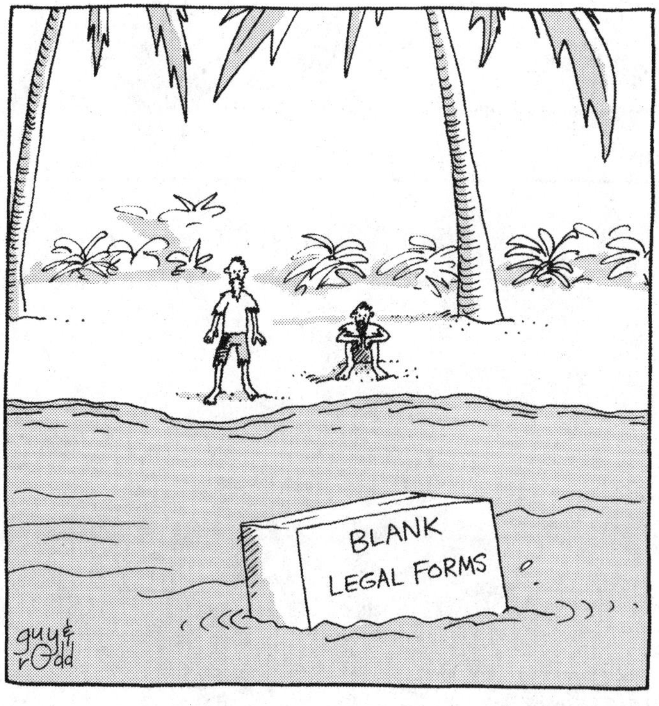
BLANK
LEGAL FORMS
guy & rodd

THE NEXT FEW YEARS WOULD BE VERY LITIGIOUS.

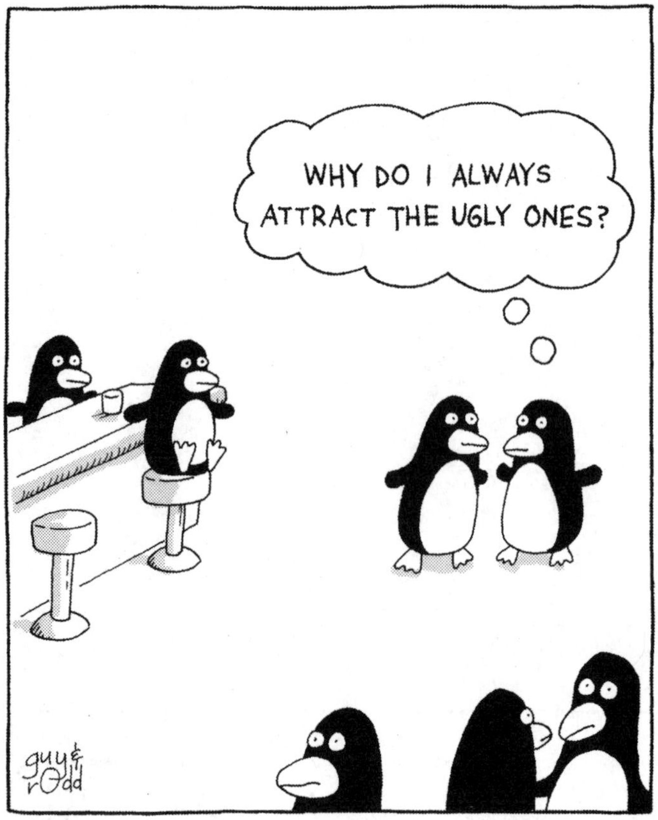
WHY DO I ALWAYS ATTRACT THE UGLY ONES?
guy & rodd

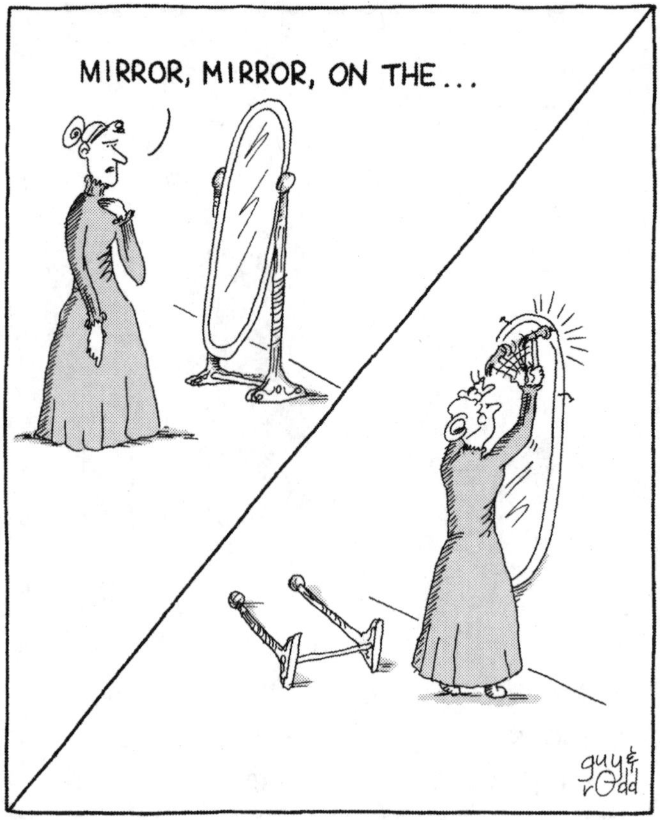
MIRROR, MIRROR, ON THE...
guy & rodd

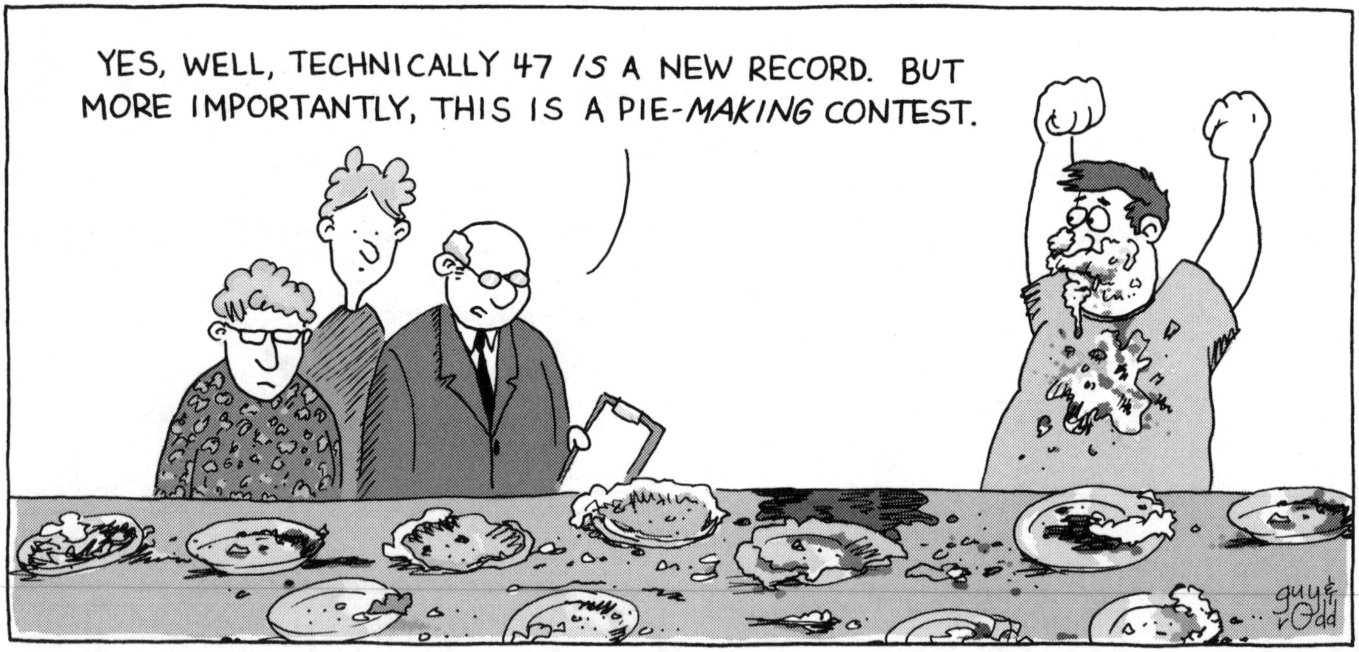
YES, WELL, TECHNICALLY 47 *IS* A NEW RECORD. BUT MORE IMPORTANTLY, THIS IS A PIE-*MAKING* CONTEST.
guy & rodd

FIRST HE FELT PRIDE, THEN CONFUSION, THEN THE
TERRIBLE DOUBTS BEGAN TO SEEP IN... HAD HE
FORGOTTEN, ONCE AGAIN, TO TELL DARRYL THEY
WERE GOING TO PLAY HIDE AND SEEK?

"THE LAST THING HE SAID WAS 'I'M GOING TO GO
LOOK UP THE WORD "DICTIONARY" IN THE
DICTIONARY', AND THEN THE UNIVERSE KIND OF
COLLAPSED AROUND HIM."

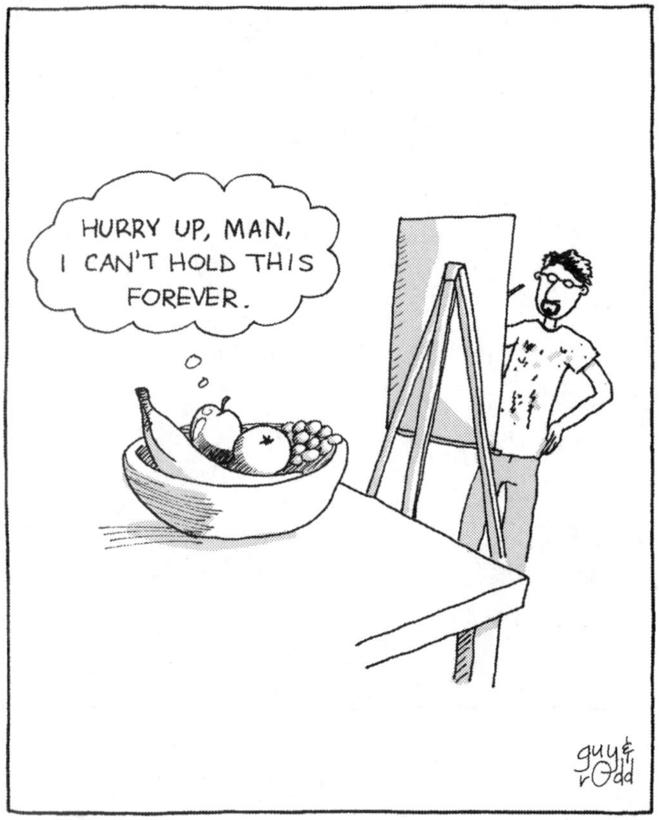
HURRY UP, MAN, I CAN'T HOLD THIS FOREVER.
guy & rOdd

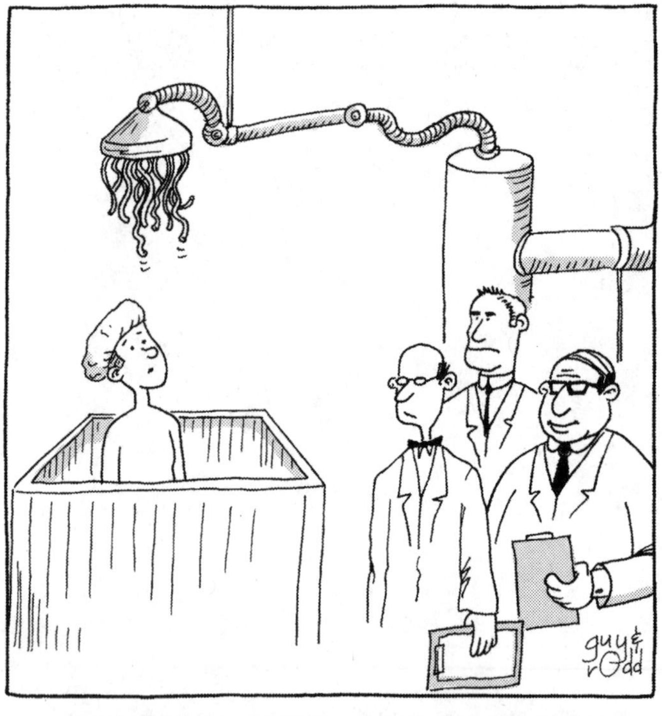
guy & rOdd

BEFORE THEY SETTLED ON WATER, SHOWER PIONEERS EXPERIMENTED WITH A NUMBER OF ALTERNATIVES, INCLUDING SPAGHETTI.

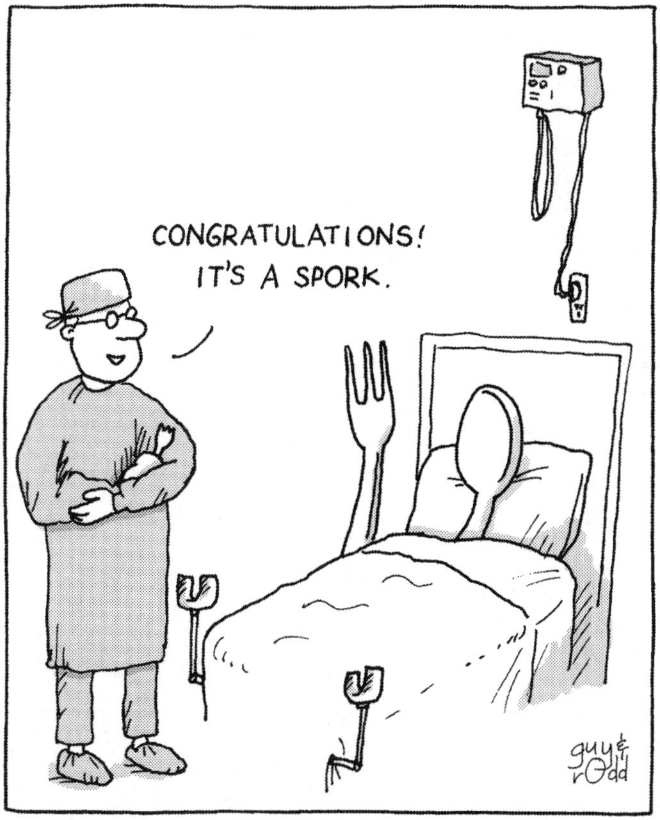
CONGRATULATIONS! IT'S A SPORK.
guy & rOdd

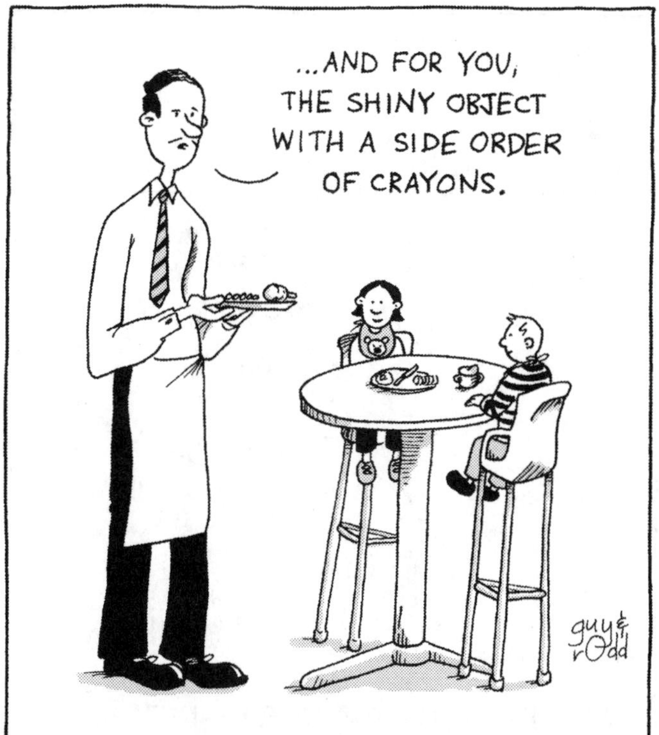
...AND FOR YOU, THE SHINY OBJECT WITH A SIDE ORDER OF CRAYONS.
guy & rOdd
TODDLER RESTAURANTS

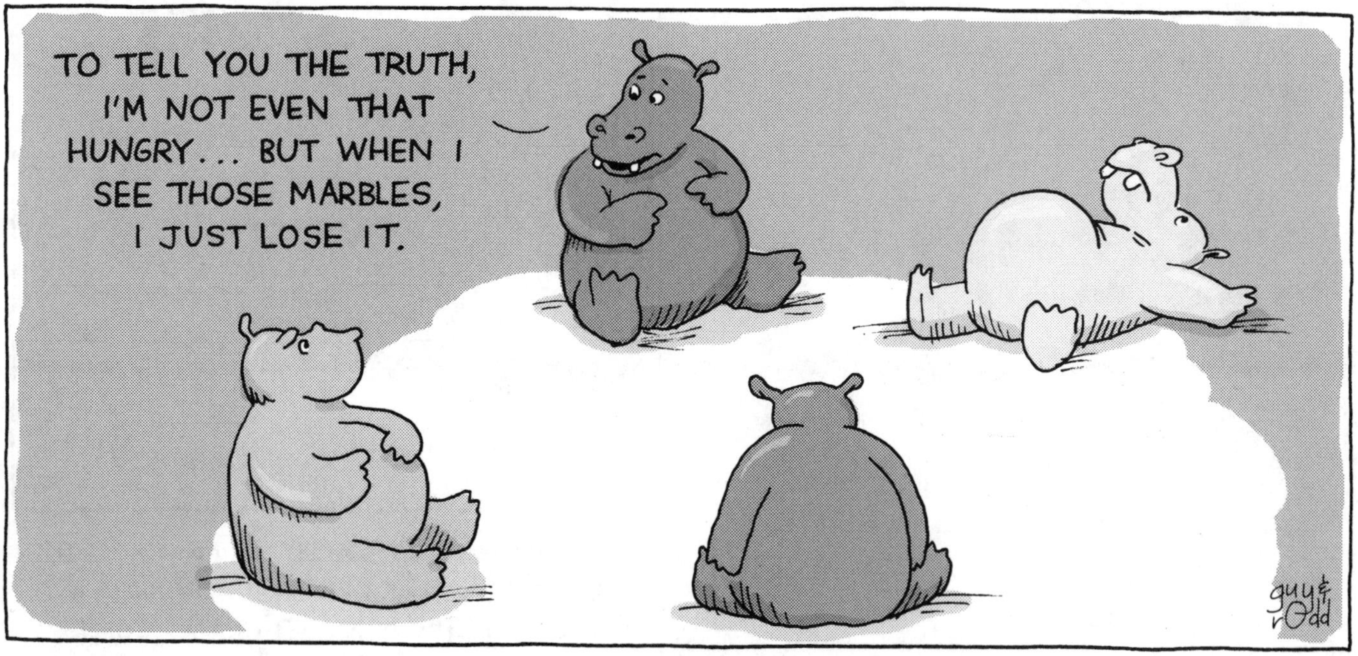
TO TELL YOU THE TRUTH, I'M NOT EVEN THAT HUNGRY... BUT WHEN I SEE THOSE MARBLES, I JUST LOSE IT.
guy & rOdd

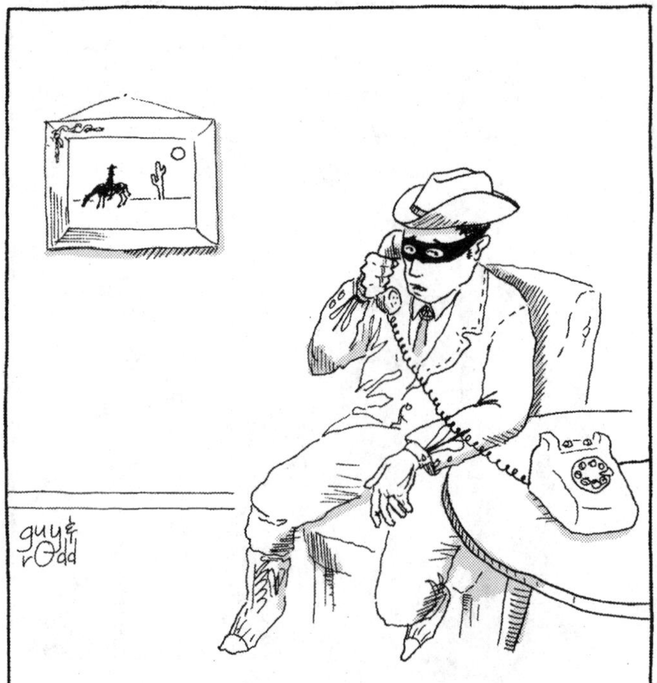
guy & rOdd

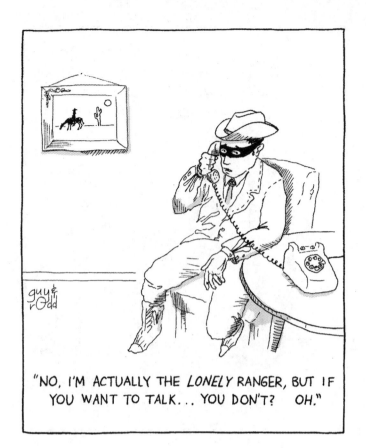

"NO, I'M ACTUALLY THE *LONELY* RANGER, BUT IF YOU WANT TO TALK... YOU DON'T? OH."

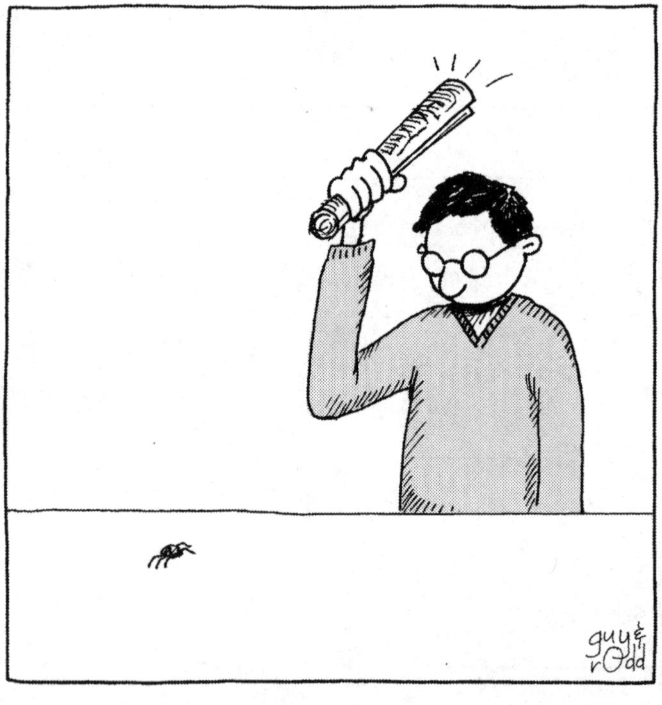
guy & rOdd

EVER SINCE HE WAS A LITTLE MAGAZINE HE HAD BEEN DEATHLY AFRAID OF SPIDERS, AND HE DIDN'T LIKE WHERE THIS WAS GOING.

SUDDENLY JOHN REALIZED HE DIDN'T WANT PAPER OR PLASTIC. HE WANTED SOMETHING NEW...SOMETHING FANTASTIC.

"I'M SORRY JAKE... I'M STARVING TO DEATH, MY HAIR'S A MESS, AND I JUST DON'T FEEL LIKE POSING ANYMORE."

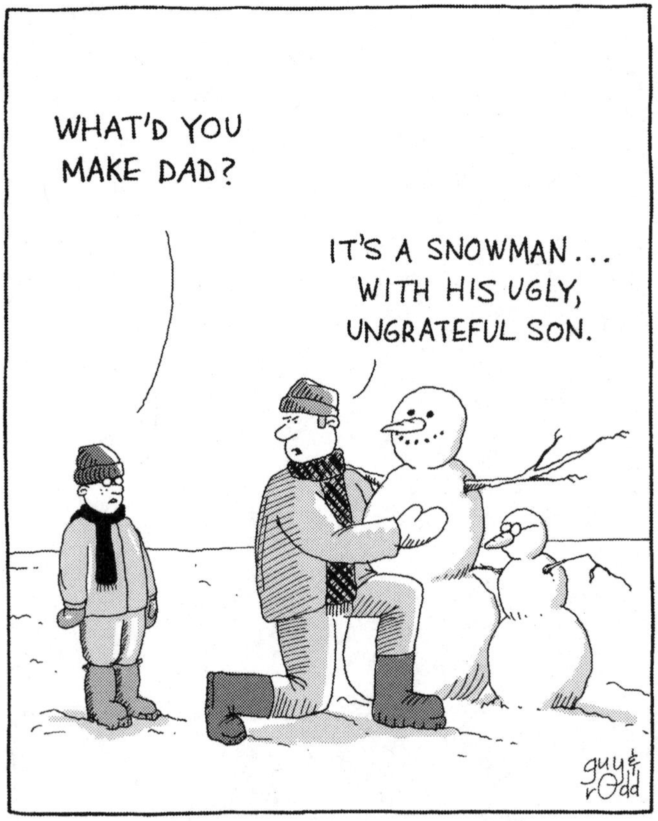
WHAT'D YOU MAKE DAD?
IT'S A SNOWMAN... WITH HIS UGLY, UNGRATEFUL SON.
guy & rOdd

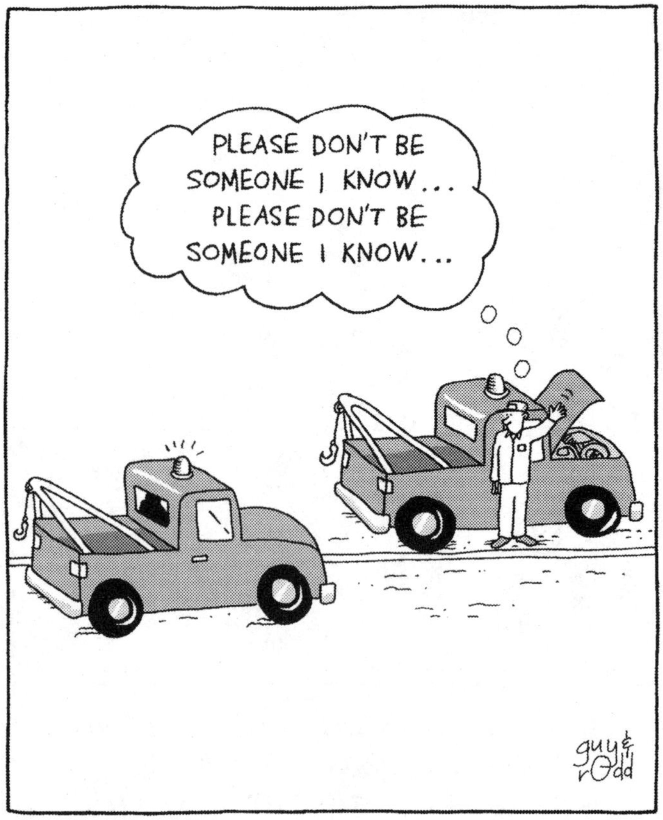
PLEASE DON'T BE SOMEONE I KNOW... PLEASE DON'T BE SOMEONE I KNOW...
guy & rOdd

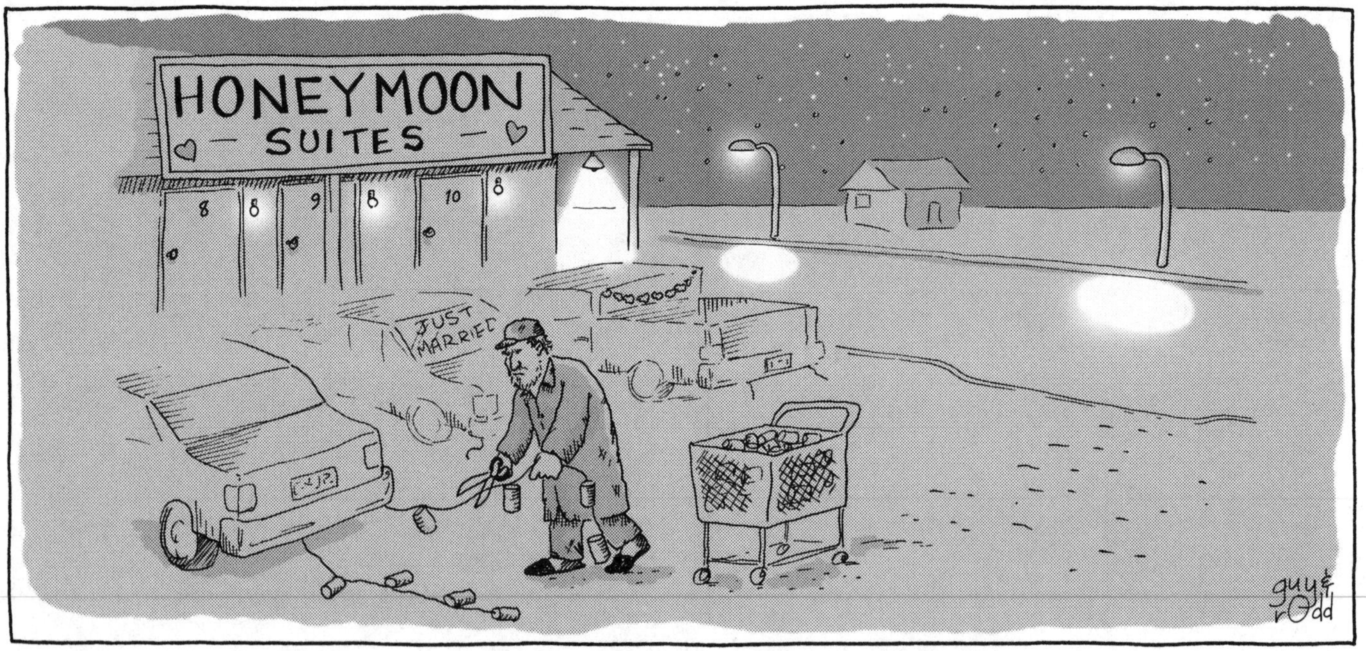
HONEYMOON SUITES
JUST MARRIED
guy & rOdd

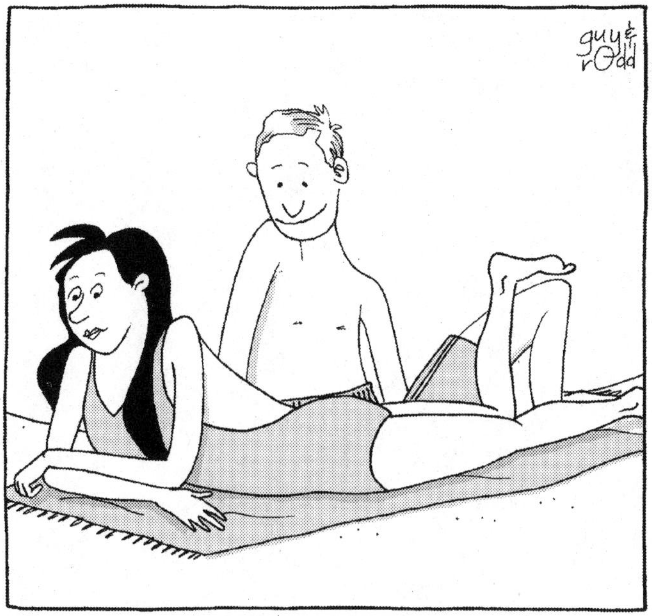

THEY WERE YOUNG AND IN LOVE, AND HAROLD WOULD SPEND WHOLE WEEKENDS COUNTING THE FRECKLES ON ARLENE'S BACK. OF COURSE THEY WERE ALSO INCREDIBLY STUPID... ARLENE ONLY HAD SEVEN FRECKLES.

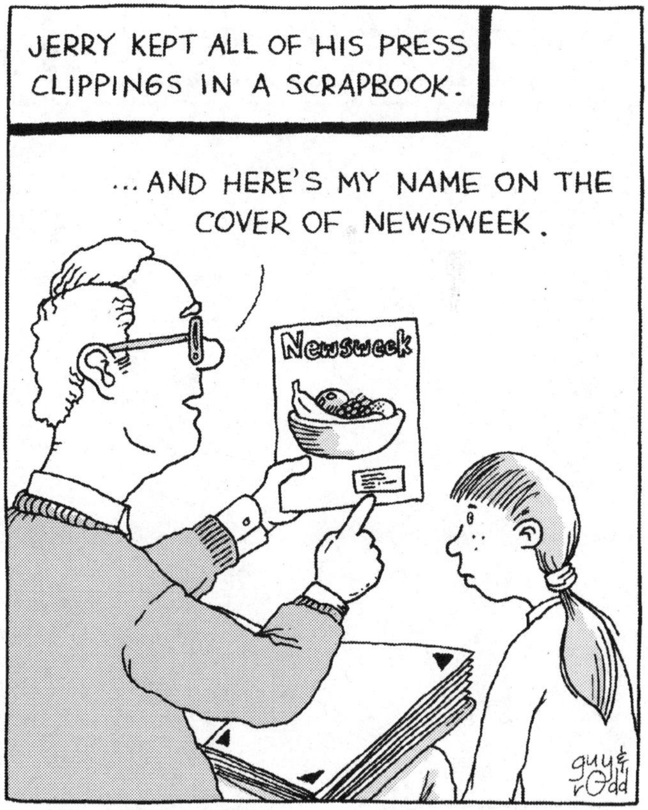
JERRY KEPT ALL OF HIS PRESS CLIPPINGS IN A SCRAPBOOK.
...AND HERE'S MY NAME ON THE COVER OF NEWSWEEK.
Newsweek

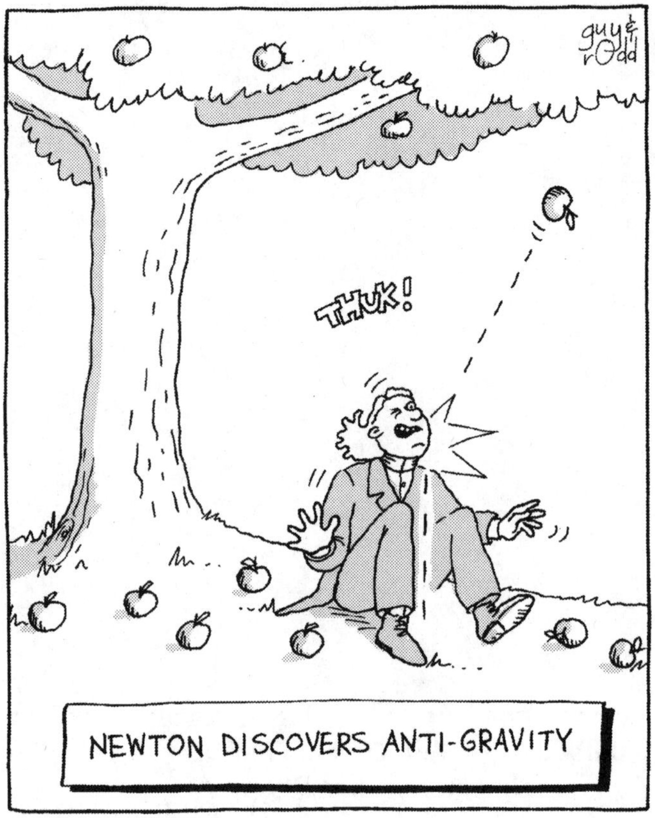
guy & rOdd
THUK!
NEWTON DISCOVERS ANTI-GRAVITY

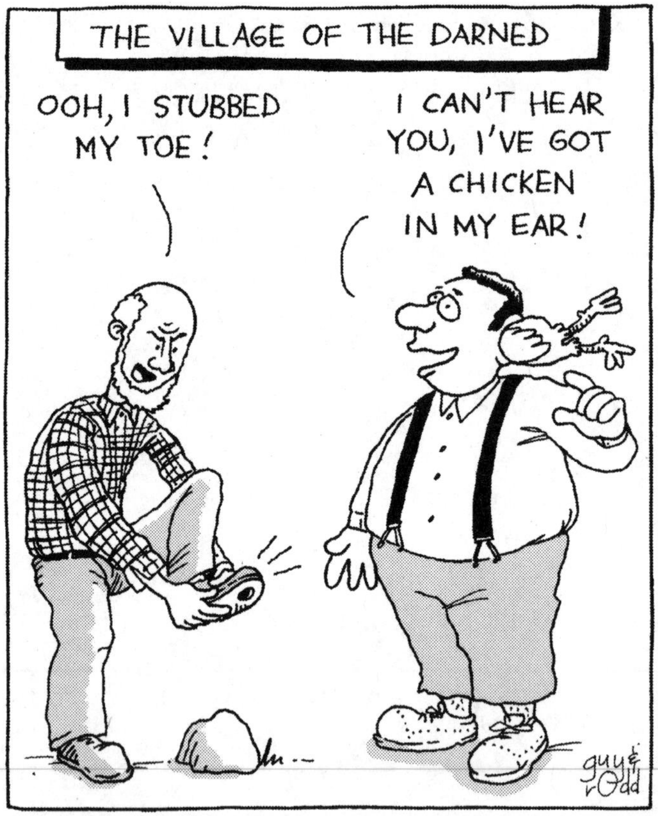
THE VILLAGE OF THE DARNED
OOH, I STUBBED MY TOE!
I CAN'T HEAR YOU, I'VE GOT A CHICKEN IN MY EAR!
guy & rOdd

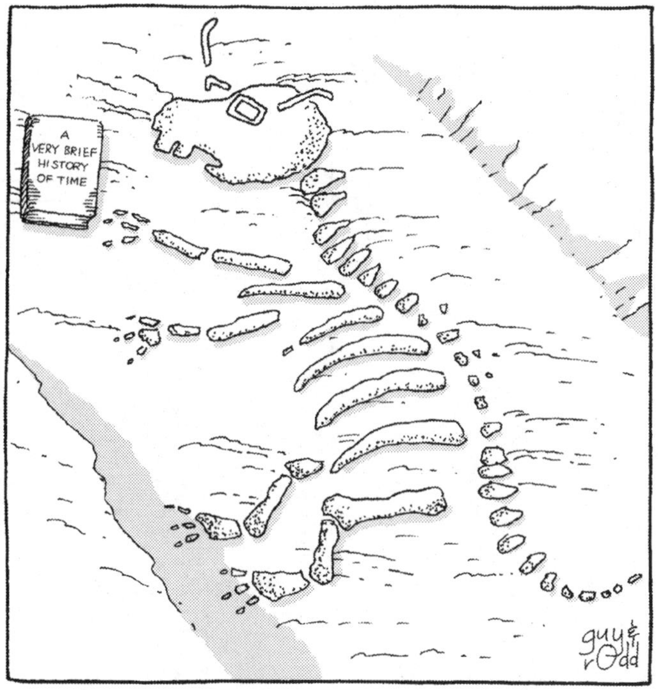
A VERY BRIEF HISTORY OF TIME
guy & rOdd

ON A HOT DAY IN 1941, SCIENTISTS UNCOVERED THE ONLY KNOWN REMAINS OF THE ELUSIVE NERDOSAURUS REX.

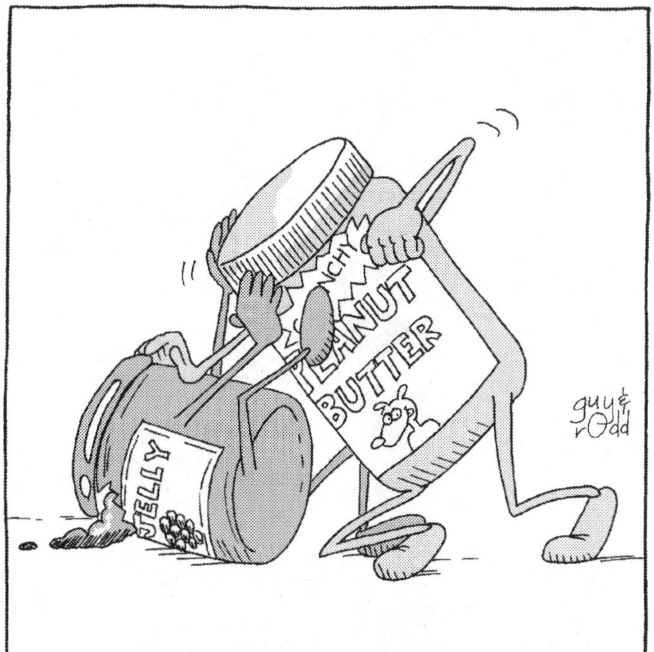
BUTTER
JELLY
guy & rOdd

IT TURNS OUT THEY DON'T GO TOGETHER SO WELL.

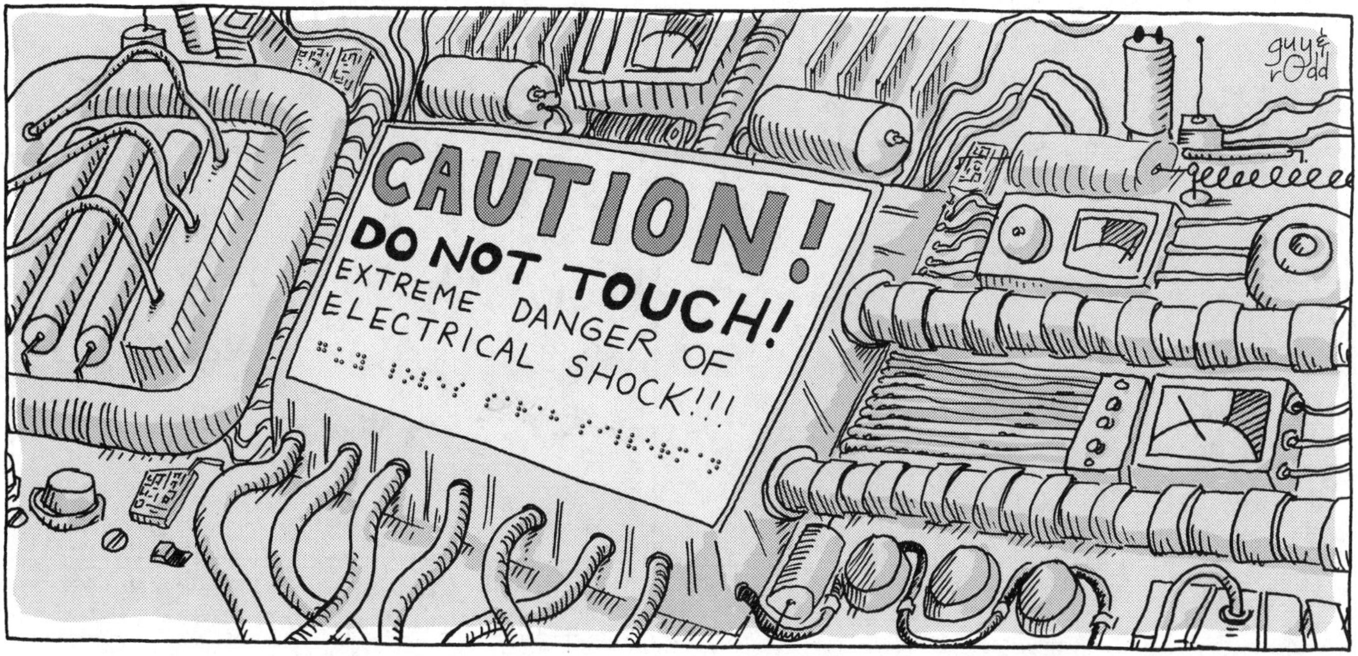
CAUTION!
DO NOT TOUCH!
EXTREME DANGER OF ELECTRICAL SHOCK!!!
guy & rOdd

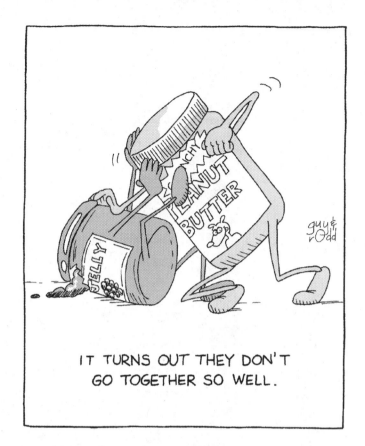

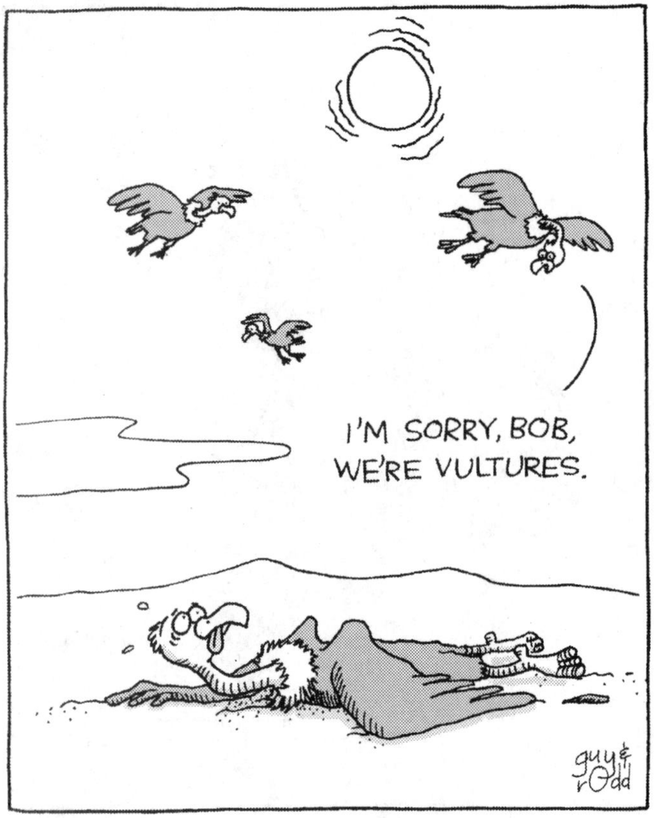
I'M SORRY, BOB,
WE'RE VULTURES.
guy & rOdd

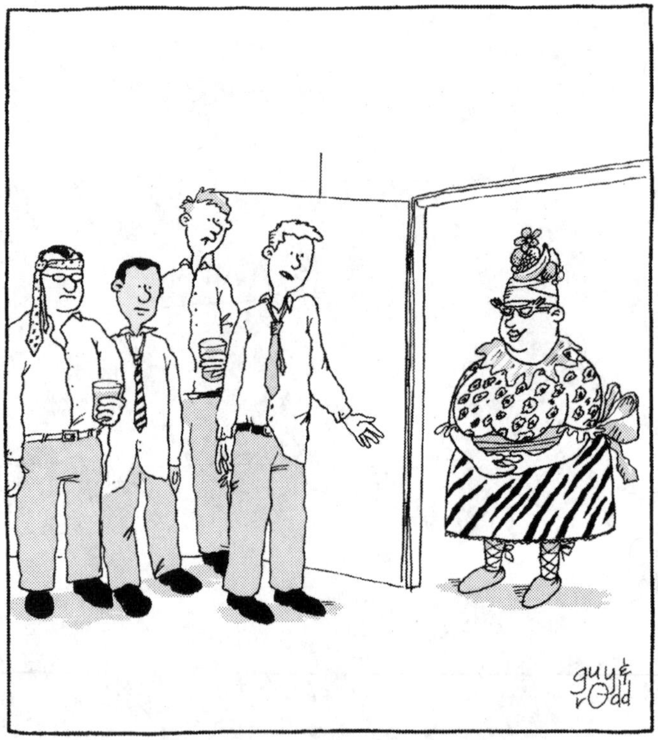
guy & rOdd

"OH, SO WHEN YOU SAID YOU WERE AN EXOTIC DANCER YOU MEANT, WELL . . . EXOTIC."

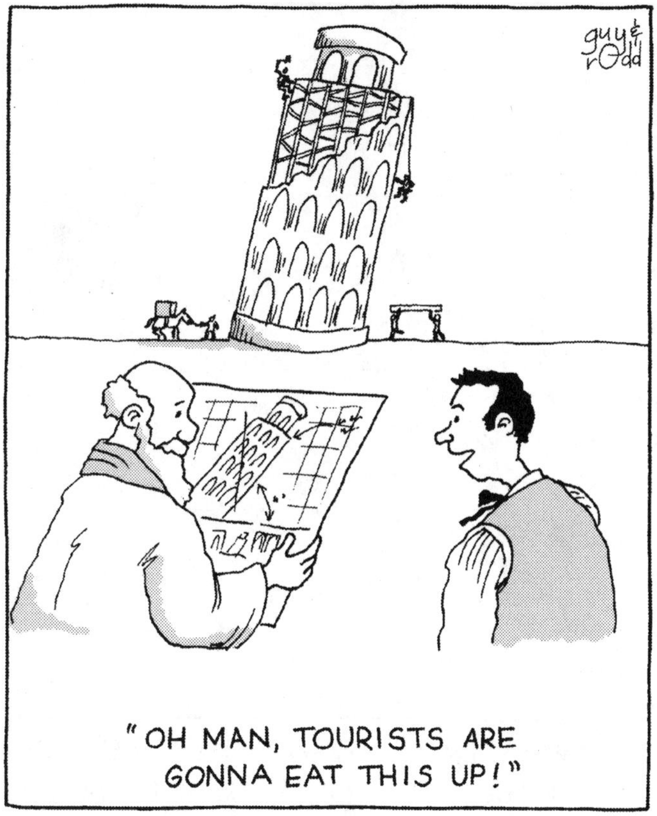
guy & rOdd
"OH MAN, TOURISTS ARE GONNA EAT THIS UP!"

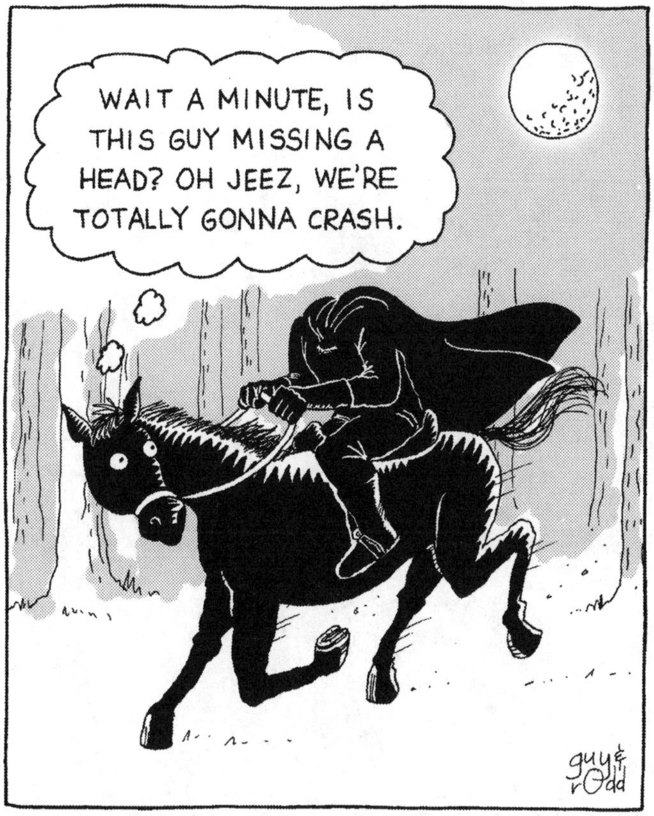
WAIT A MINUTE, IS THIS GUY MISSING A HEAD? OH JEEZ, WE'RE TOTALLY GONNA CRASH.
guy & rOdd

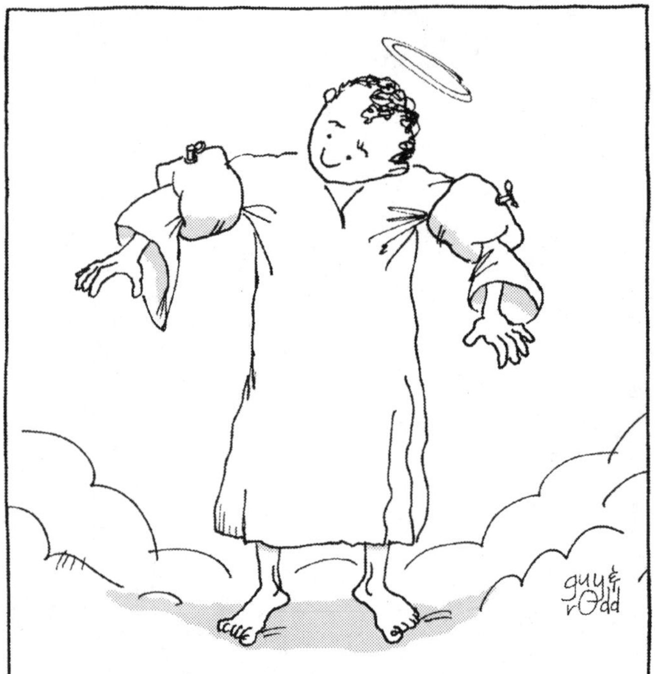

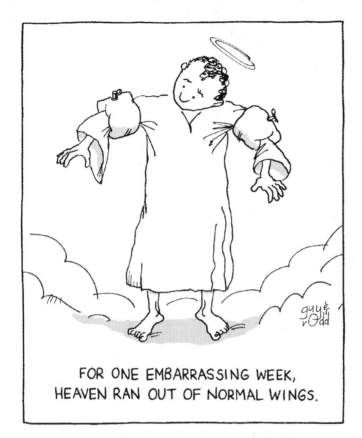

FOR ONE EMBARRASSING WEEK,
HEAVEN RAN OUT OF NORMAL WINGS.

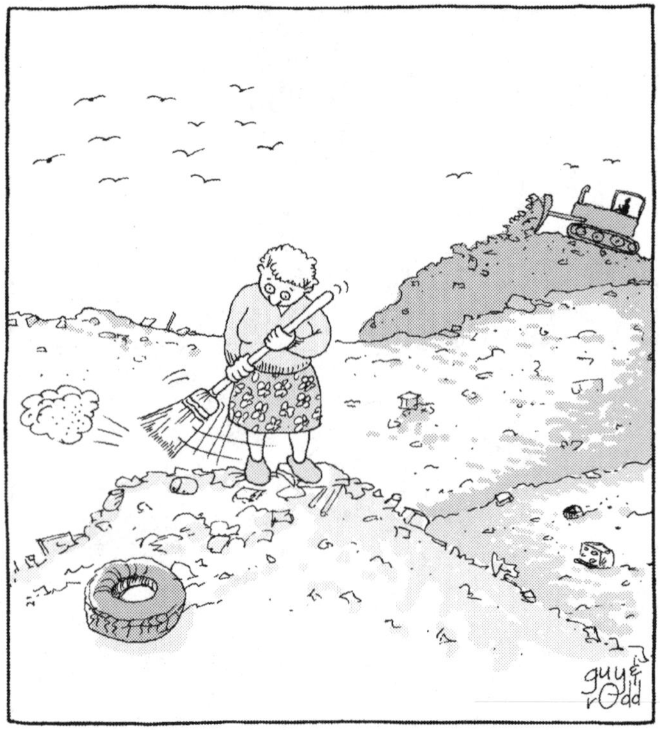

SLOWLY, ALMOST IMPERCEPTIBLY, FEELINGS
OF FUTILITY STARTED TO CREEP IN.

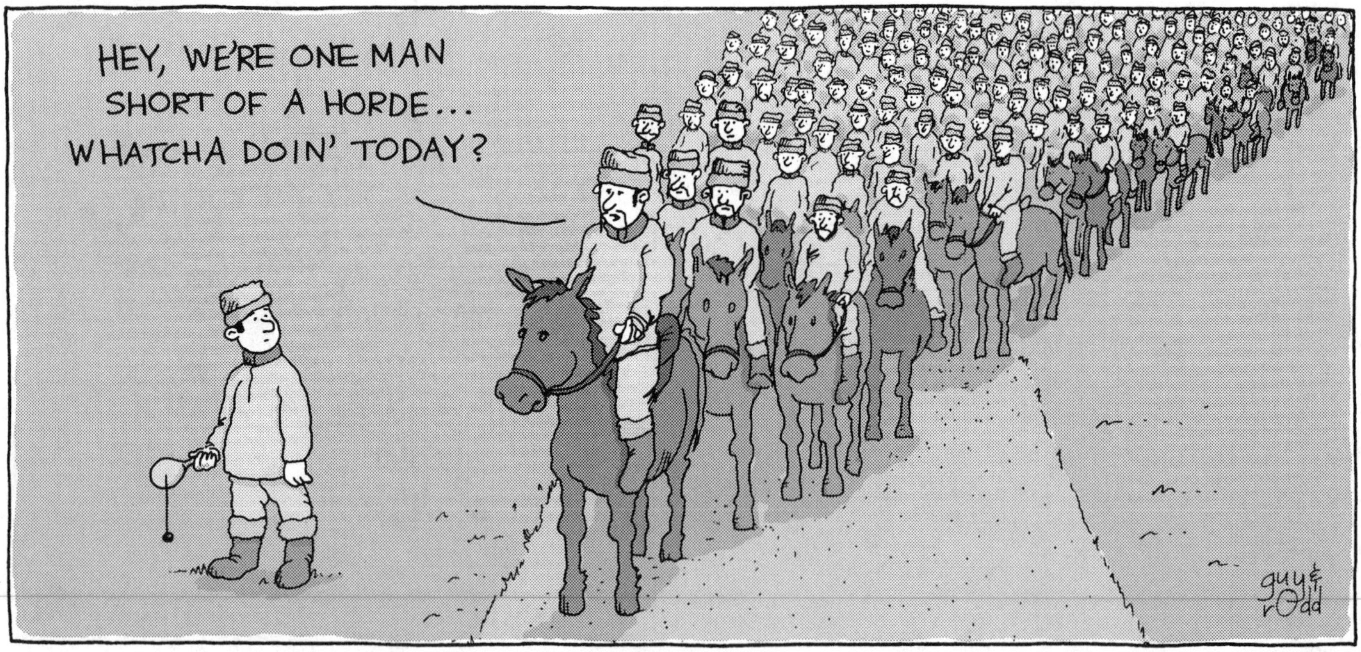
HEY, WE'RE ONE MAN SHORT OF A HORDE... WHATCHA DOIN' TODAY?

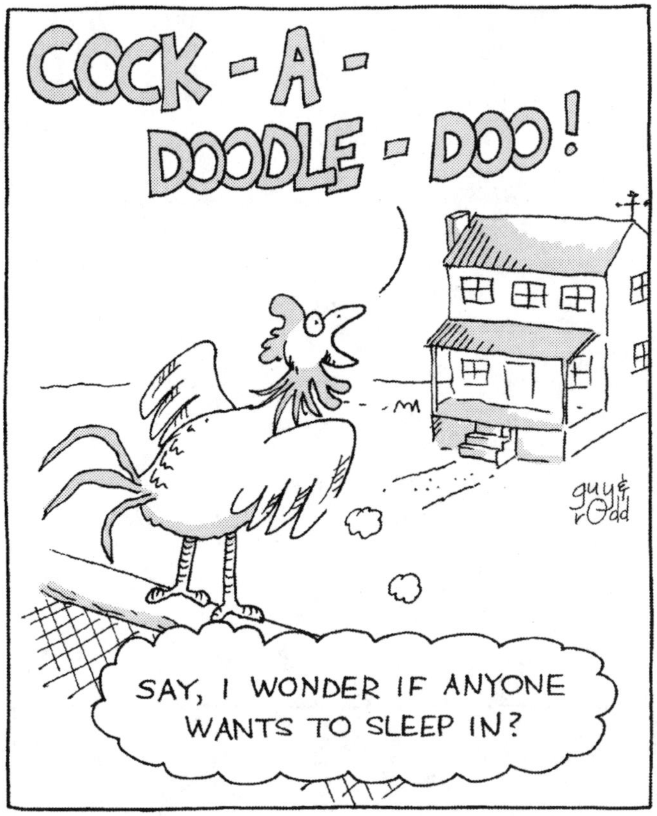
COCK-A-DOODLE-DOO!
SAY, I WONDER IF ANYONE WANTS TO SLEEP IN?
guy & rOdd

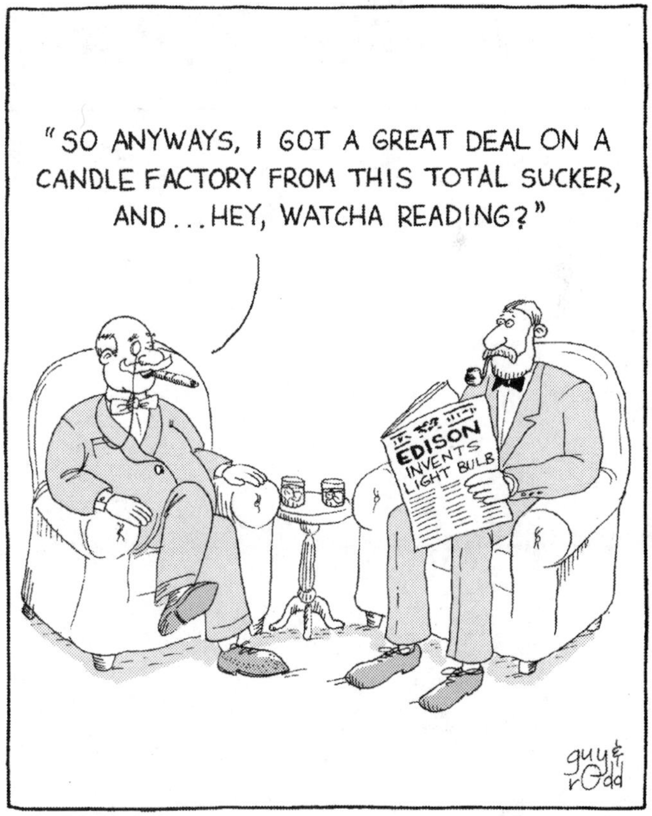
"SO ANYWAYS, I GOT A GREAT DEAL ON A CANDLE FACTORY FROM THIS TOTAL SUCKER, AND...HEY, WATCHA READING?"
EDISON INVENTS LIGHT BULB
guy & rOdd

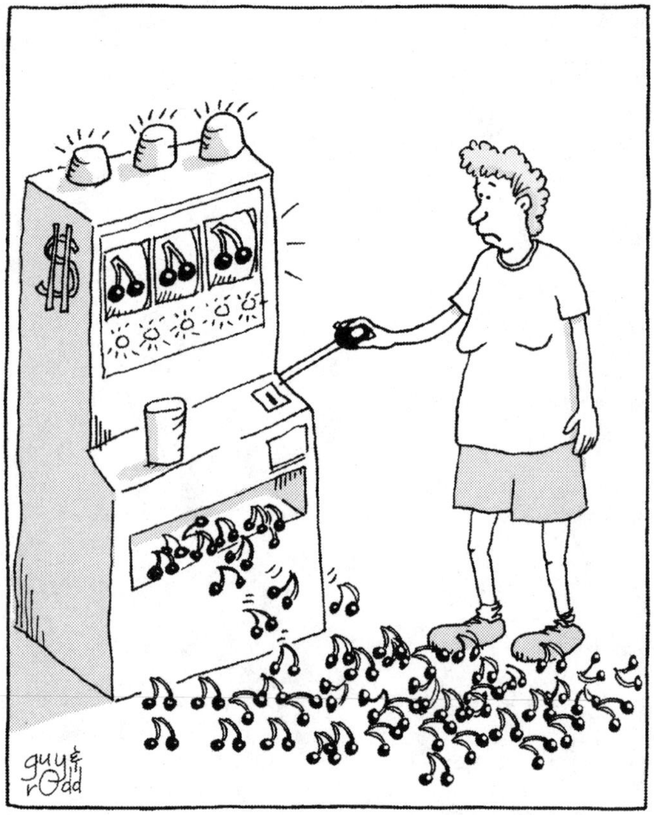
guy & rOdd

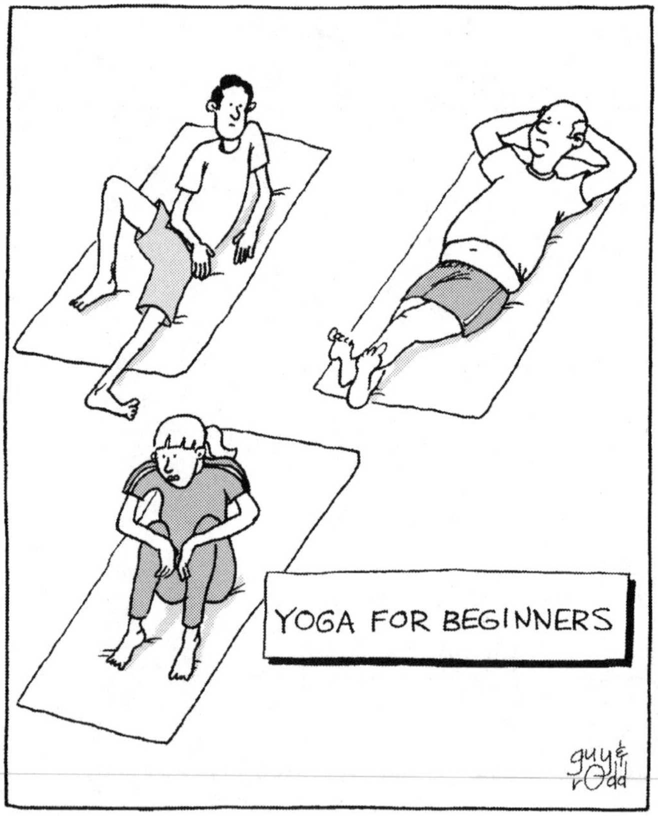
YOGA FOR BEGINNERS
guy & rOdd

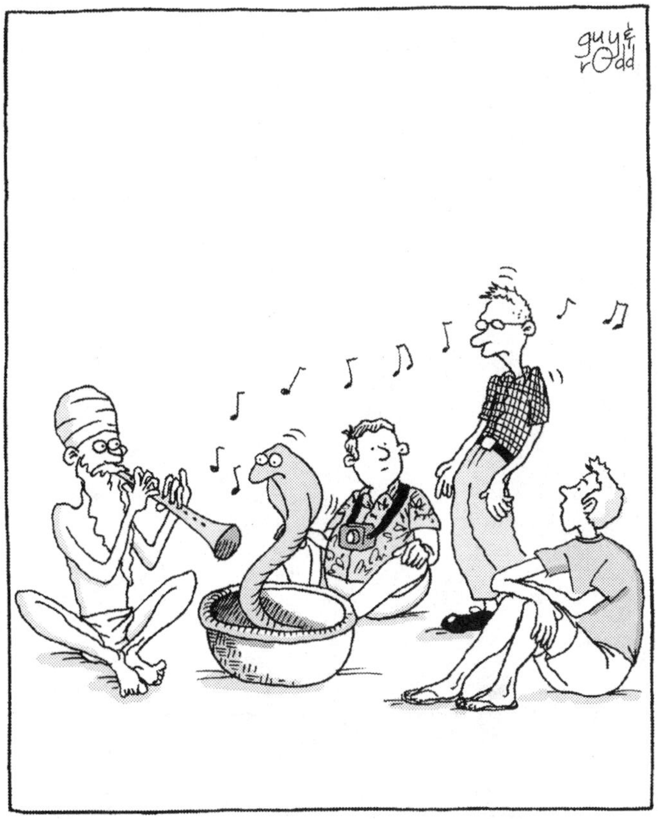
guy & rOdd

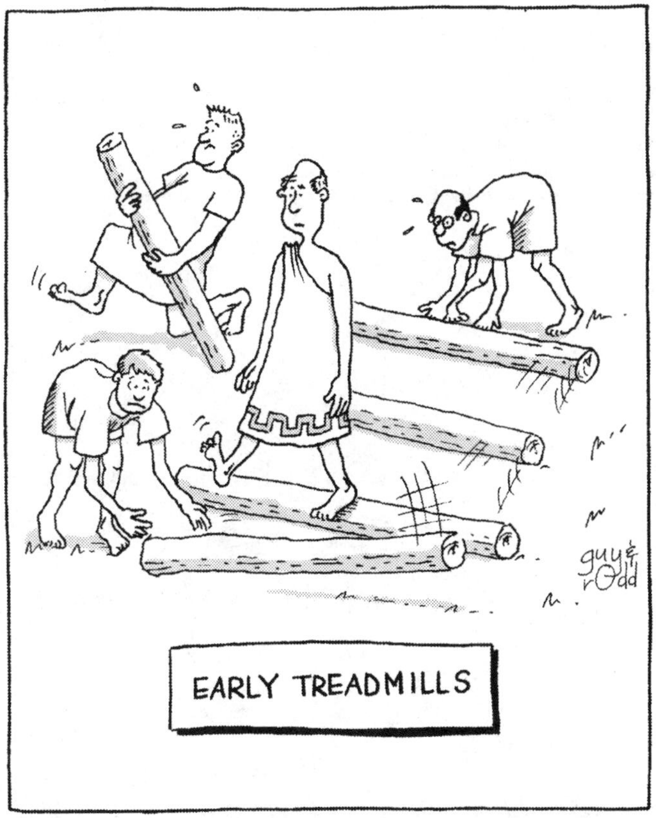
guy & rOdd
EARLY TREADMILLS

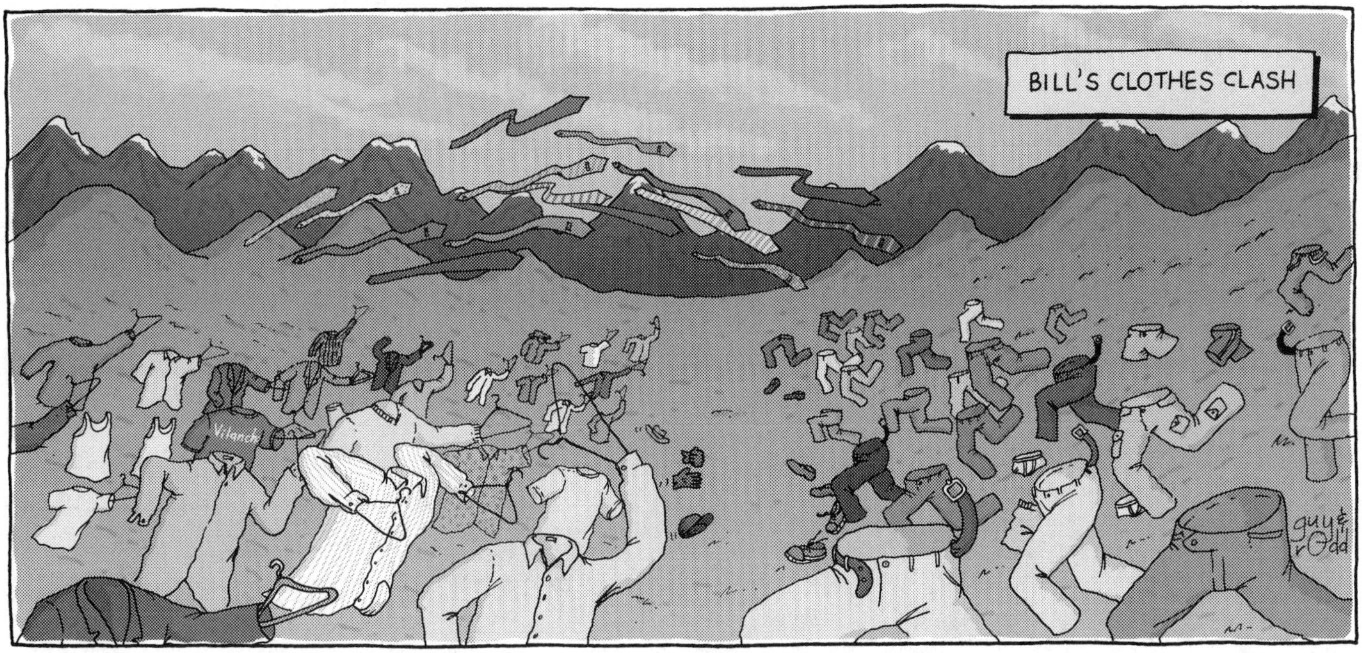
BILL'S CLOTHES CLASH
Vilanch
guy & rOdd

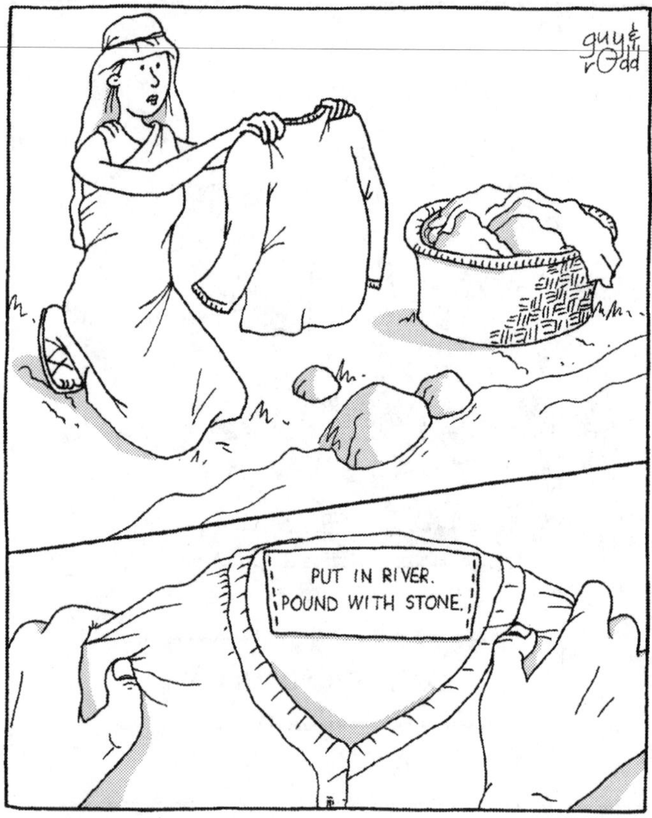
guy & rOdd
PUT IN RIVER.
POUND WITH STONE.

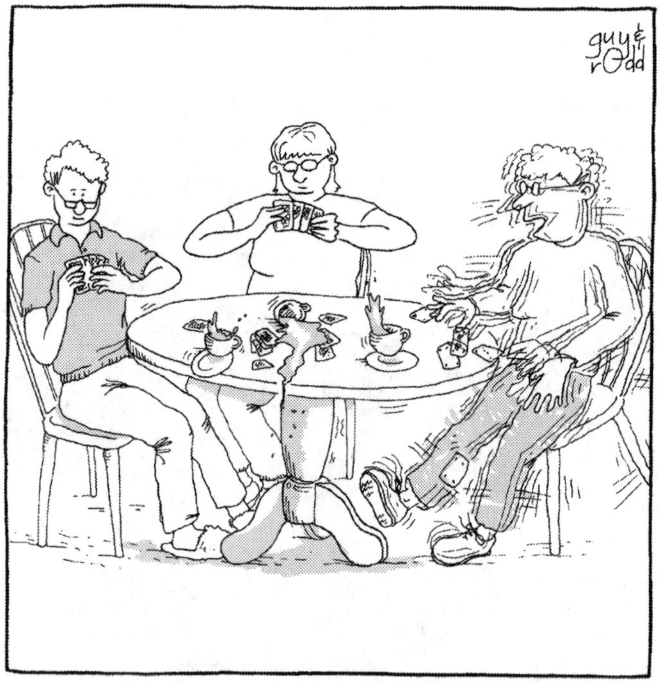
guy & rOdd

FOR SEVERAL MINUTES, NORMA'S BODY IS POSSESSED BY THE SPIRIT OF HER DEAD WASHING MACHINE.

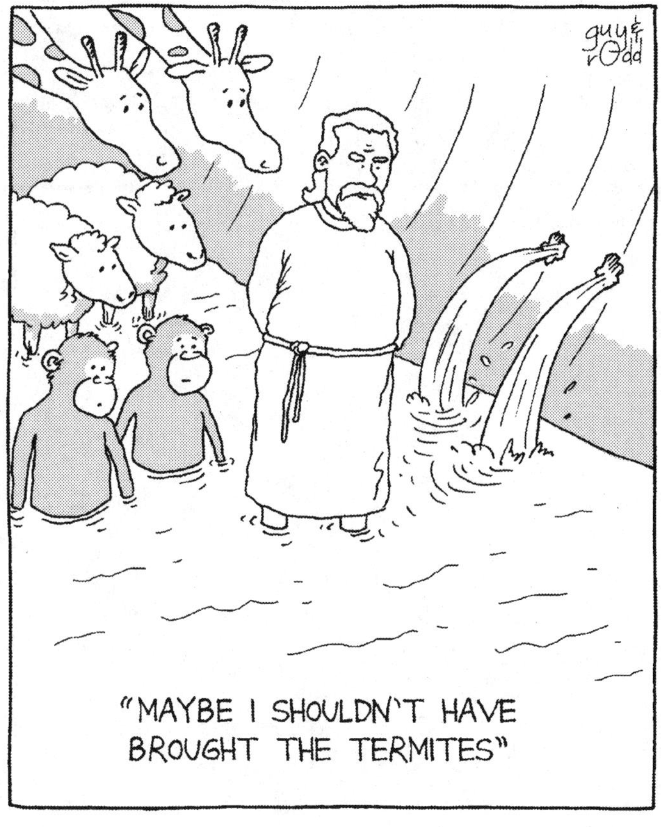
guy & rOdd

"MAYBE I SHOULDN'T HAVE BROUGHT THE TERMITES"

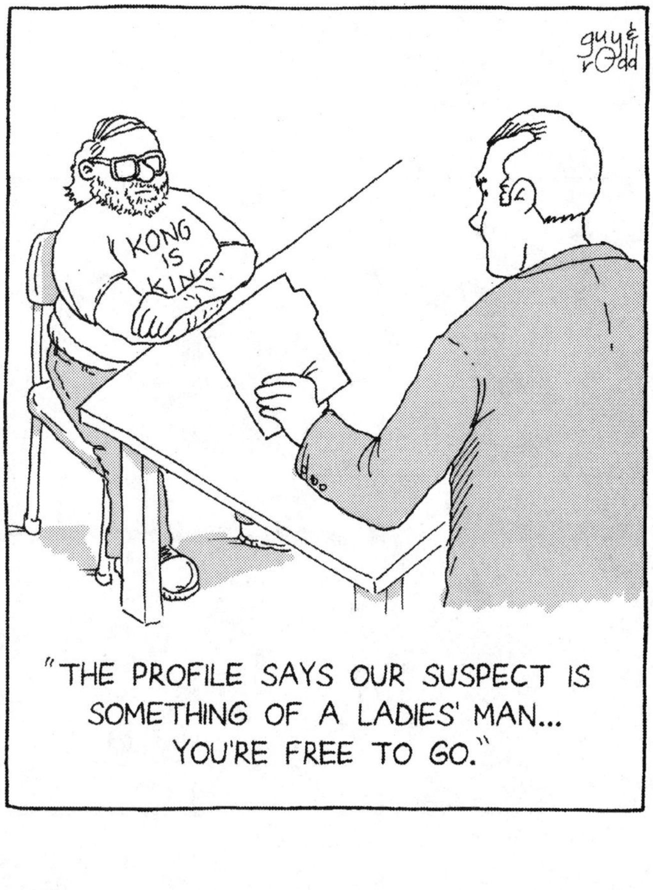
guy & rOdd
KONG IS

"THE PROFILE SAYS OUR SUSPECT IS SOMETHING OF A LADIES' MAN... YOU'RE FREE TO GO."

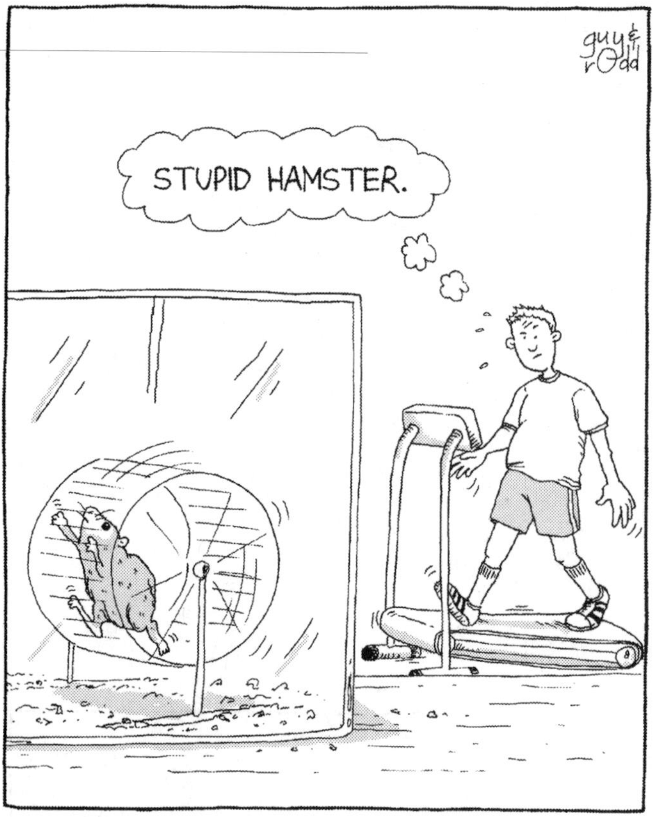
guy & rodd
STUPID HAMSTER.

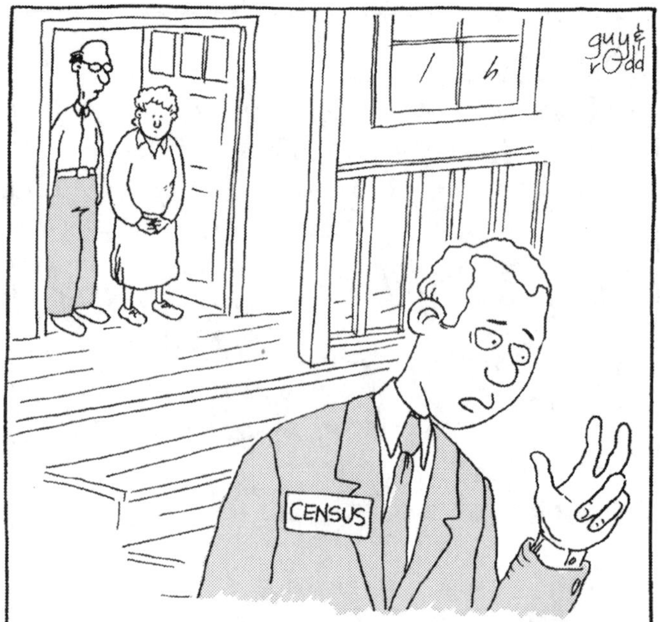
guy & rodd
CENSUS

"FOUR MILLION, EIGHT HUNDRED SEVENTEEN THOUSAND SIXTY THREE ... TWO? WAIT... FOUR ... WAIT, OH BOY, I PROBABLY SHOULD HAVE BEEN WRITING THIS DOWN."

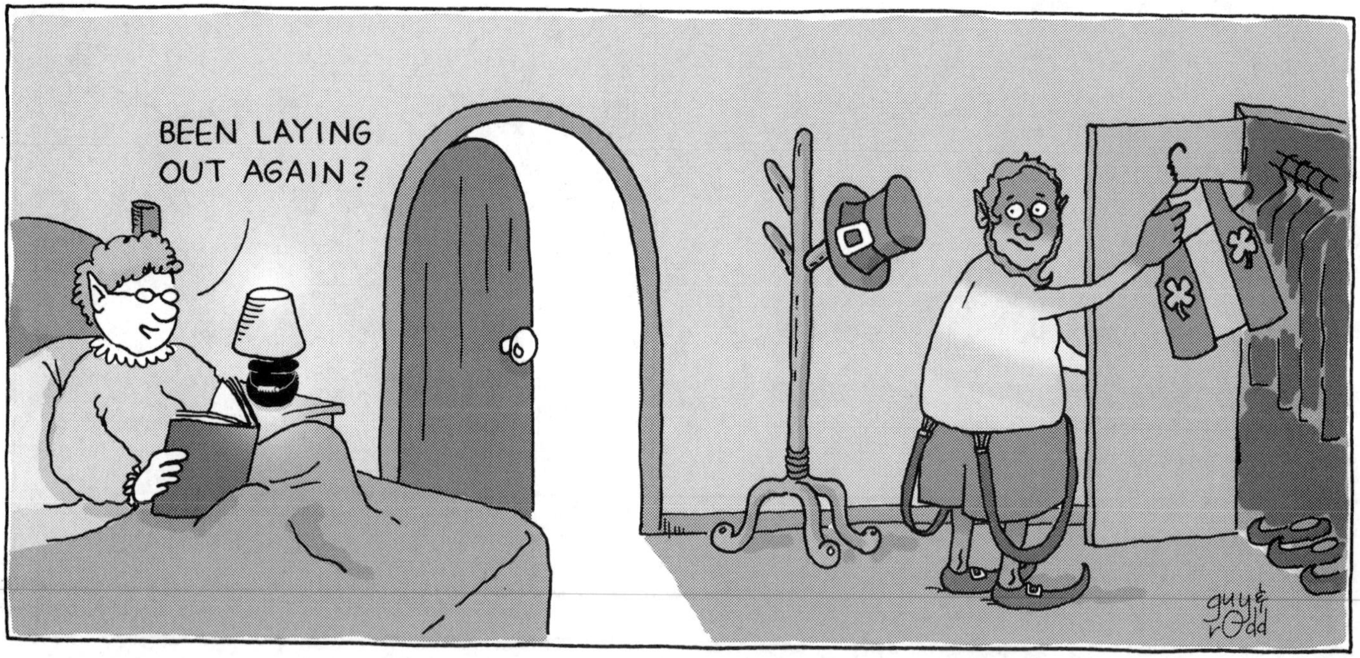
BEEN LAYING OUT AGAIN?
guy & rodd

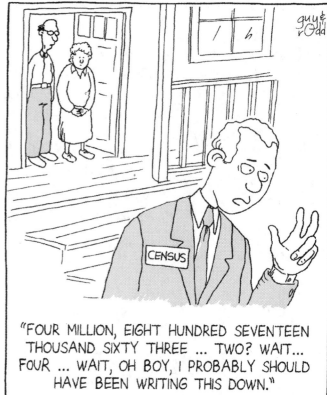

"NOW THAT YOU'RE IO, WE CAN TELL YOU
THE TRUTH: BEAUTY ISN'T ACTUALLY
IN THE EYE OF THE BEHOLDER,
THERE ARE INTERNATIONAL STANDARDS...
AND YOU HAVEN'T MET THEM."

"...A RACCOON, SURE, EVEN A SKUNK
WOULD BE OK, BUT THE CAT?!"

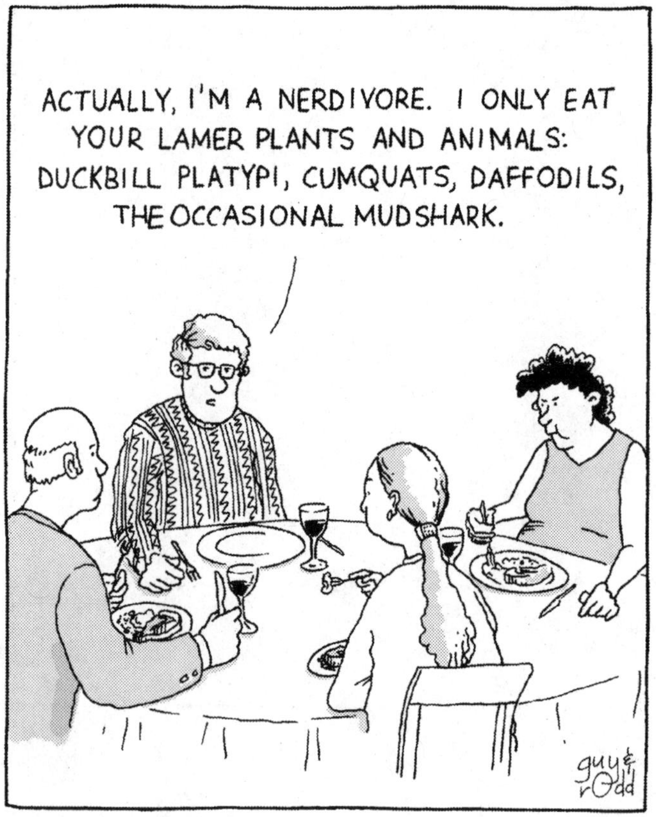
ACTUALLY, I'M A NERDIVORE. I ONLY EAT YOUR LAMER PLANTS AND ANIMALS: DUCKBILL PLATYPI, CUMQUATS, DAFFODILS, THE OCCASIONAL MUDSHARK.
guy & rodd

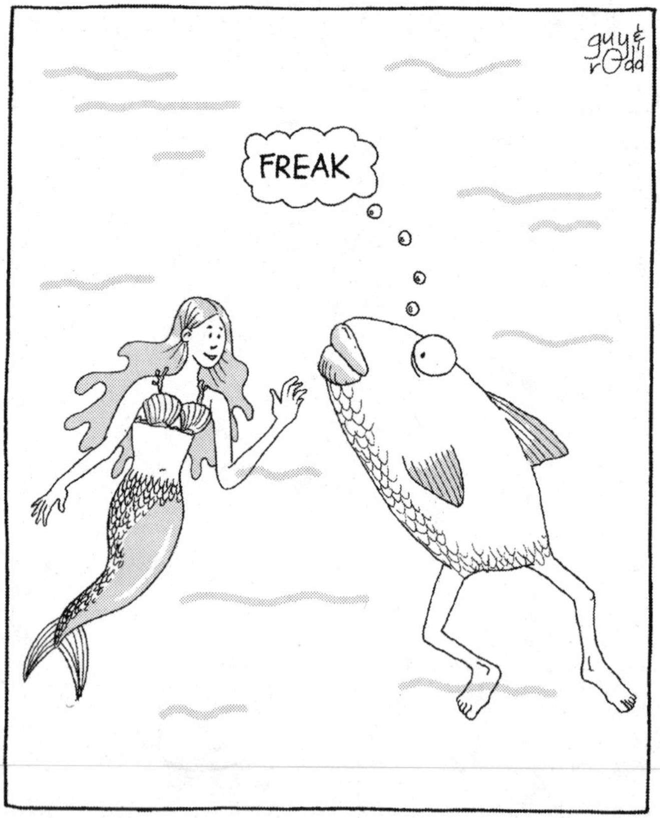
guy & rodd
FREAK

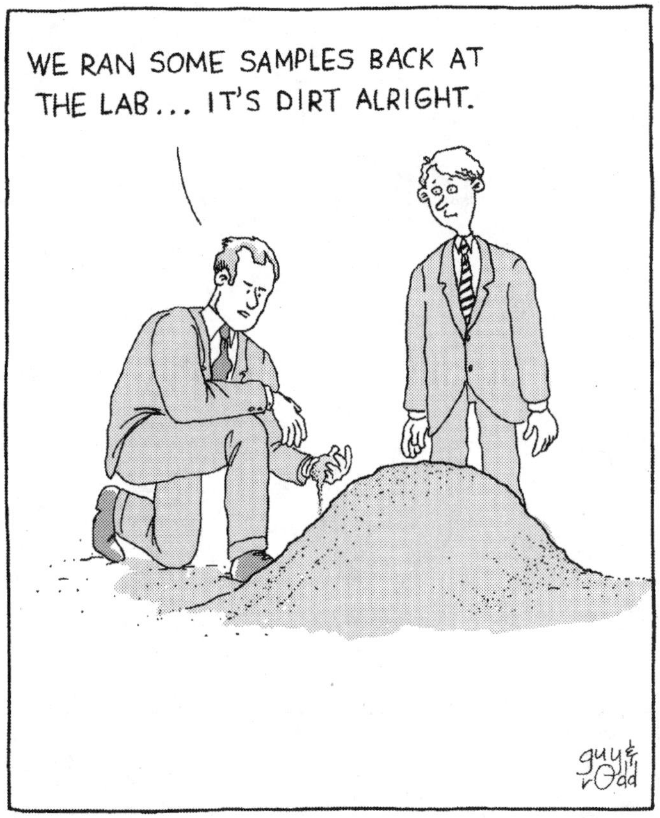
WE RAN SOME SAMPLES BACK AT THE LAB... IT'S DIRT ALRIGHT.

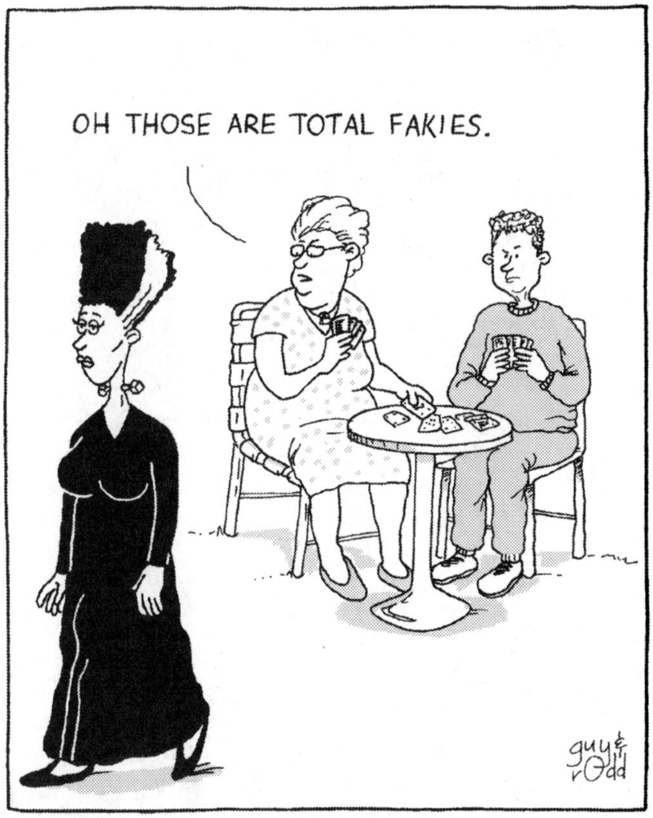
OH THOSE ARE TOTAL FAKIES.

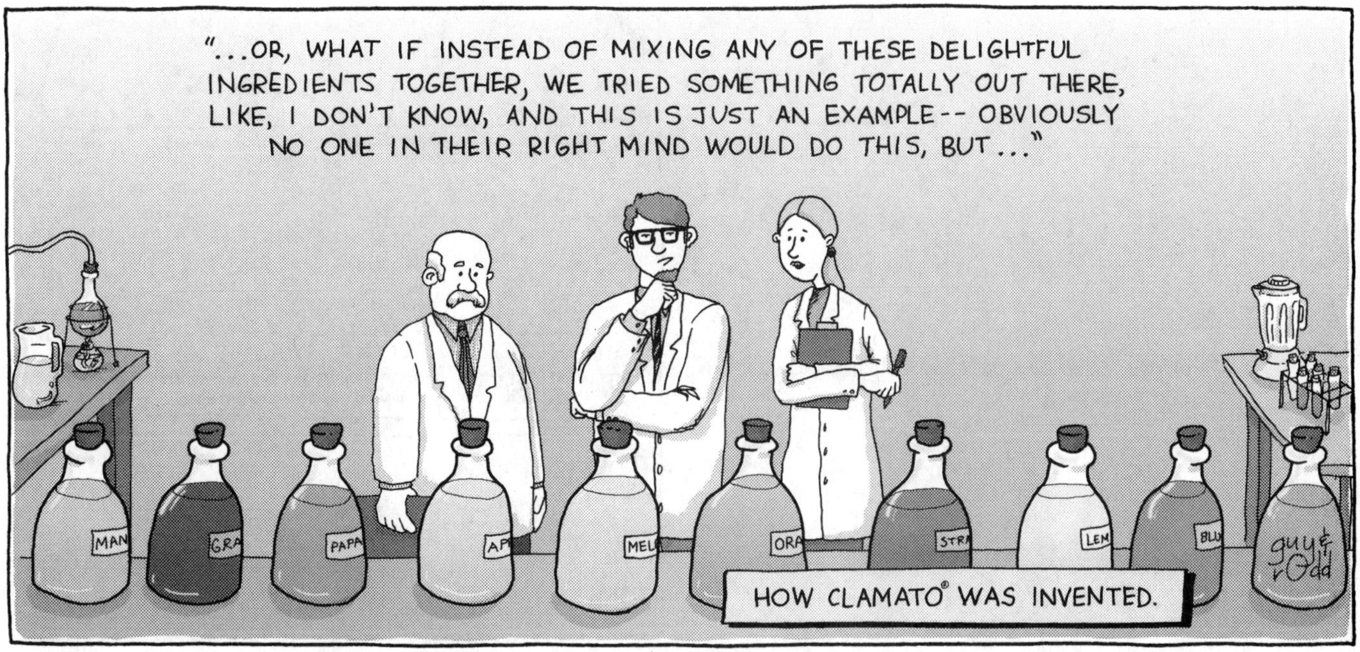
"...OR, WHAT IF INSTEAD OF MIXING ANY OF THESE DELIGHTFUL INGREDIENTS TOGETHER, WE TRIED SOMETHING TOTALLY OUT THERE, LIKE, I DON'T KNOW, AND THIS IS JUST AN EXAMPLE-- OBVIOUSLY NO ONE IN THEIR RIGHT MIND WOULD DO THIS, BUT..."
MAN
GRA
PAPA
AP
MEL
ORA
STR
LEM
BLU
HOW CLAMATO® WAS INVENTED.

"LOOK AT THAT PLUMAGE.
HE MUST BE THE ALPHA MALE."

MY CHILD IS AN HONOR STUDENT AT
GLASSLICKER ELEMENTARY SCHOOL

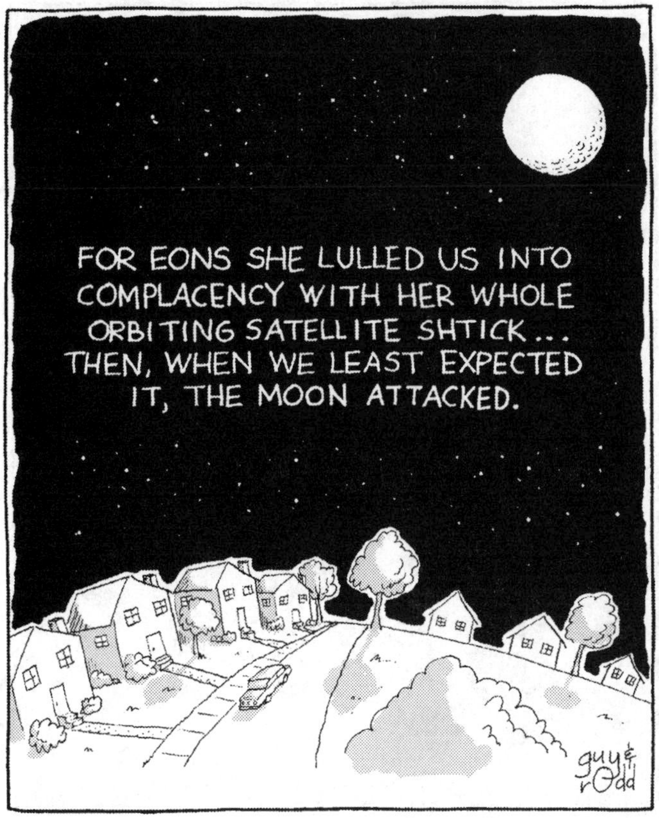
FOR EONS SHE LULLED US INTO COMPLACENCY WITH HER WHOLE ORBITING SATELLITE SHTICK... THEN, WHEN WE LEAST EXPECTED IT, THE MOON ATTACKED.
guy & rOdd

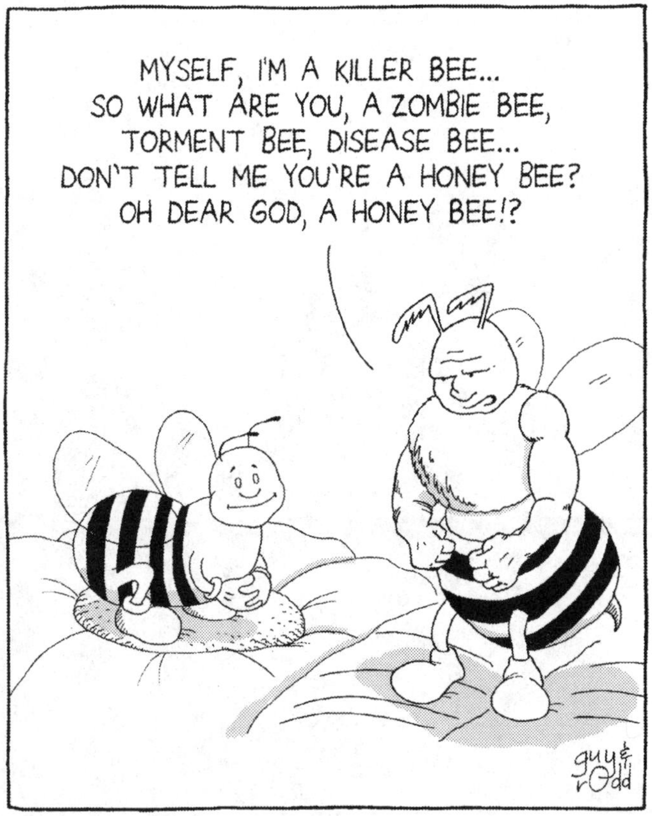
MYSELF, I'M A KILLER BEE... SO WHAT ARE YOU, A ZOMBIE BEE, TORMENT BEE, DISEASE BEE... DON'T TELL ME YOU'RE A HONEY BEE? OH DEAR GOD, A HONEY BEE!?
guy & rOdd

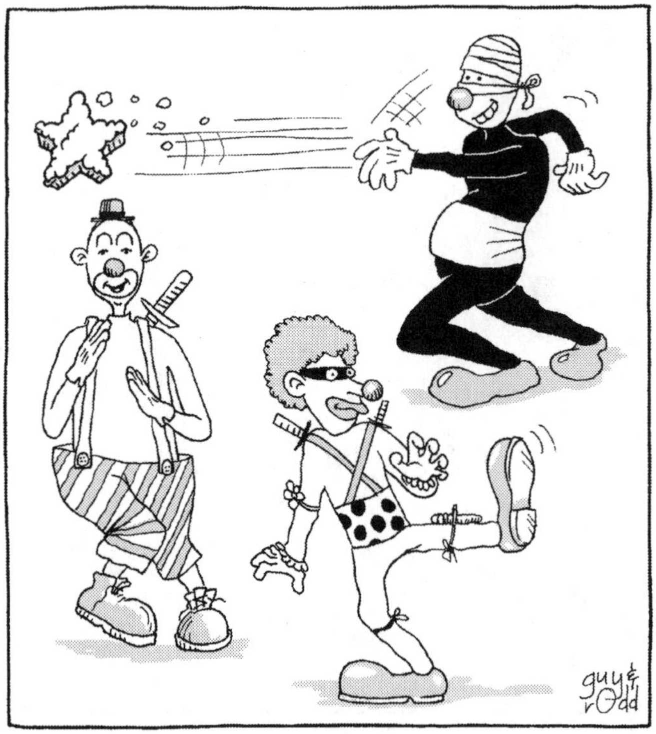
guy & rOdd

THE DEADLY NINJA CLOWNS
OF GUANGZHOU PROVINCE

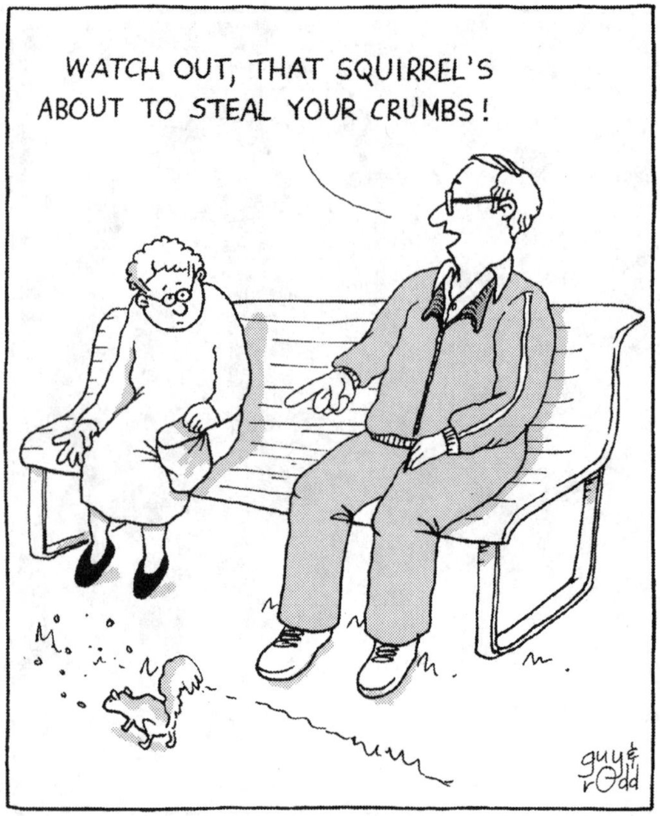
WATCH OUT, THAT SQUIRREL'S ABOUT TO STEAL YOUR CRUMBS!
guy & rOdd

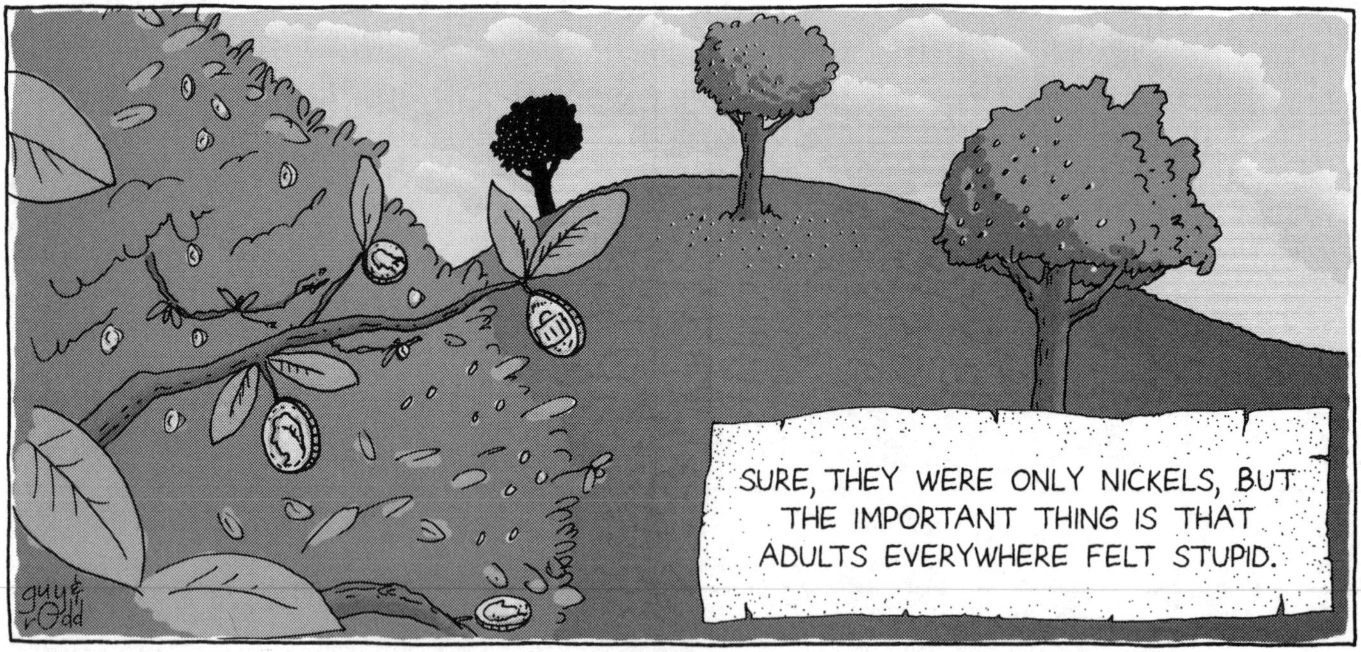
SURE, THEY WERE ONLY NICKELS, BUT THE IMPORTANT THING IS THAT ADULTS EVERYWHERE FELT STUPID.
guy & rOdd

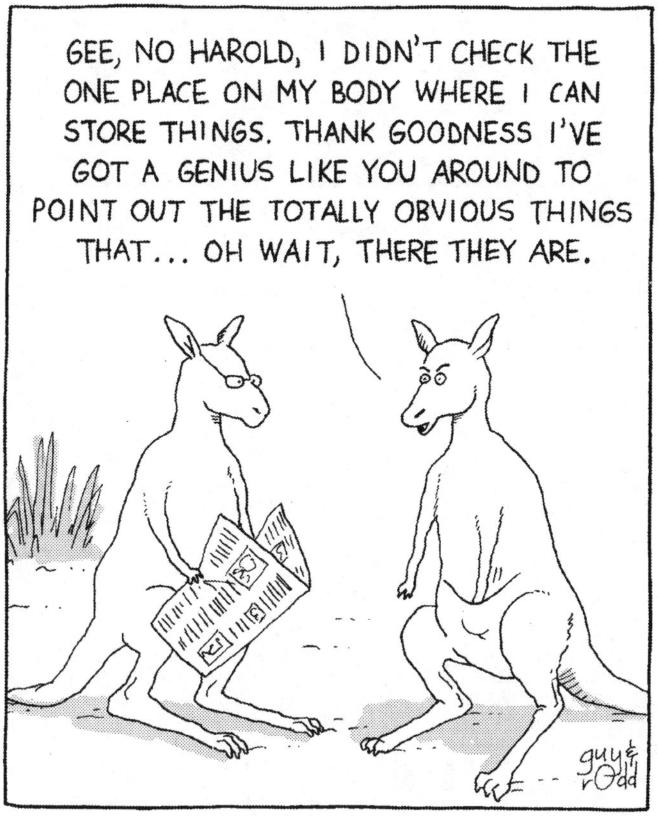
GEE, NO HAROLD, I DIDN'T CHECK THE ONE PLACE ON MY BODY WHERE I CAN STORE THINGS. THANK GOODNESS I'VE GOT A GENIUS LIKE YOU AROUND TO POINT OUT THE TOTALLY OBVIOUS THINGS THAT... OH WAIT, THERE THEY ARE.
guy & rodd

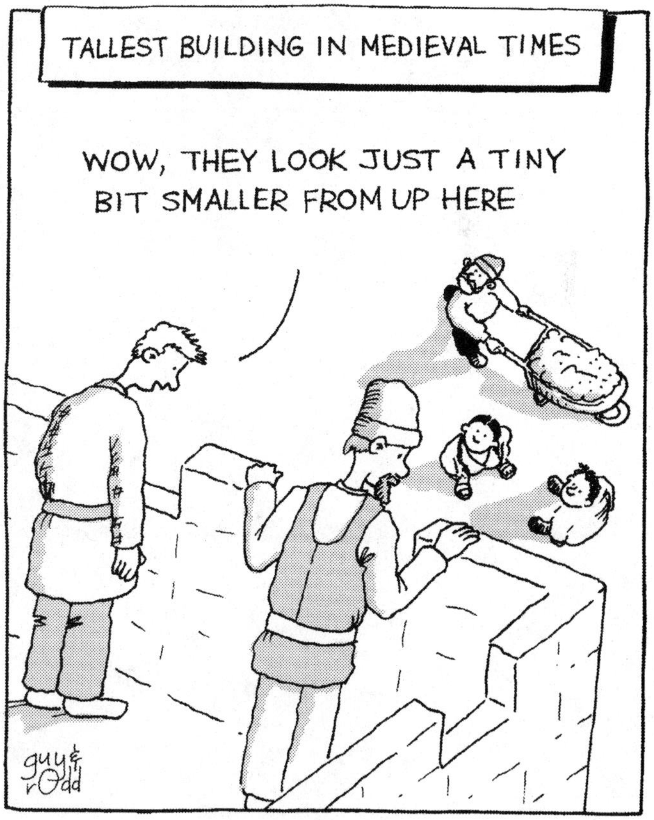
TALLEST BUILDING IN MEDIEVAL TIMES
WOW, THEY LOOK JUST A TINY BIT SMALLER FROM UP HERE
guy & rodd

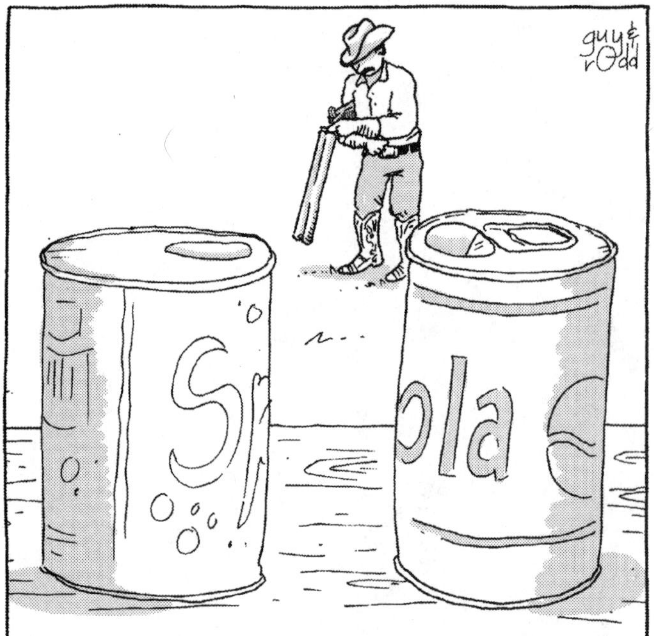
guy & rOdd
Sp
ola

"YOU'RE THE GREATEST CAN I'VE EVER MET. I JUST KNOW WE'LL GROW OLD TOGETHER ON THIS FENCE POST!"

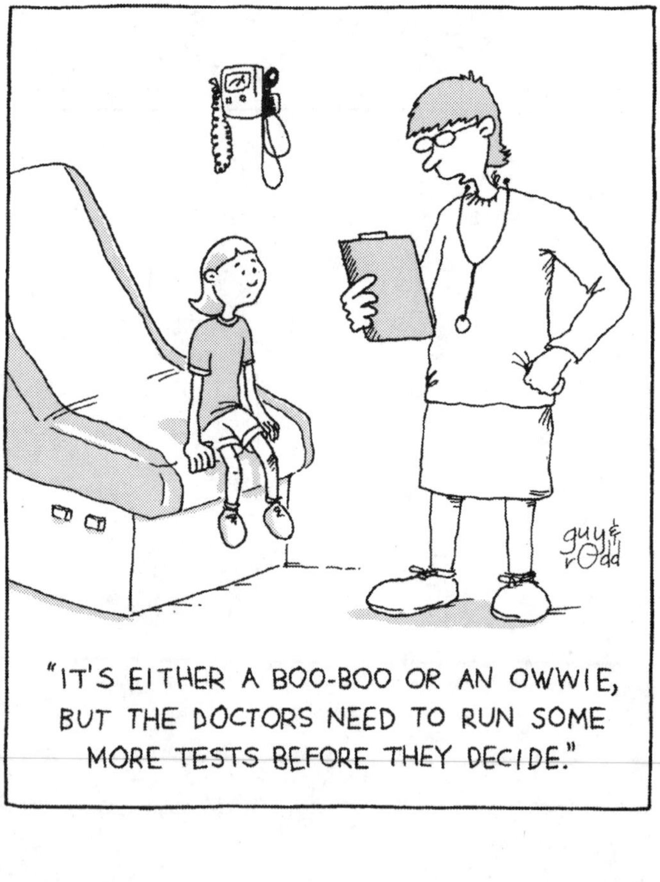
guy & rOdd

"IT'S EITHER A BOO-BOO OR AN OWWIE, BUT THE DOCTORS NEED TO RUN SOME MORE TESTS BEFORE THEY DECIDE."

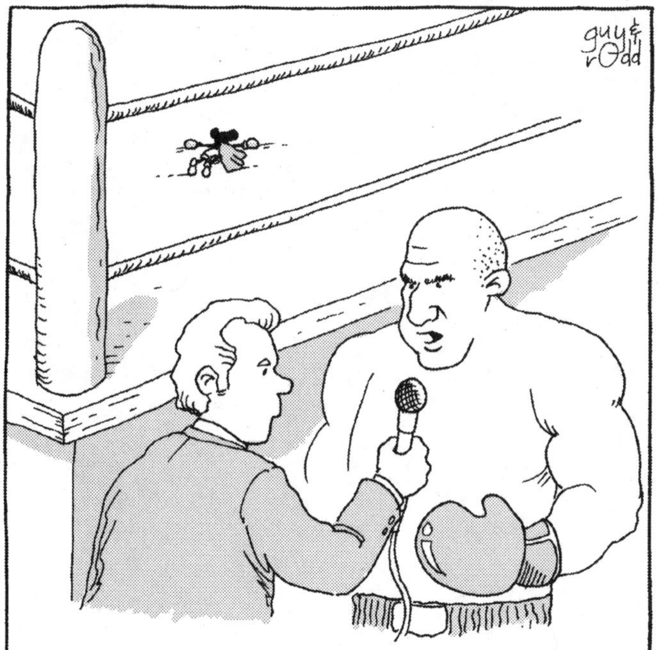

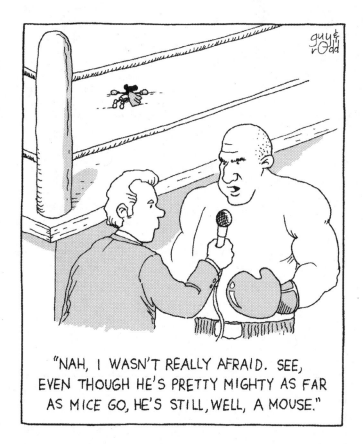

"NAH, I WASN'T REALLY AFRAID. SEE, EVEN THOUGH HE'S PRETTY MIGHTY AS FAR AS MICE GO, HE'S STILL, WELL, A MOUSE."

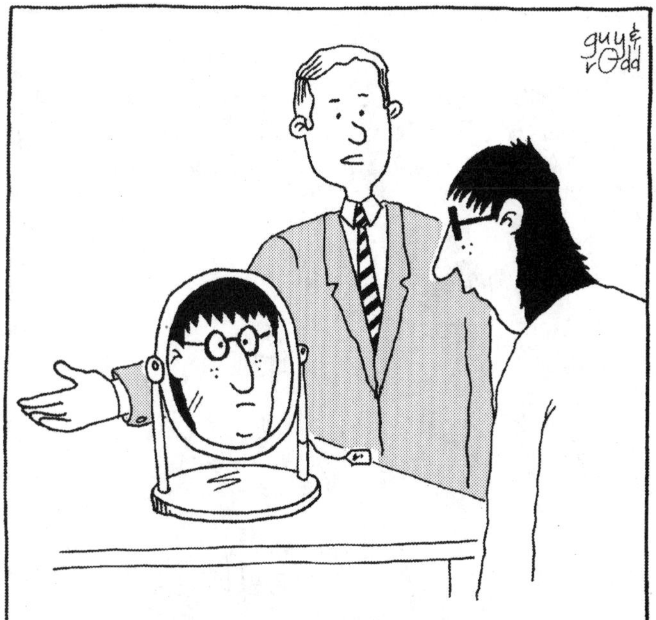

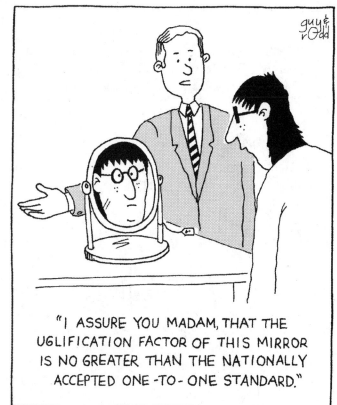

"I ASSURE YOU MADAM, THAT THE UGLIFICATION FACTOR OF THIS MIRROR IS NO GREATER THAN THE NATIONALLY ACCEPTED ONE-TO-ONE STANDARD."

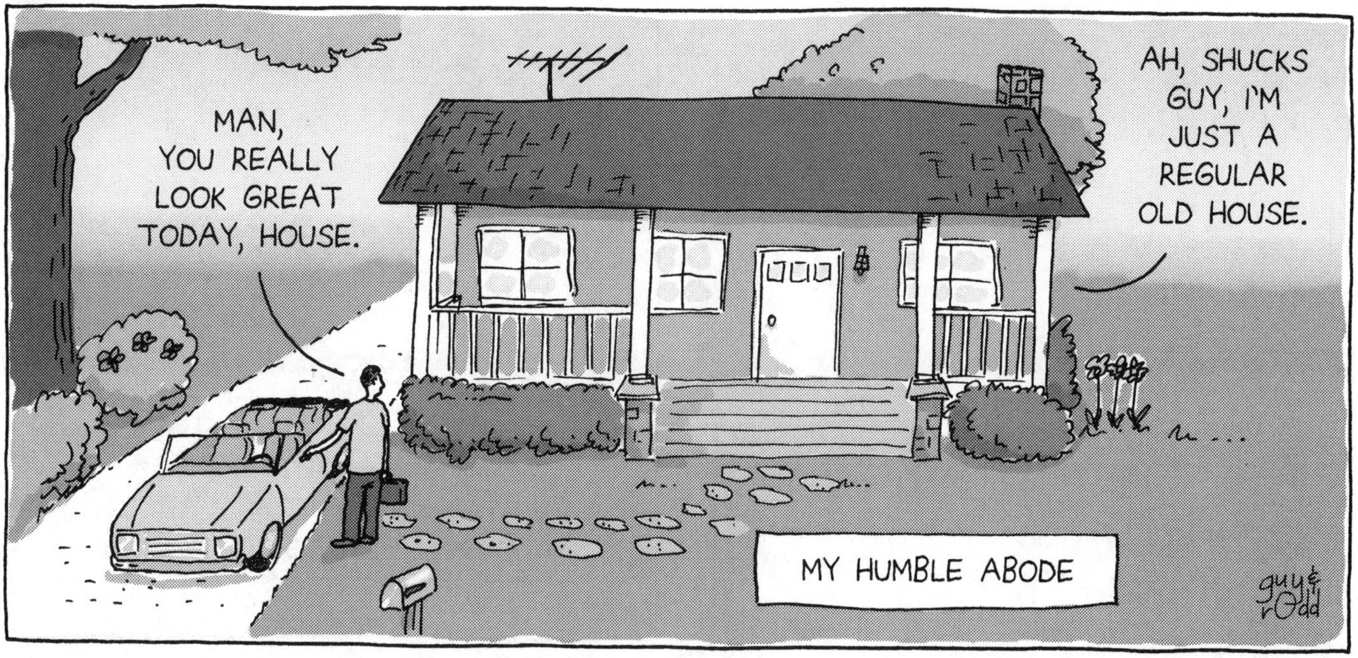
MAN, YOU REALLY LOOK GREAT TODAY, HOUSE.
AH, SHUCKS GUY, I'M JUST A REGULAR OLD HOUSE.
MY HUMBLE ABODE

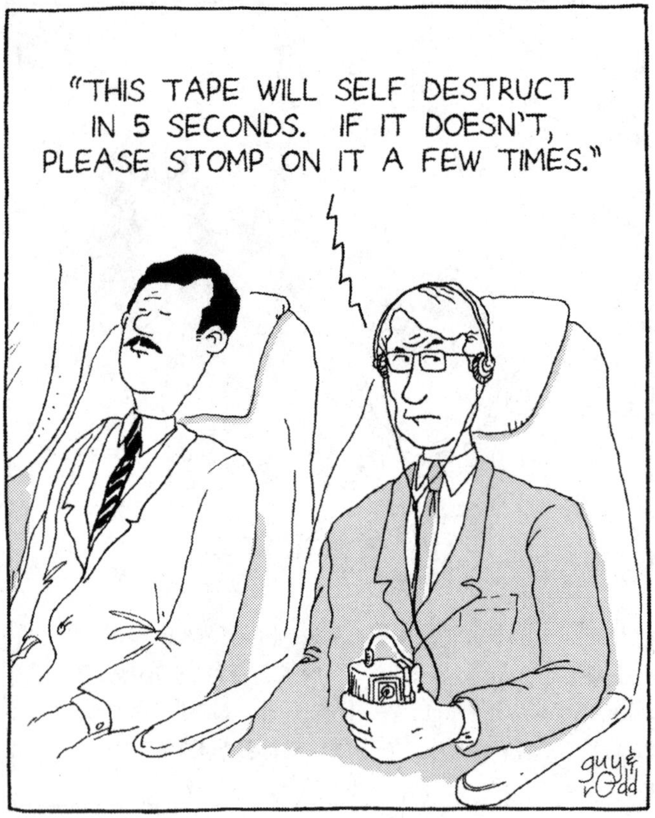
"THIS TAPE WILL SELF DESTRUCT IN 5 SECONDS. IF IT DOESN'T, PLEASE STOMP ON IT A FEW TIMES."
guy & rodd

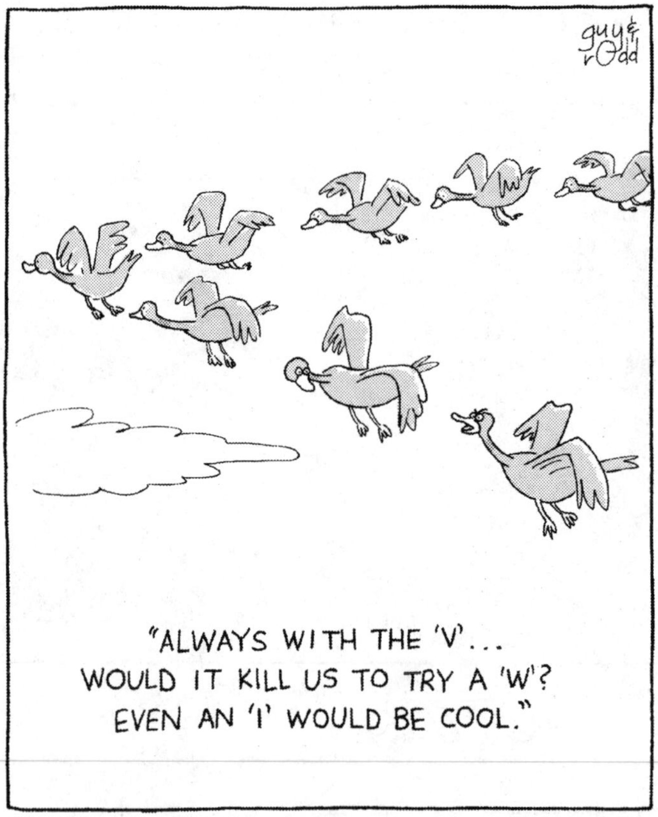
guy & rodd
"ALWAYS WITH THE 'V'... WOULD IT KILL US TO TRY A 'W'? EVEN AN 'I' WOULD BE COOL."

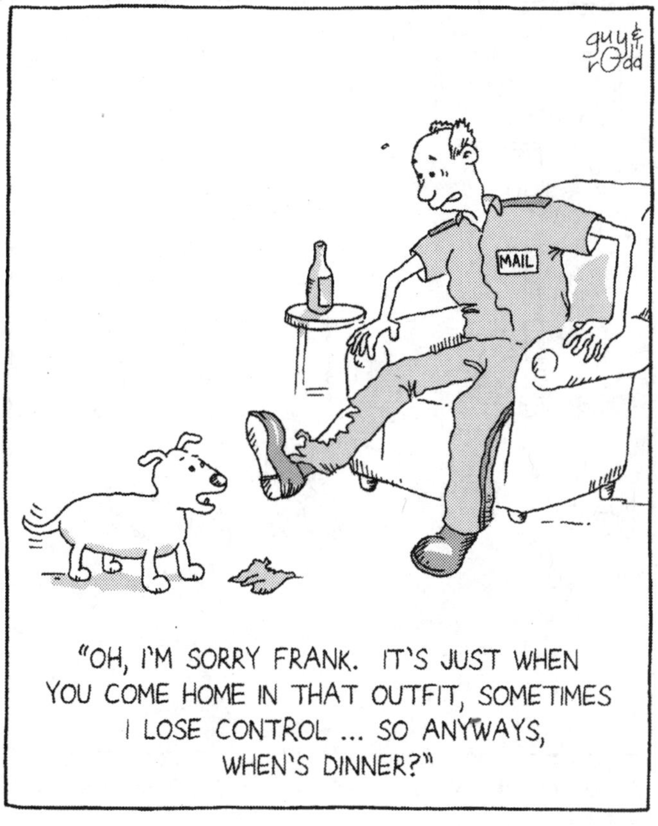
guy & rOdd
MAIL

"OH, I'M SORRY FRANK. IT'S JUST WHEN YOU COME HOME IN THAT OUTFIT, SOMETIMES I LOSE CONTROL ... SO ANYWAYS, WHEN'S DINNER?"

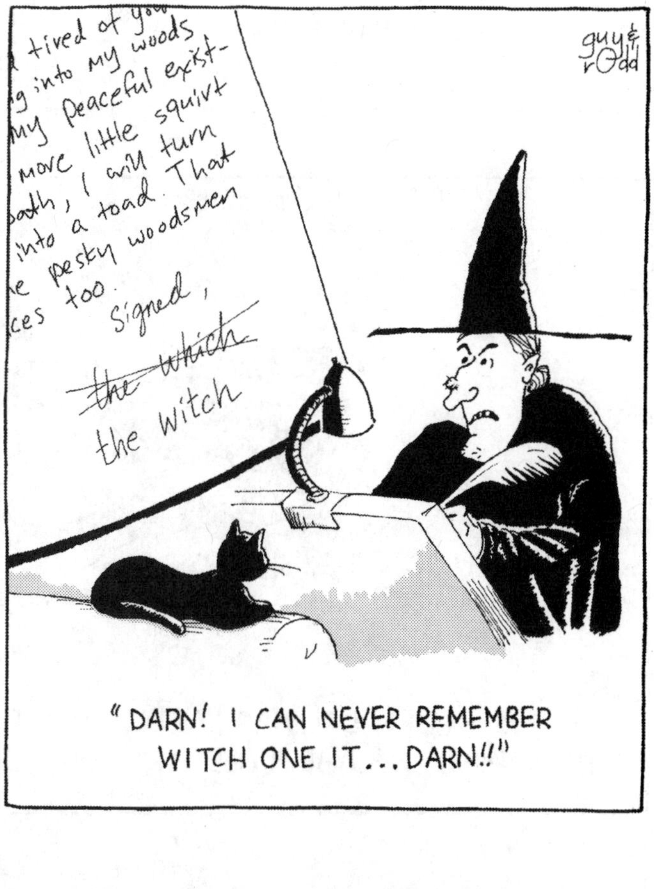
guy & rOdd
tired of you
g into my woods
my peaceful exist-
more little squirt
path, I will turn
into a toad. That
e pesky woodsmen
ces too.
Signed,
the which
the witch

"DARN! I CAN NEVER REMEMBER WITCH ONE IT... DARN!!"

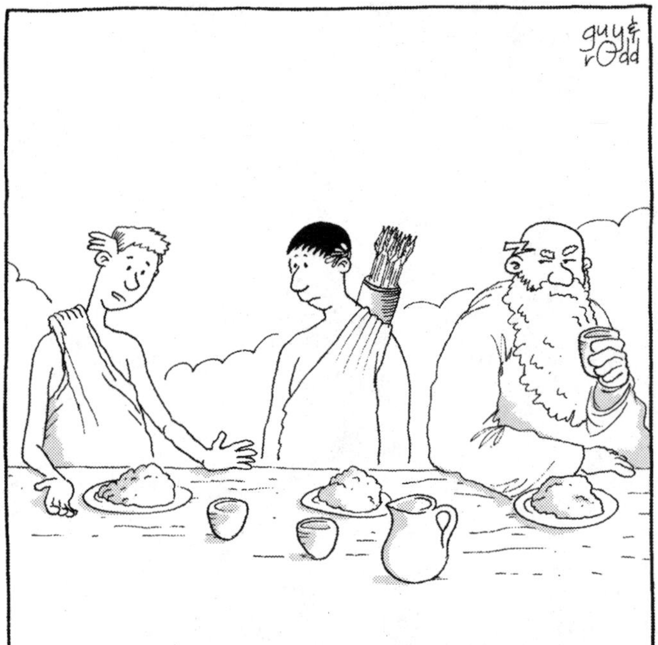
guy & rOdd

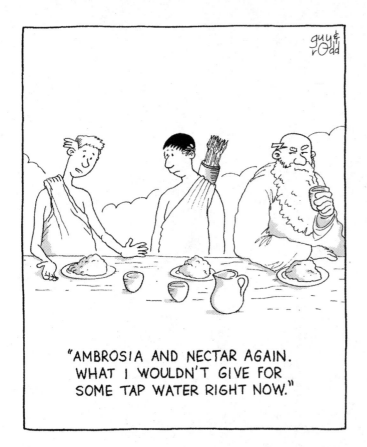

"AMBROSIA AND NECTAR AGAIN. WHAT I WOULDN'T GIVE FOR SOME TAP WATER RIGHT NOW."

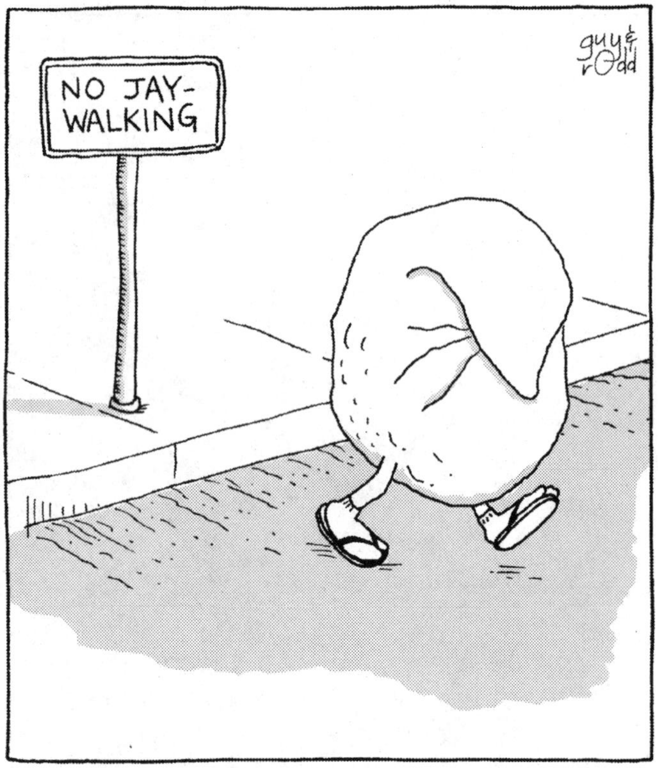
guy & rOdd
NO JAY-
WALKING

WON-TON DISREGARD FOR THE LAW

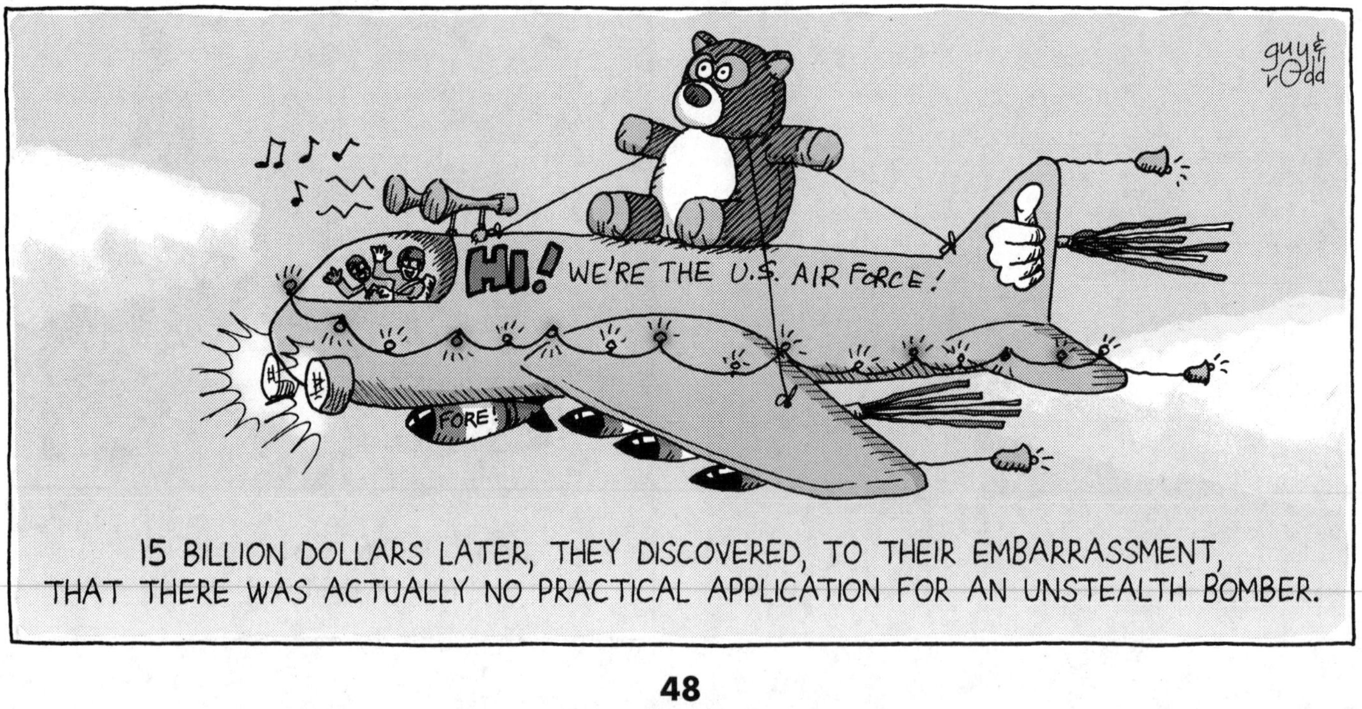
guy & rOdd
HI! WE'RE THE U.S. AIR FORCE!
FORE!

15 BILLION DOLLARS LATER, THEY DISCOVERED, TO THEIR EMBARRASSMENT, THAT THERE WAS ACTUALLY NO PRACTICAL APPLICATION FOR AN UNSTEALTH BOMBER.

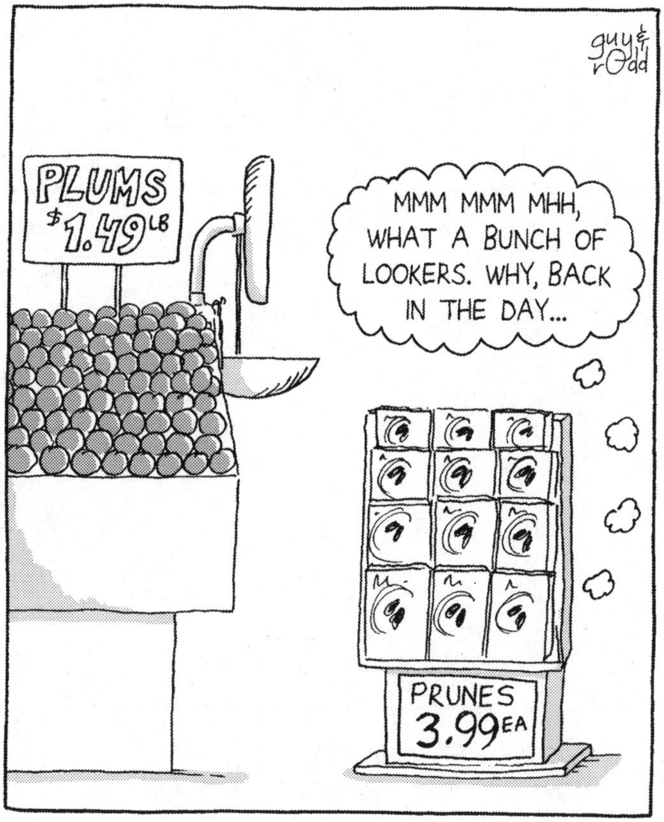
guy & rodd
PLUMS $1.49 LB
MMM MMM MHH, WHAT A BUNCH OF LOOKERS. WHY, BACK IN THE DAY...
PRUNES 3.99 EA

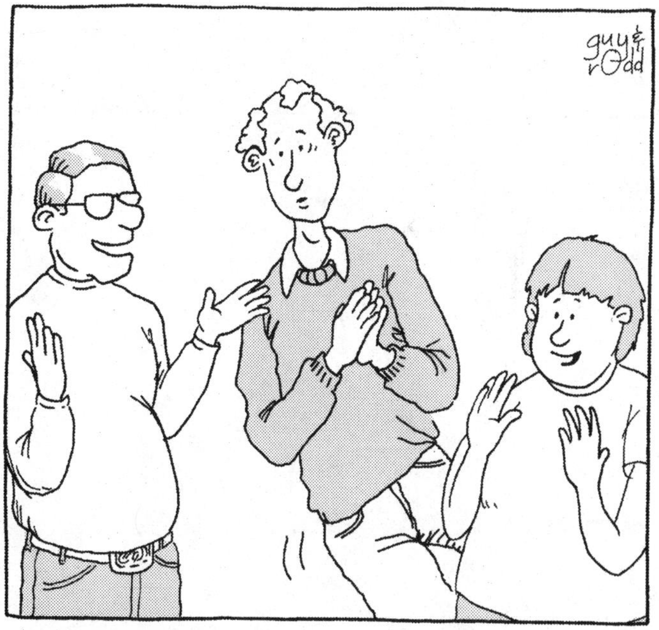
guy & rodd

WHILE SINGING THE POPULAR SONG, CLAY WAS DISTURBED TO DISCOVER THAT HIS THIGH BONE WASN'T CONNECTED TO HIS HIP BONE, THAT IT WAS, IN FACT, CONNECTED TO NOTHING.

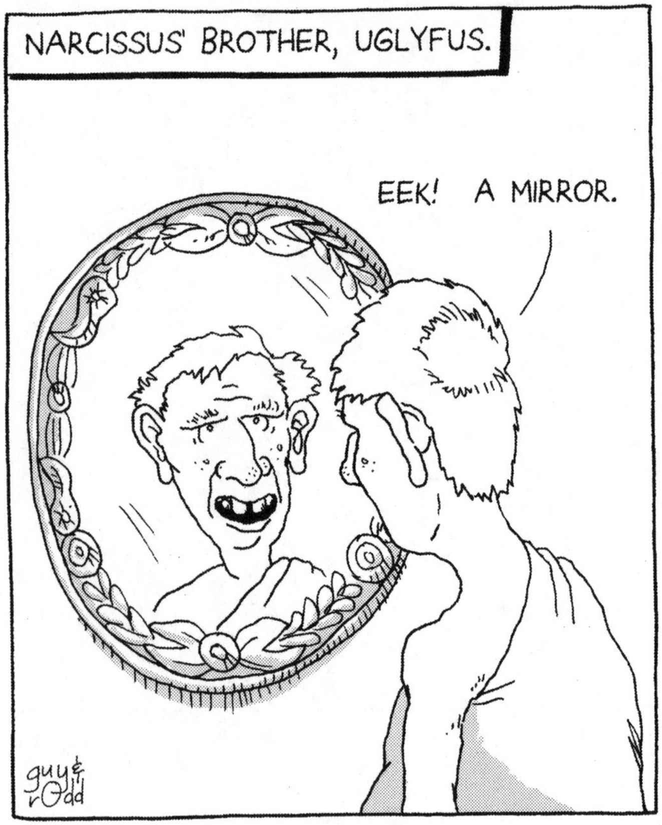
NARCISSUS' BROTHER, UGLYFUS.
EEK! A MIRROR.
guy & rodd

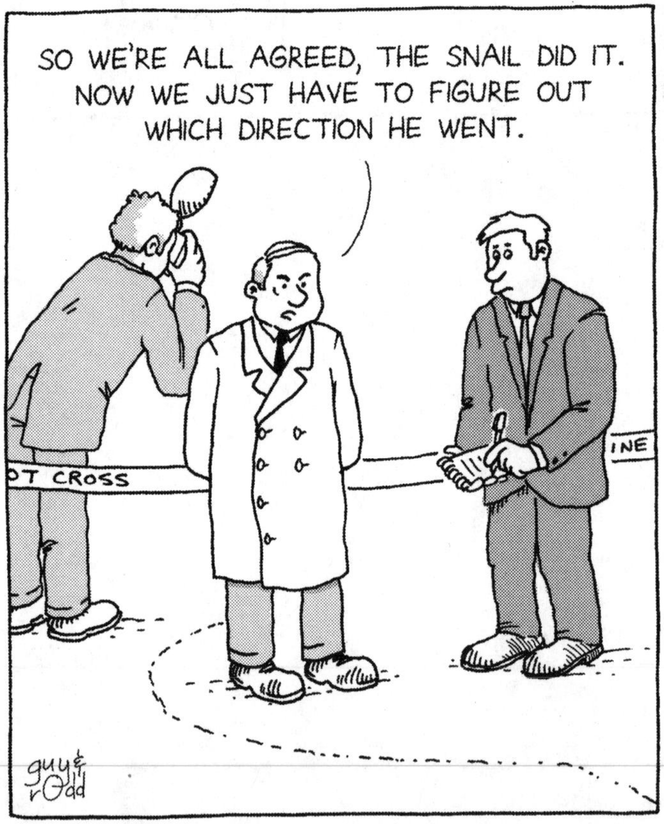
SO WE'RE ALL AGREED, THE SNAIL DID IT. NOW WE JUST HAVE TO FIGURE OUT WHICH DIRECTION HE WENT.
OT CROSS
INE
guy & rodd

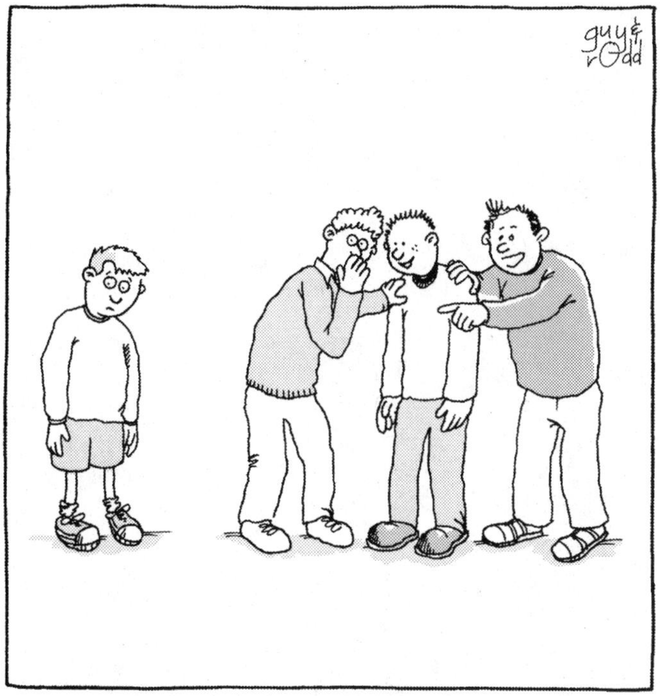

YOUNG GREG DISCOVERS IN THE SAME DAY THAT HE IS A HOMO SAPIEN AND HIS EPIDERMIS IS SHOWING.

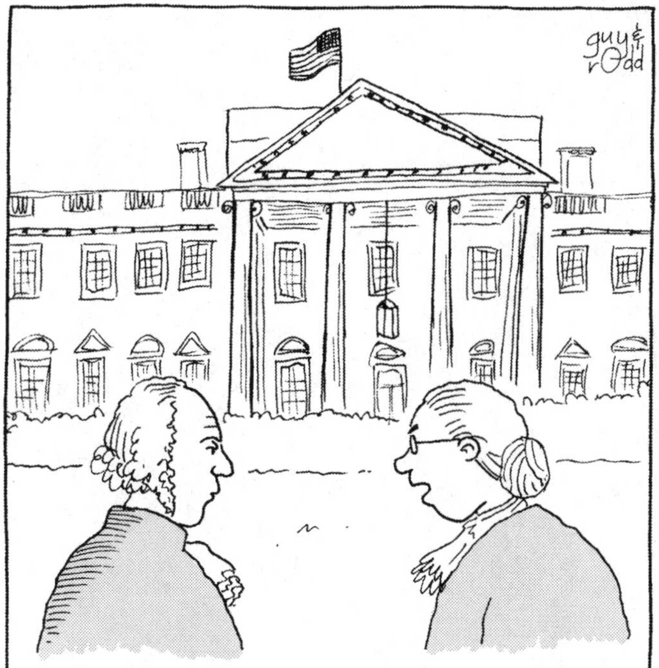

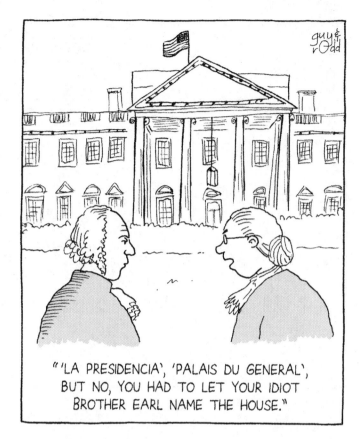

"'LA PRESIDENCIA', 'PALAIS DU GENERAL', BUT NO, YOU HAD TO LET YOUR IDIOT BROTHER EARL NAME THE HOUSE."

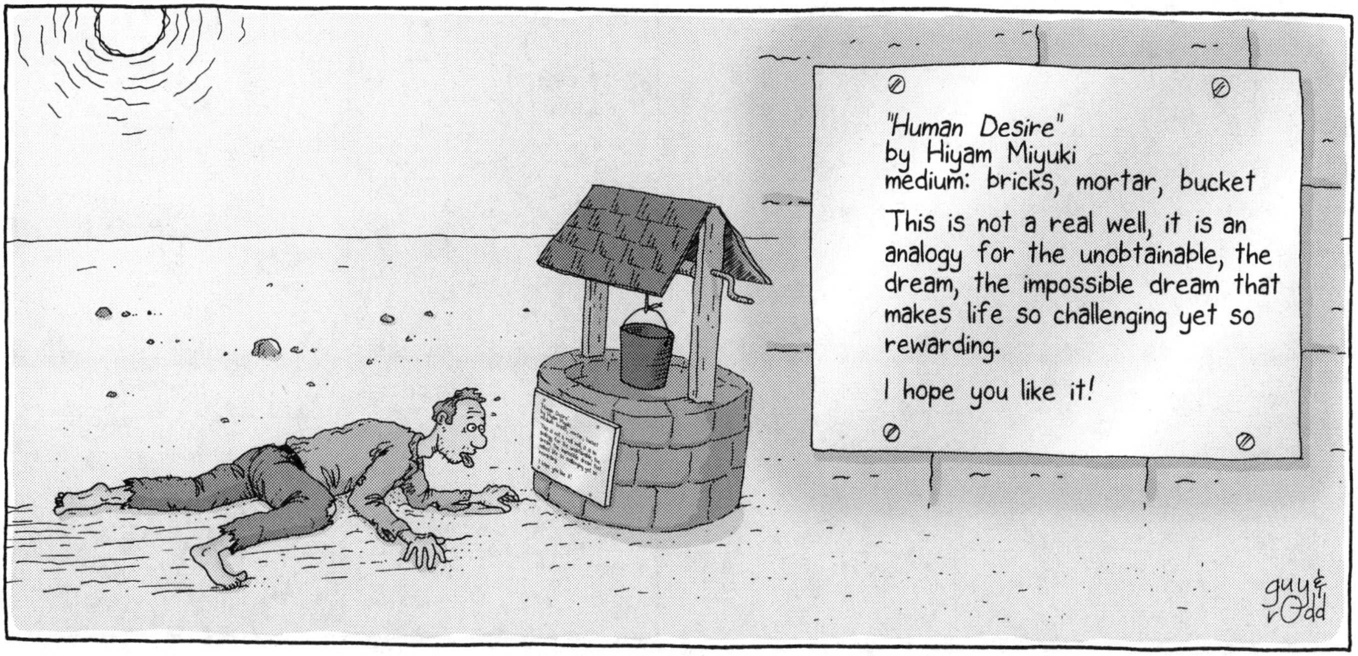
"Human Desire"
by Hiyam Miyuki
medium: bricks, mortar, bucket
This is not a real well, it is an analogy for the unobtainable, the dream, the impossible dream that makes life so challenging yet so rewarding.
I hope you like it!

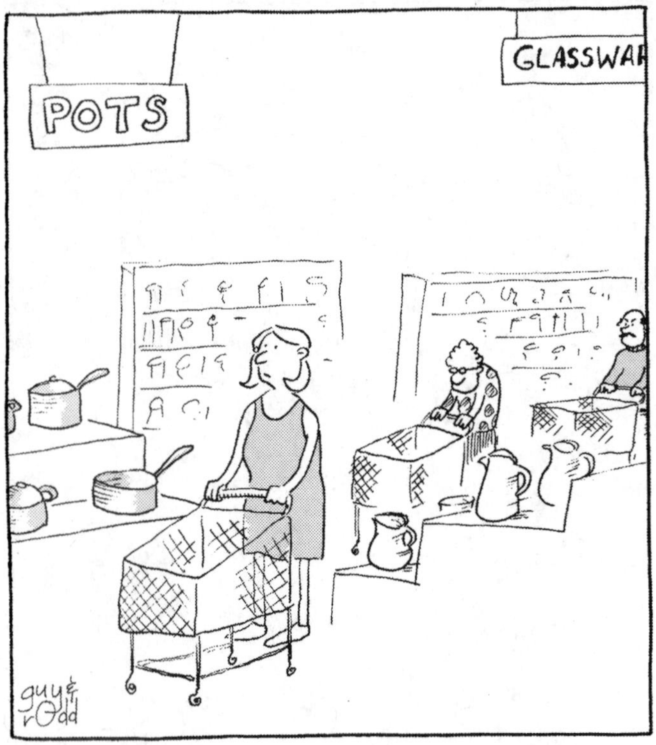
GLASSWAR
POTS

DYSLEXICS ARE THE LEADING CAUSE OF TRAFFIC JAMS AT KITCHEN STORES.

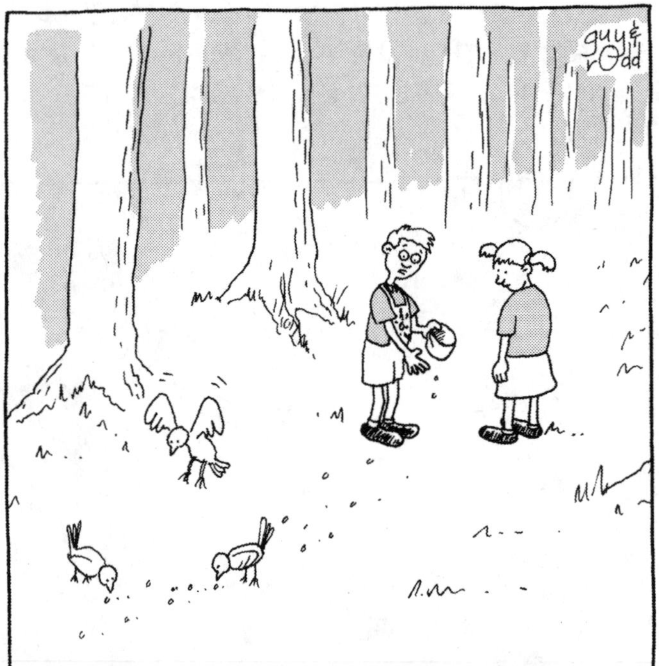

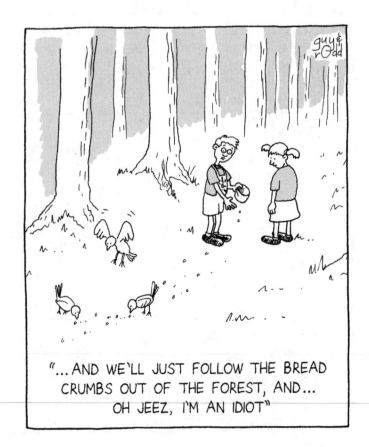

"...AND WE'LL JUST FOLLOW THE BREAD CRUMBS OUT OF THE FOREST, AND... OH JEEZ, I'M AN IDIOT"

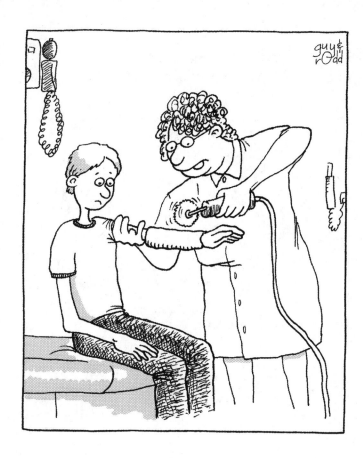

"EXCUSE ME, BUT WHICH AISLE DID YOU FIND THOSE ON?"

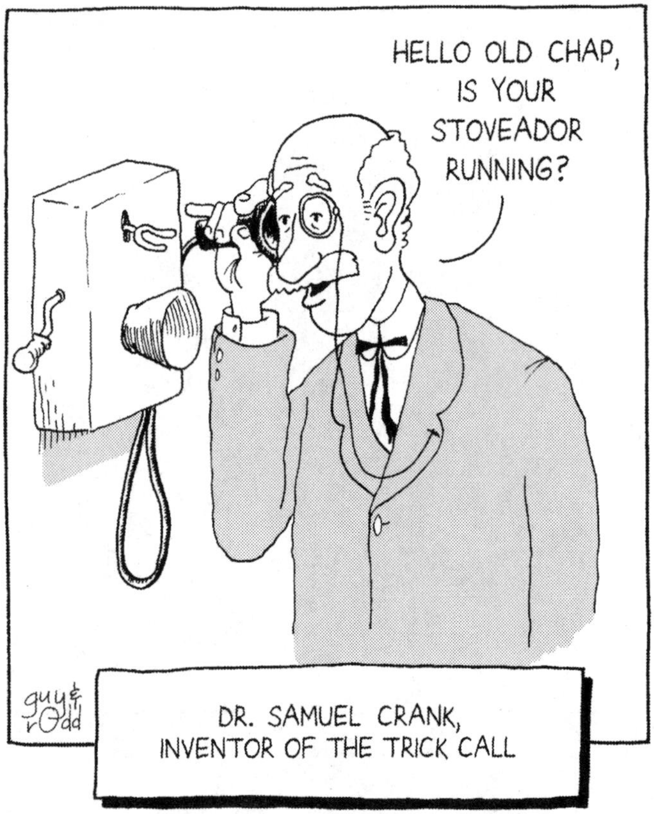
HELLO OLD CHAP, IS YOUR STOVEADOR RUNNING?
DR. SAMUEL CRANK, INVENTOR OF THE TRICK CALL

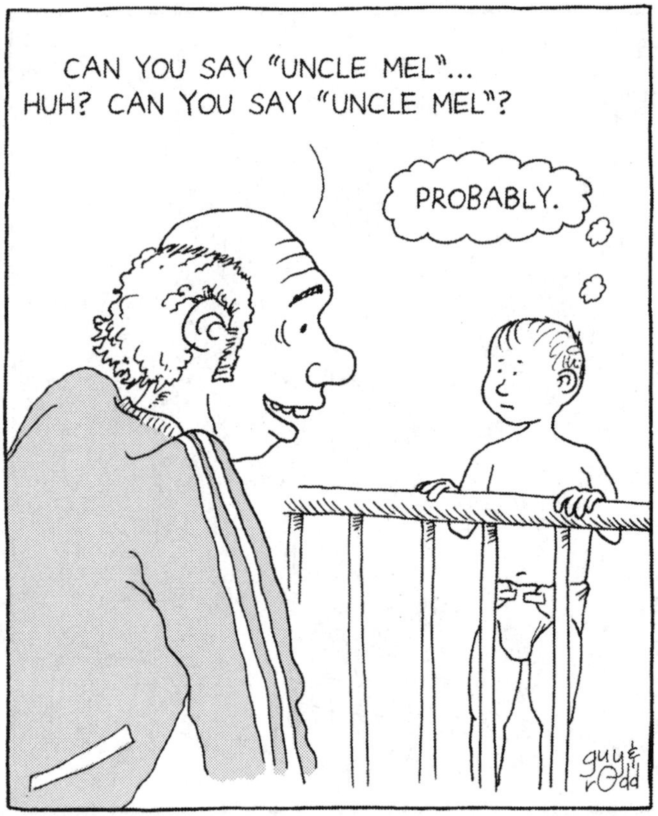
CAN YOU SAY "UNCLE MEL"... HUH? CAN YOU SAY "UNCLE MEL"?
PROBABLY.

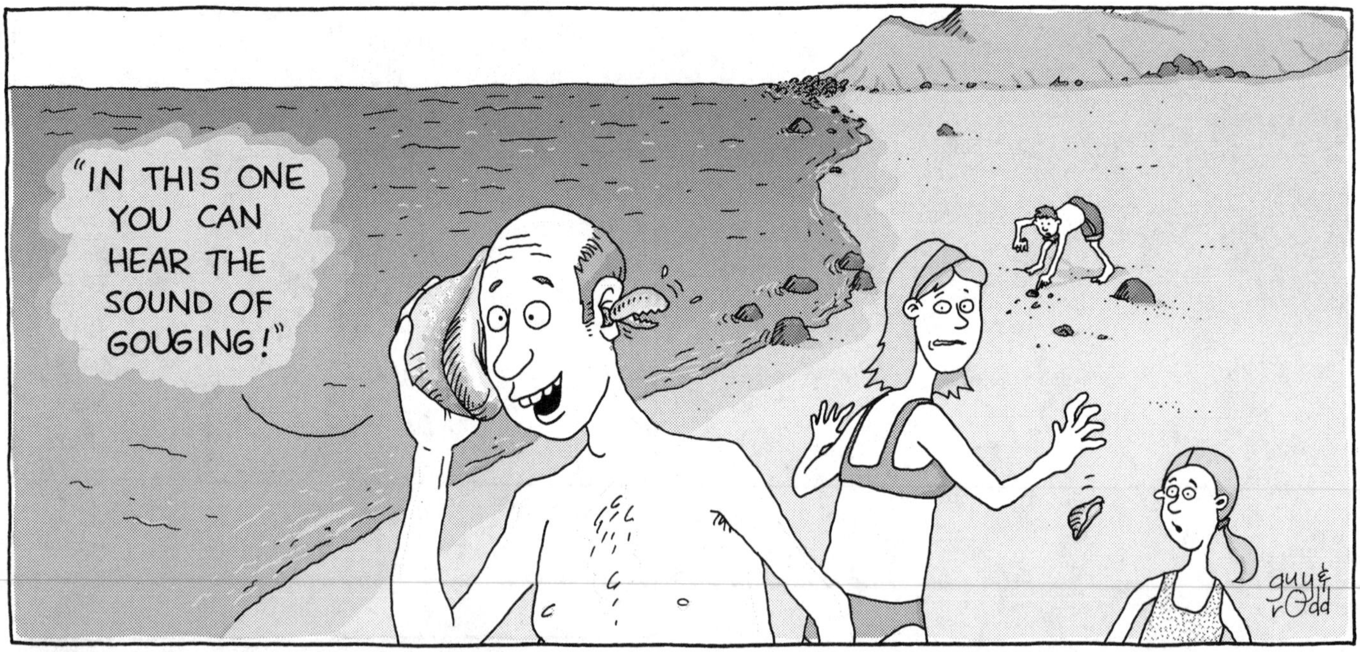
"IN THIS ONE YOU CAN HEAR THE SOUND OF GOUGING!"

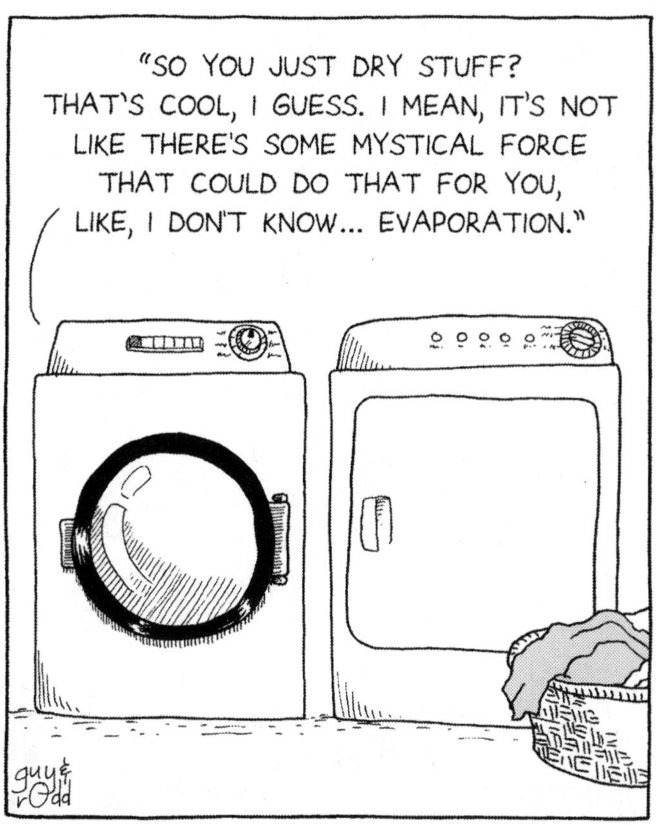
guy & rOdd

"SO YOU JUST DRY STUFF? THAT'S COOL, I GUESS. I MEAN, IT'S NOT LIKE THERE'S SOME MYSTICAL FORCE THAT COULD DO THAT FOR YOU, LIKE, I DON'T KNOW... EVAPORATION."

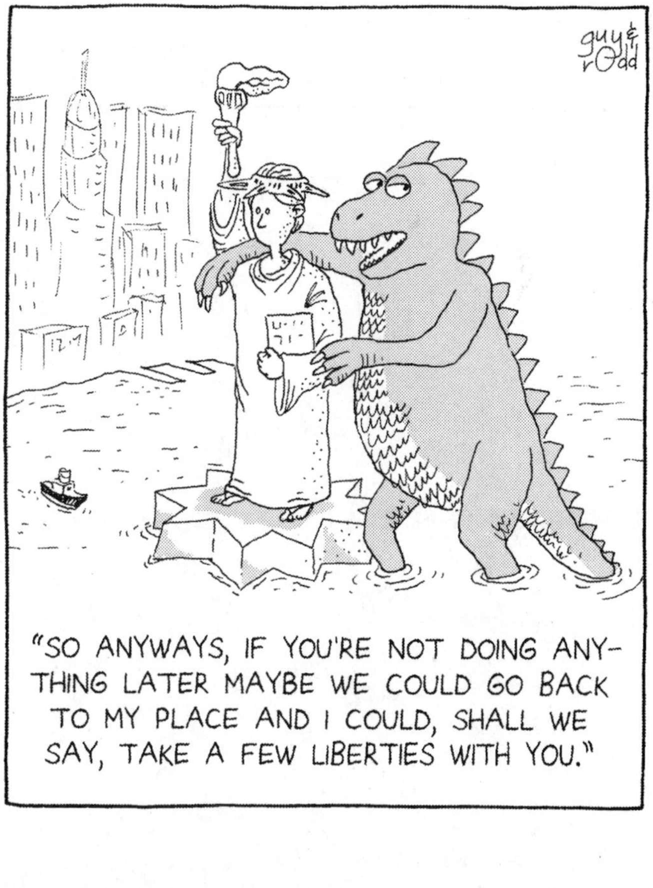
guy & rOdd

"SO ANYWAYS, IF YOU'RE NOT DOING ANYTHING LATER MAYBE WE COULD GO BACK TO MY PLACE AND I COULD, SHALL WE SAY, TAKE A FEW LIBERTIES WITH YOU."

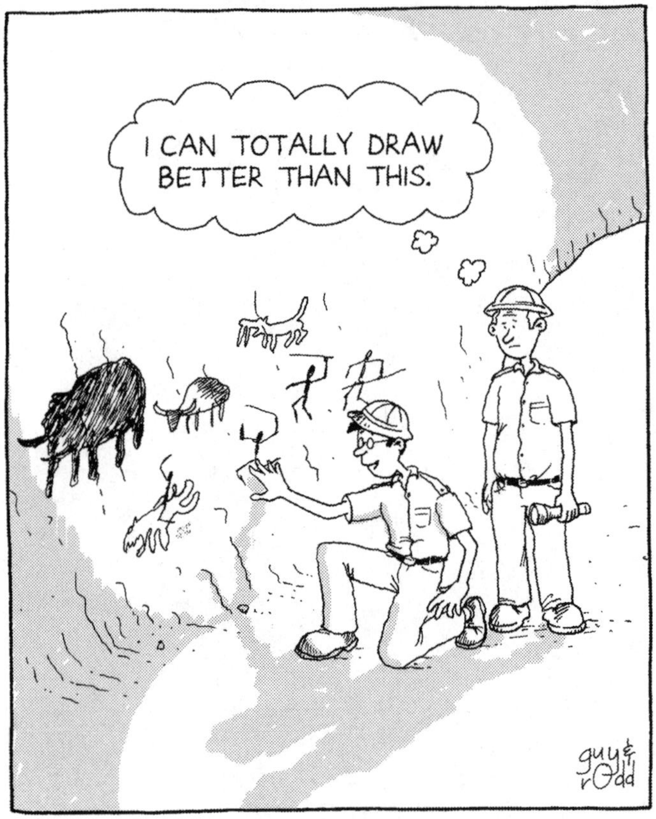
I CAN TOTALLY DRAW BETTER THAN THIS.
guy & rodd

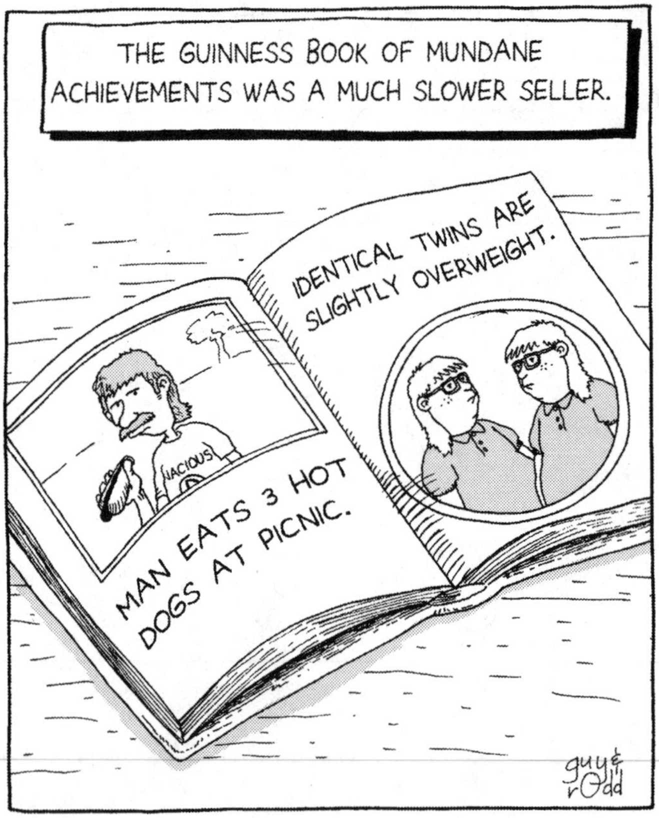
THE GUINNESS BOOK OF MUNDANE ACHIEVEMENTS WAS A MUCH SLOWER SELLER.
IDENTICAL TWINS ARE SLIGHTLY OVERWEIGHT.
MAN EATS 3 HOT DOGS AT PICNIC.
guy & rodd

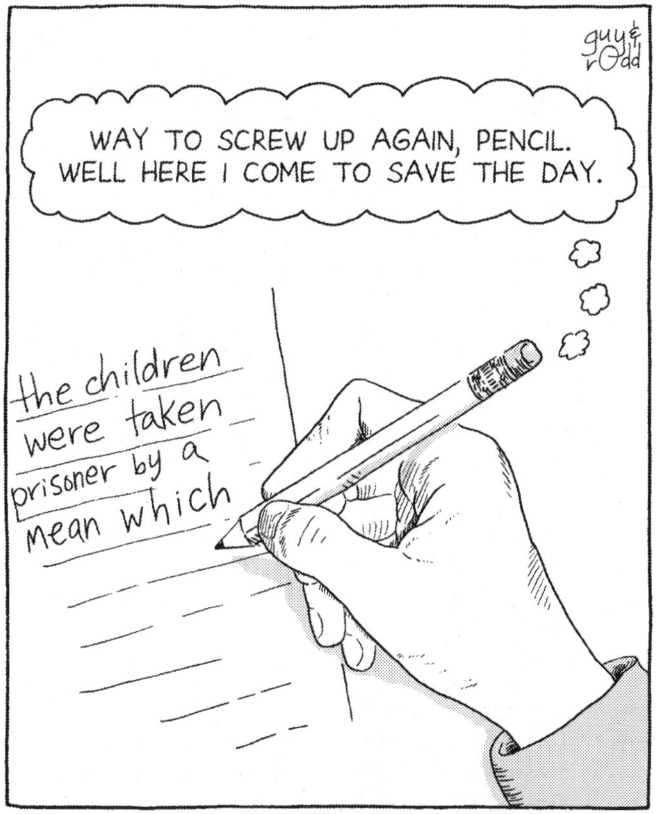
guy & rodd
WAY TO SCREW UP AGAIN, PENCIL. WELL HERE I COME TO SAVE THE DAY.
the children were taken prisoner by a mean which

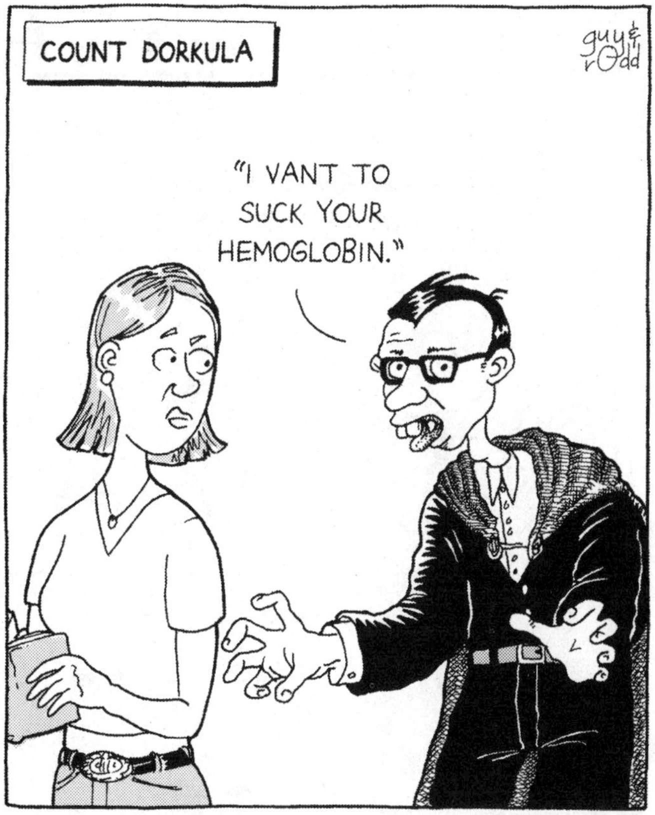
COUNT DORKULA
guy & rodd
"I VANT TO SUCK YOUR HEMOGLOBIN."

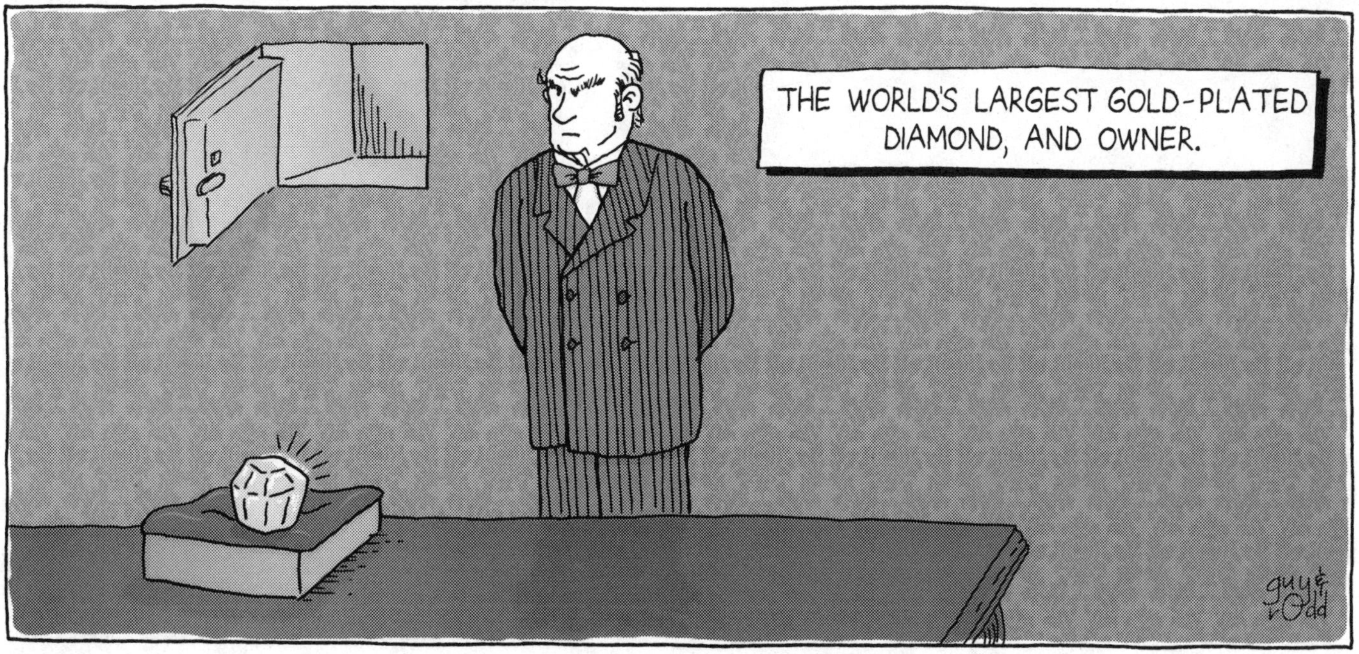
THE WORLD'S LARGEST GOLD-PLATED DIAMOND, AND OWNER.
guy & rodd

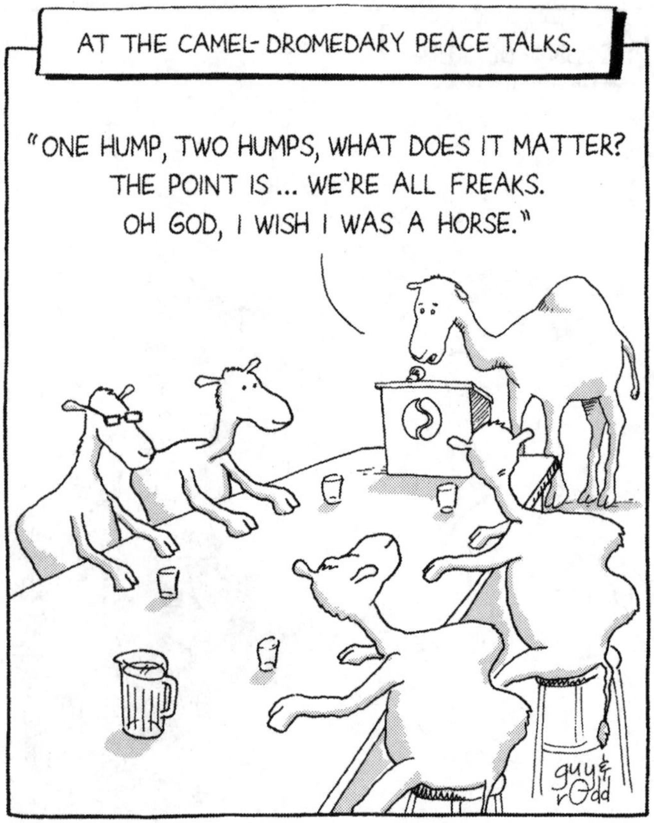
AT THE CAMEL-DROMEDARY PEACE TALKS.
"ONE HUMP, TWO HUMPS, WHAT DOES IT MATTER? THE POINT IS ... WE'RE ALL FREAKS. OH GOD, I WISH I WAS A HORSE."
guy & rodd

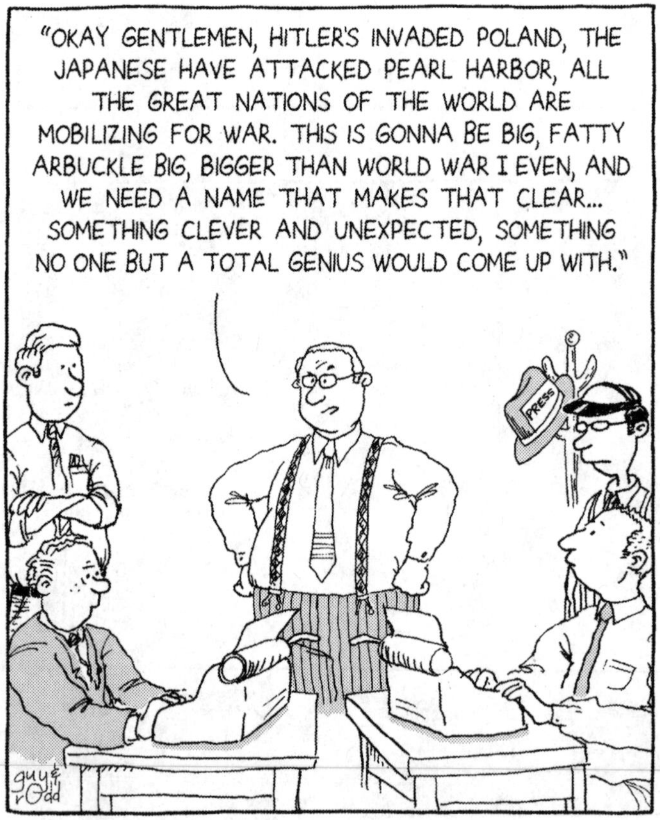
"OKAY GENTLEMEN, HITLER'S INVADED POLAND, THE JAPANESE HAVE ATTACKED PEARL HARBOR, ALL THE GREAT NATIONS OF THE WORLD ARE MOBILIZING FOR WAR. THIS IS GONNA BE BIG, FATTY ARBUCKLE BIG, BIGGER THAN WORLD WAR I EVEN, AND WE NEED A NAME THAT MAKES THAT CLEAR... SOMETHING CLEVER AND UNEXPECTED, SOMETHING NO ONE BUT A TOTAL GENIUS WOULD COME UP WITH."
PRESS
guy & rodd

PUBLICLY, GWEN WOULD PRETEND TO BE THRILLED, BUT THE TRUTH WAS THAT ALL SHE HAD REALLY WANTED TO DO WAS MAKE OUT WITH A TOAD.

AHH, CRUEL FATE. FOR YEARS WILBUR HAD DREAMED OF TASTING AN APPLE, BUT NOT LIKE THIS, NO NEVER LIKE THIS.

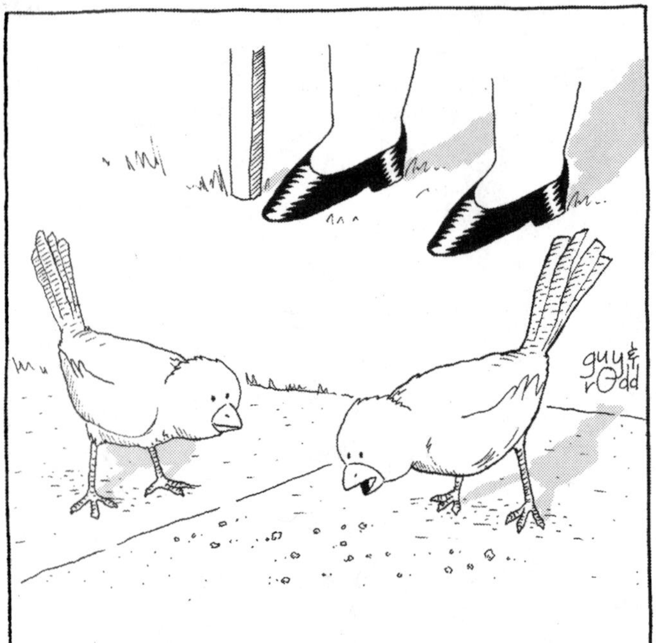

"YOU KNOW, I'M REALLY STARTING TO GET SICK OF CRUMBS. JUST ONCE I'D LIKE A FULL MEAL... WELL THOUGHT OUT, AND CAREFULLY PREPARED."

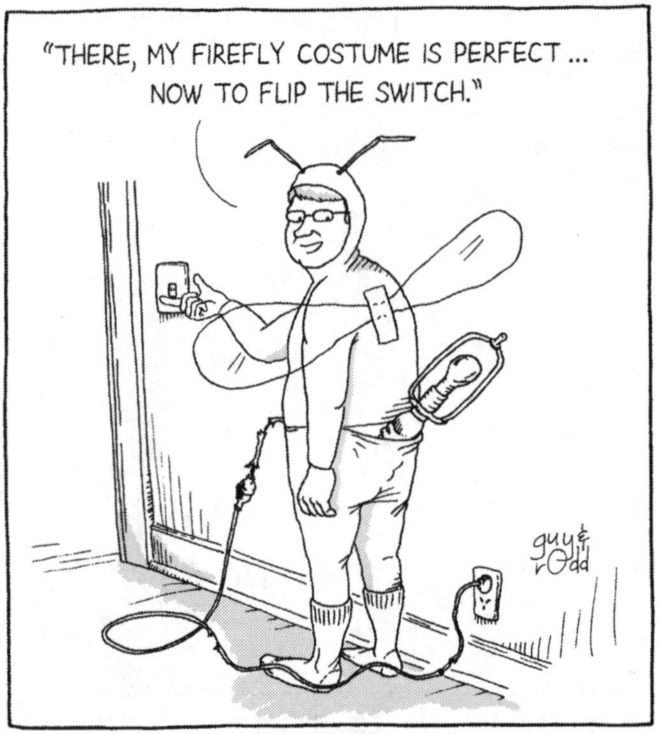
"THERE, MY FIREFLY COSTUME IS PERFECT ... NOW TO FLIP THE SWITCH."

IT WASN'T THE FIRST BAD DECISION RON O'NEAL MADE, BUT IT WOULD BE THE LAST.

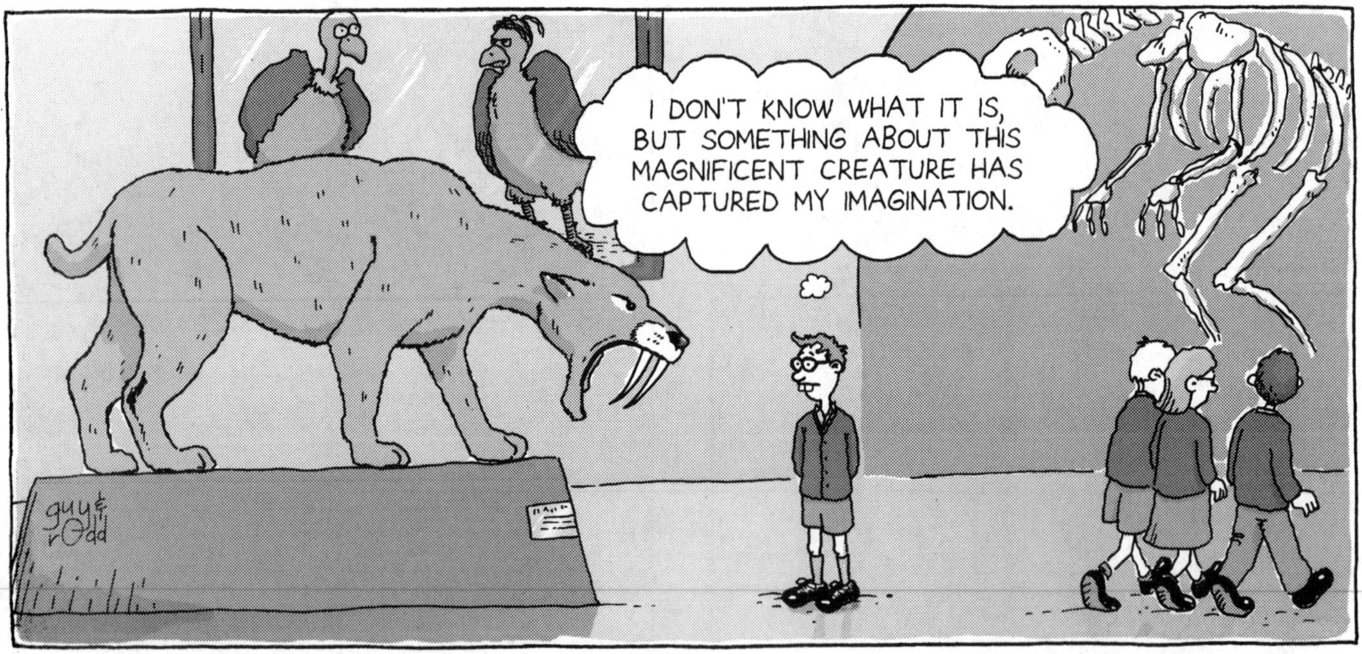
I DON'T KNOW WHAT IT IS, BUT SOMETHING ABOUT THIS MAGNIFICENT CREATURE HAS CAPTURED MY IMAGINATION.

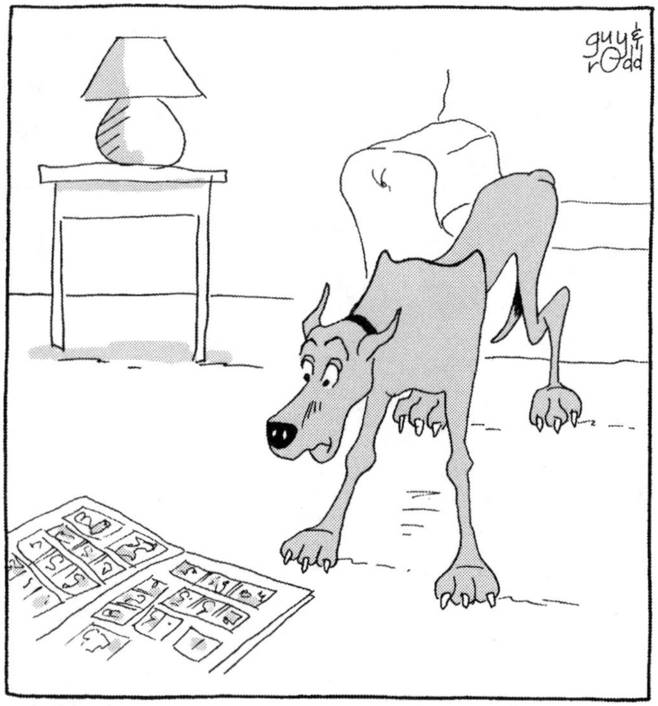
guy & rOdd

SUDDENLY, MARMADUKE DISCOVERED THAT HIS WHOLE LIFE WAS A JOKE... AND NOT A VERY FUNNY ONE EITHER.

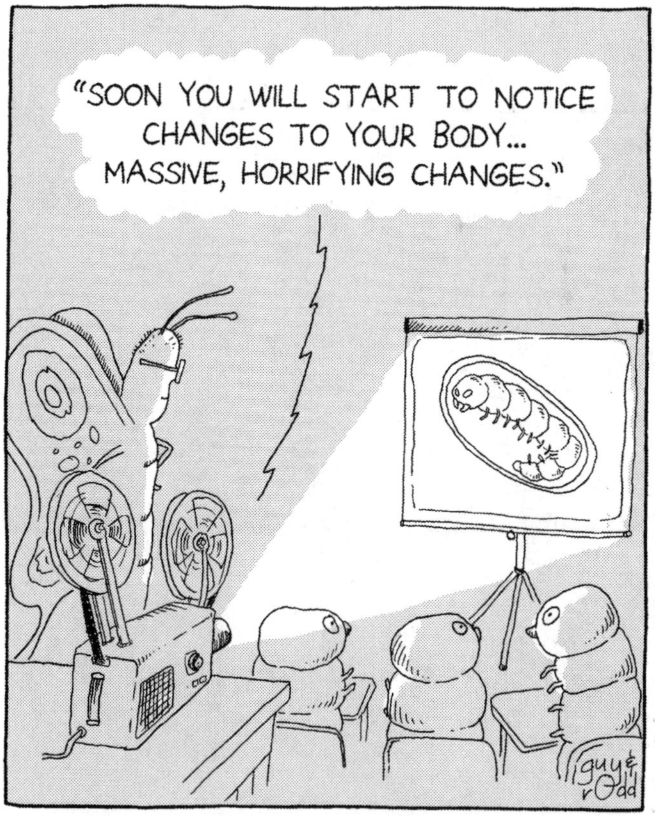
"SOON YOU WILL START TO NOTICE CHANGES TO YOUR BODY... MASSIVE, HORRIFYING CHANGES."
guy & rOdd

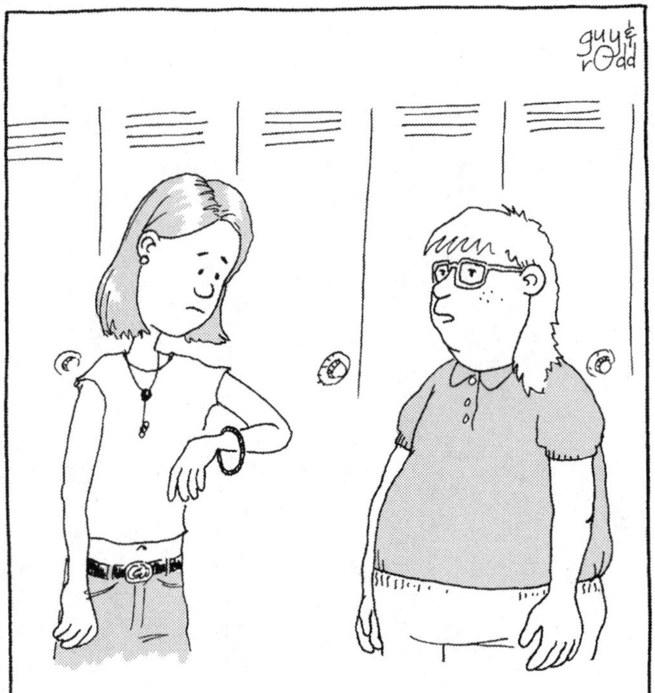

"IT'S A HATRED BRACELET. I MADE IT FOR YOU."

"... AND I WOULD HAVE GOTTEN AWAY WITH IT TOO, IF IT WASN'T FOR THOSE DANG MEDDLING KIDS... THAT AND MY INCREDIBLY STUPID PLAN. ALSO, IN RETROSPECT, I REALIZE MY COSTUME WAS, REGRETTABLY, QUITE LAME."

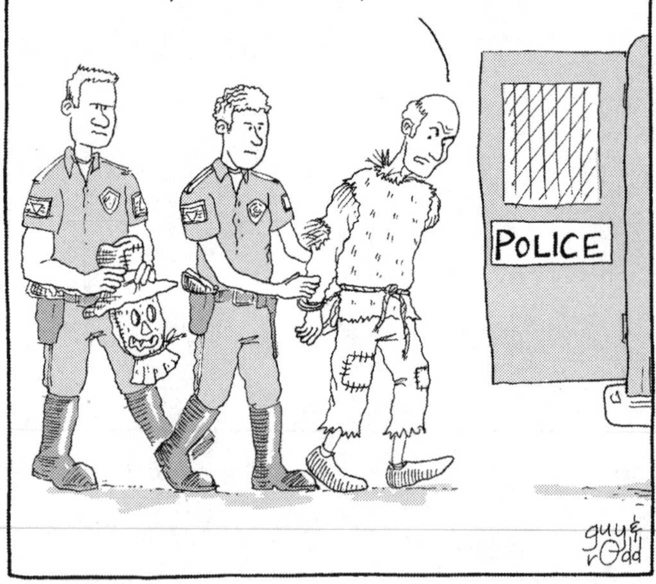
POLICE

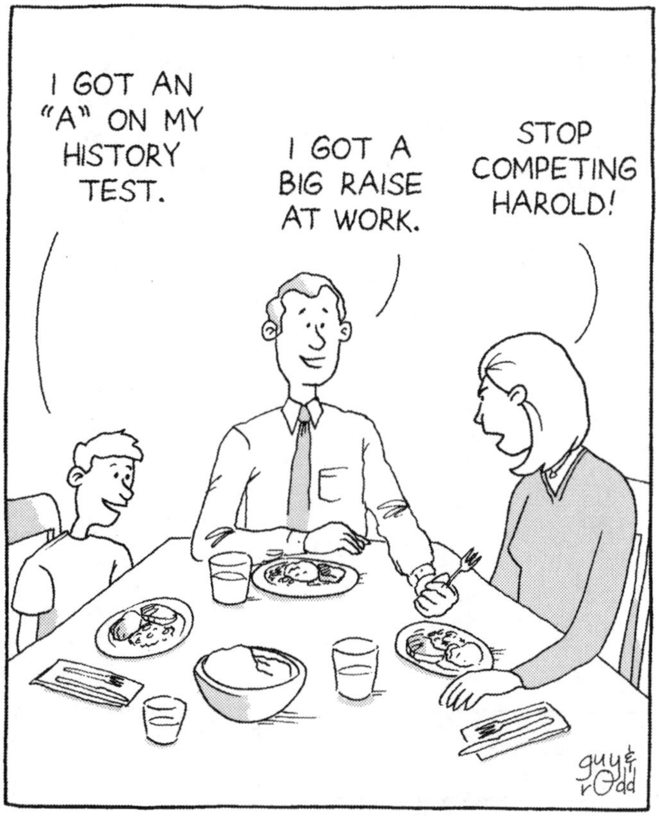
I GOT AN "A" ON MY HISTORY TEST.
I GOT A BIG RAISE AT WORK.
STOP COMPETING HAROLD!
guy & rodd

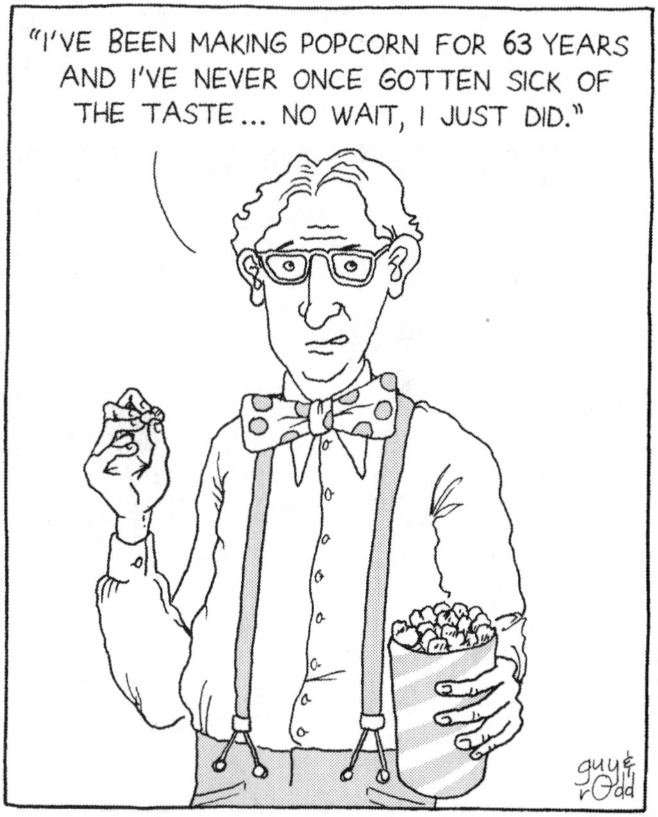
"I'VE BEEN MAKING POPCORN FOR 63 YEARS AND I'VE NEVER ONCE GOTTEN SICK OF THE TASTE... NO WAIT, I JUST DID."
guy & rodd

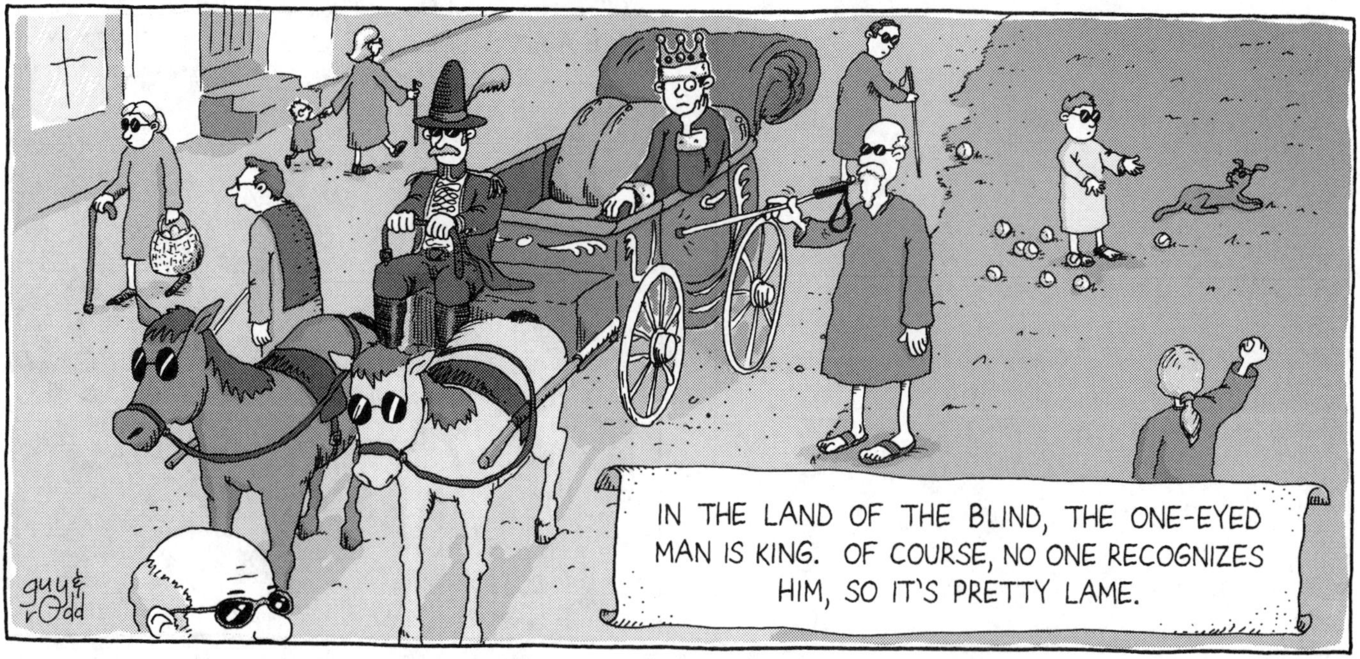
IN THE LAND OF THE BLIND, THE ONE-EYED MAN IS KING. OF COURSE, NO ONE RECOGNIZES HIM, SO IT'S PRETTY LAME.
guy & rodd

SHORTLY AFTER DISCOVERING THAT SOME OF THE LOWER PRIMATES ALSO USED TOOLS, AN EXPLORER IN ZAMBEZI DISCOVERED THEIR PATENT OFFICE.
PAtents
Patent no. 8
sorta use a rock to bang on a nut or something.
guy & rodd

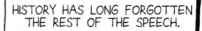

HISTORY HAS LONG FORGOTTEN THE REST OF THE SPEECH.
"GIVE ME LIBERTY OR GIVE ME DEATH... OR CHICKS, YOUNG CHICKS WHO KNOW HOW TO HAVE A GOOD TIME. OR GADGETS, OR, LIKE, MONEY. OR A REALLY NICE COAT, BLUE MAYBE ..."
guy & rodd

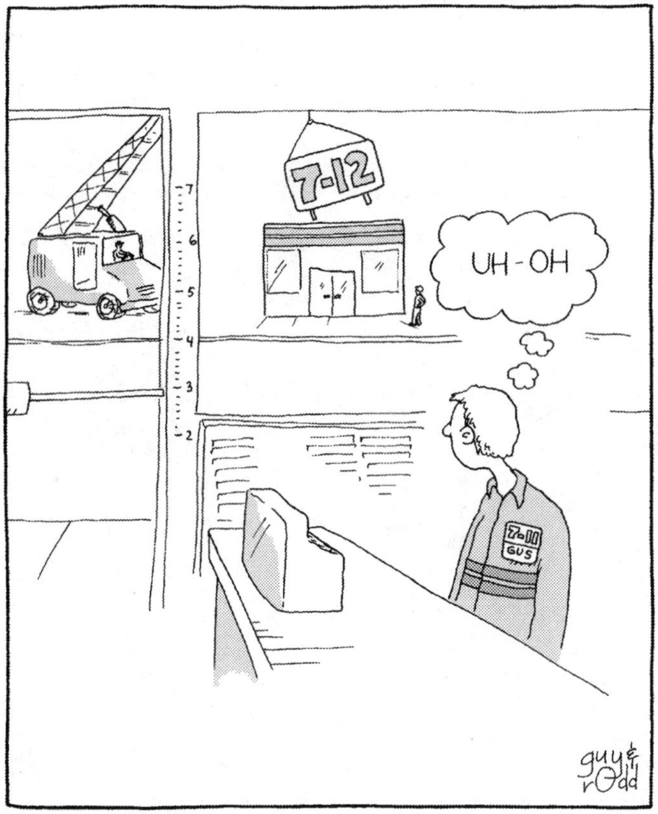
7-12
UH-OH
7-11
GUS
guy & rodd

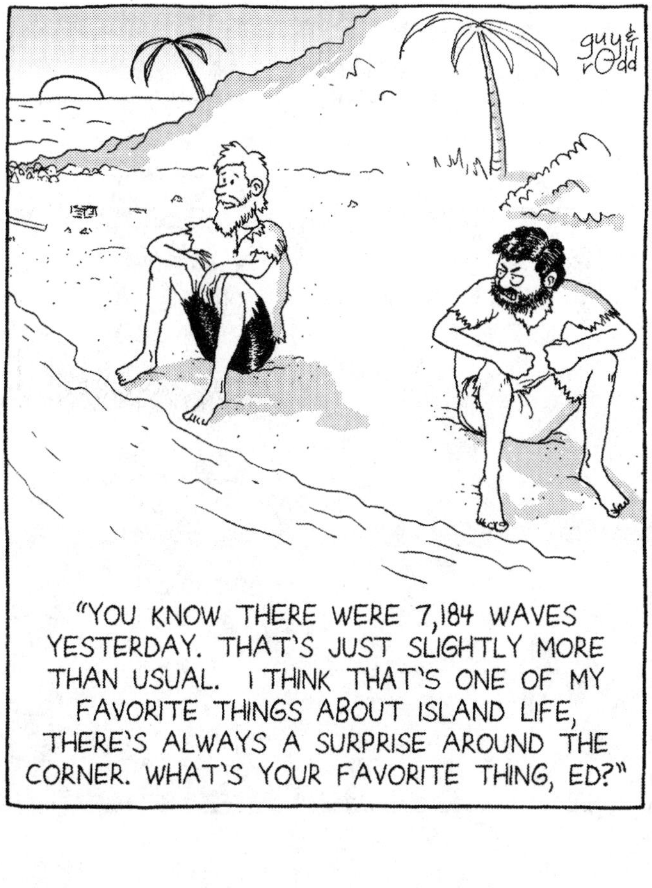
guy & rodd

"YOU KNOW THERE WERE 7,184 WAVES YESTERDAY. THAT'S JUST SLIGHTLY MORE THAN USUAL. I THINK THAT'S ONE OF MY FAVORITE THINGS ABOUT ISLAND LIFE, THERE'S ALWAYS A SURPRISE AROUND THE CORNER. WHAT'S YOUR FAVORITE THING, ED?"

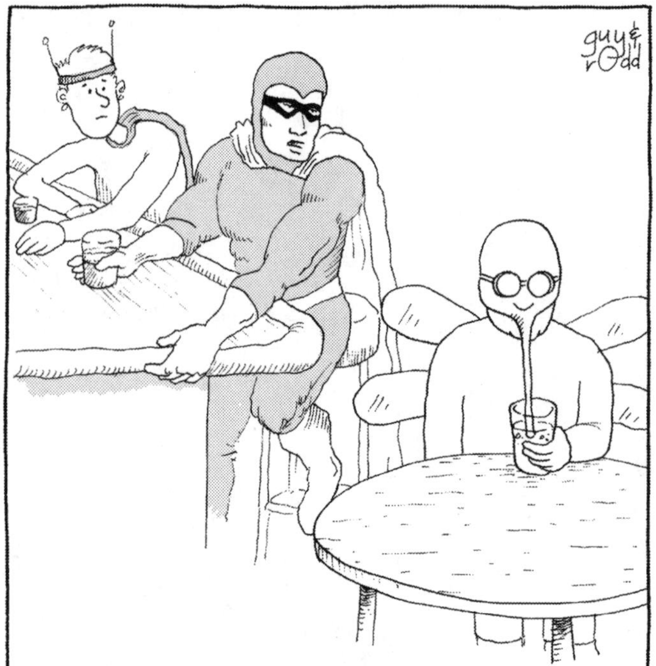

"OH HIM, THAT'S MOSQUITO MAN ... HE'S ANNOYING ALRIGHT, BUT PRETTY HARMLESS AS FAR AS SUPER VILLAINS GO."

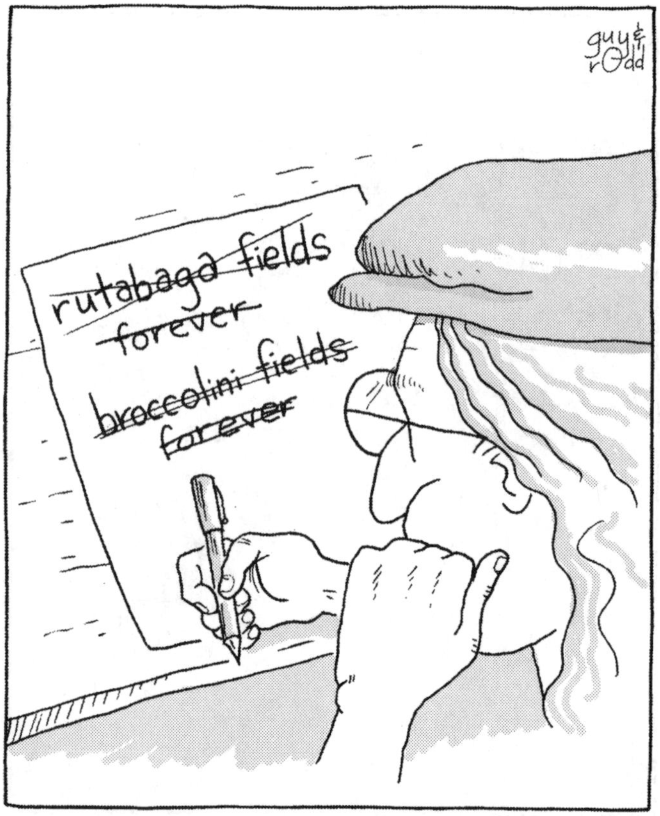
rutabaga fields
forever
broccolini fields
forever

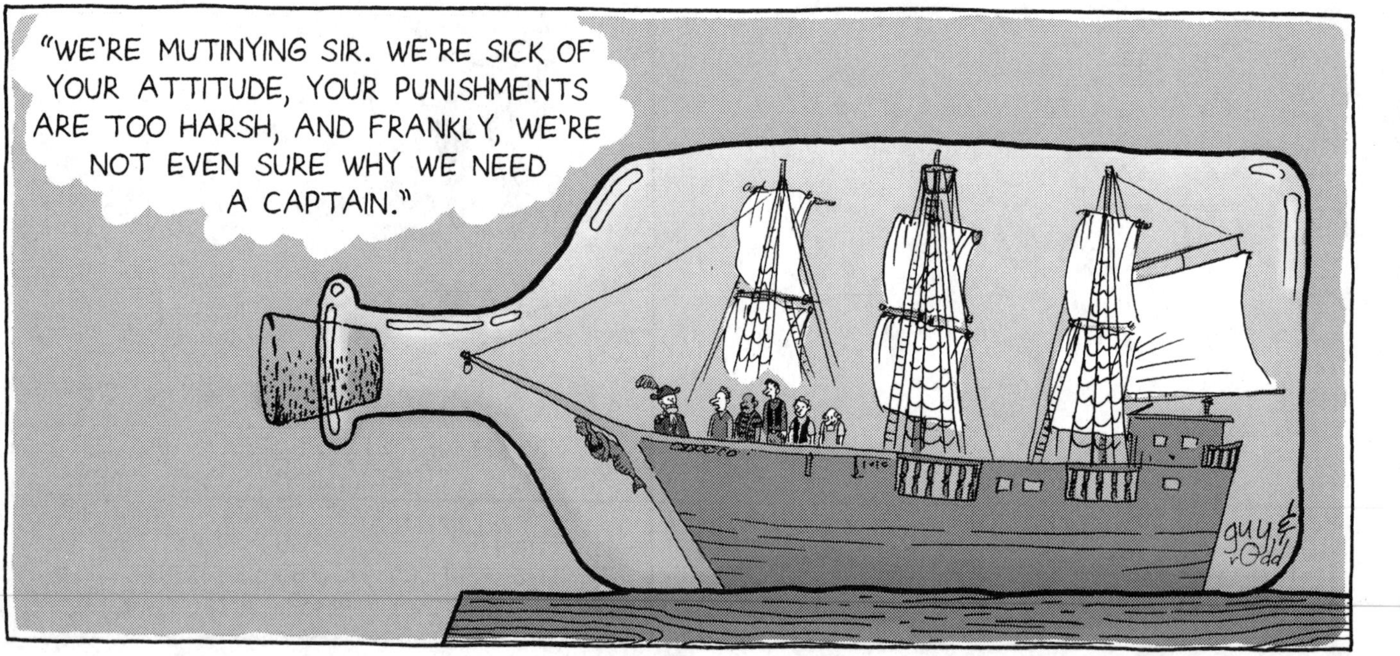
"WE'RE MUTINYING SIR. WE'RE SICK OF YOUR ATTITUDE, YOUR PUNISHMENTS ARE TOO HARSH, AND FRANKLY, WE'RE NOT EVEN SURE WHY WE NEED A CAPTAIN."

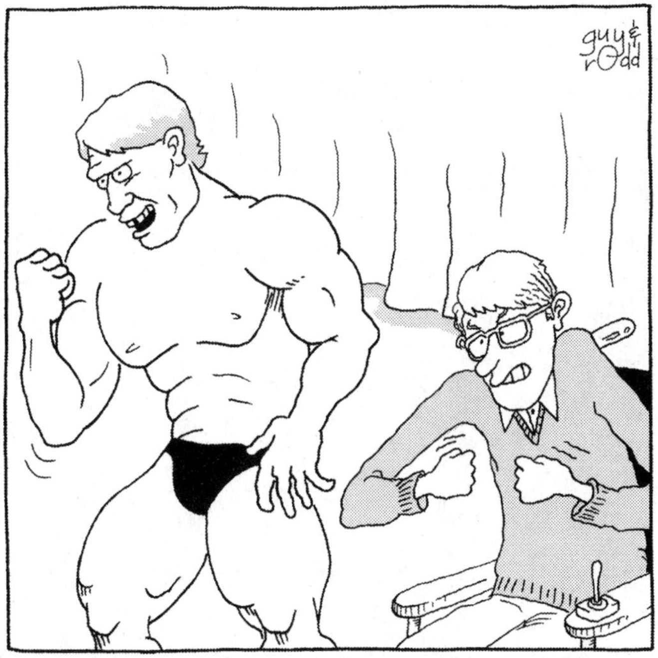
guy & rOdd

IN 1970, HAVING ASSUMED IT WAS A SCIENCE COMPETITION, STEPHEN HAWKING WAS DEVASTATED WHEN HE LOST THE TITLE OF "MR. UNIVERSE" TO A COMPLETE IDIOT.

"HEY, DO WE EVEN NEED THESE TUNNELS? WHAT IF WE'RE JUST DOING THIS TO AMUSE THESE PEOPLE?"

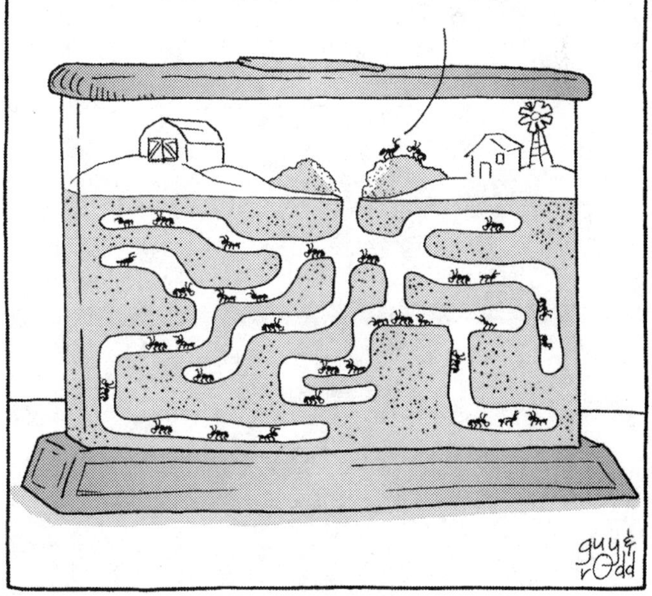
guy & rOdd

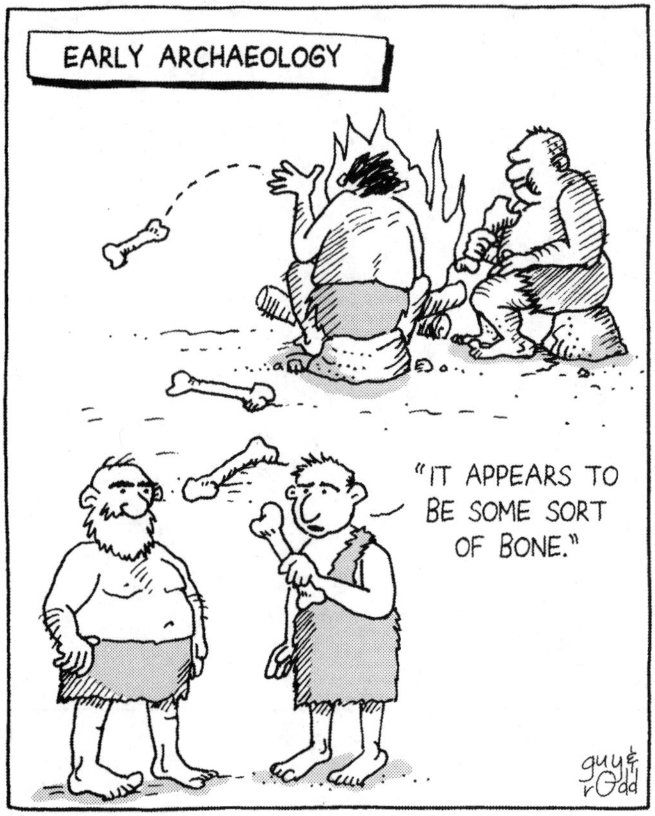
EARLY ARCHAEOLOGY
"IT APPEARS TO BE SOME SORT OF BONE."
guy & rodd

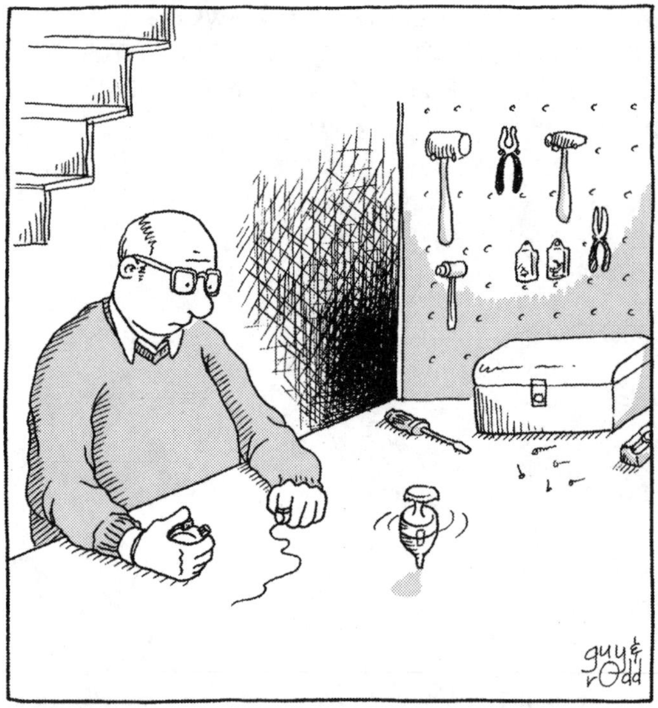
guy & rodd

FOR YEARS HE HAD SPENT EVERY FREE MOMENT WORKING ON HIS PERPETUAL MOTION MACHINE. SO FAR, HE WAS UP TO 18 SECONDS.

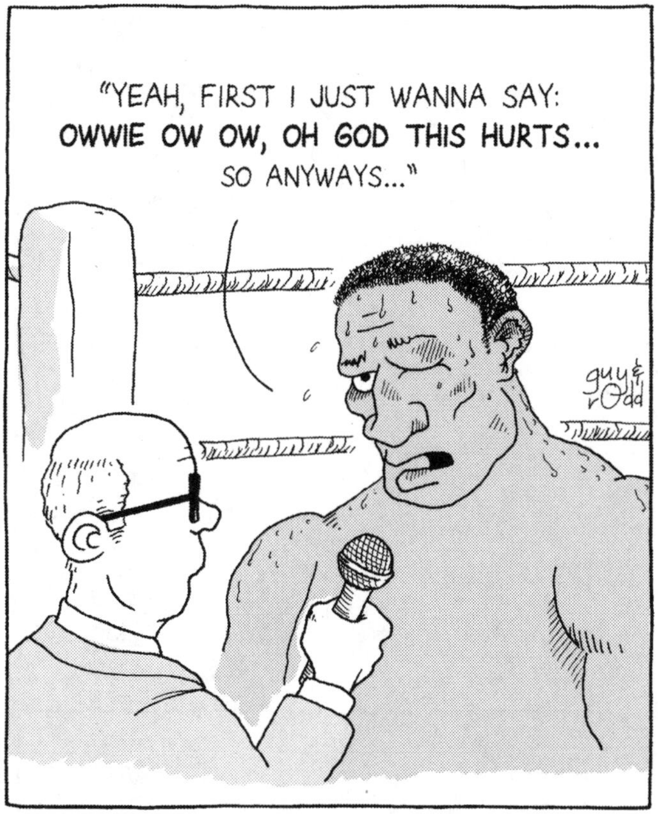

"YEAH, FIRST I JUST WANNA SAY:
OWWIE OW OW, OH GOD THIS HURTS...
SO ANYWAYS..."

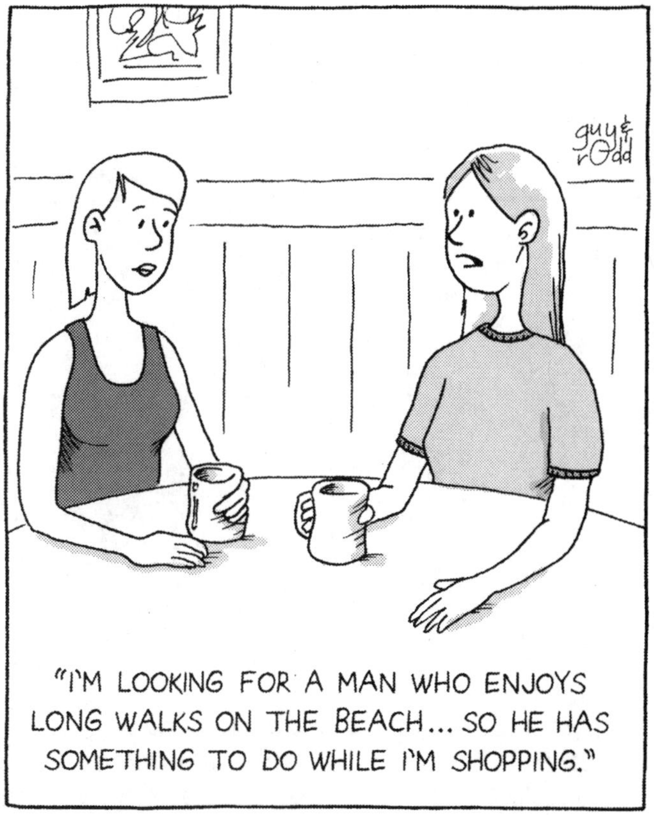

"I'M LOOKING FOR A MAN WHO ENJOYS LONG WALKS ON THE BEACH... SO HE HAS SOMETHING TO DO WHILE I'M SHOPPING."

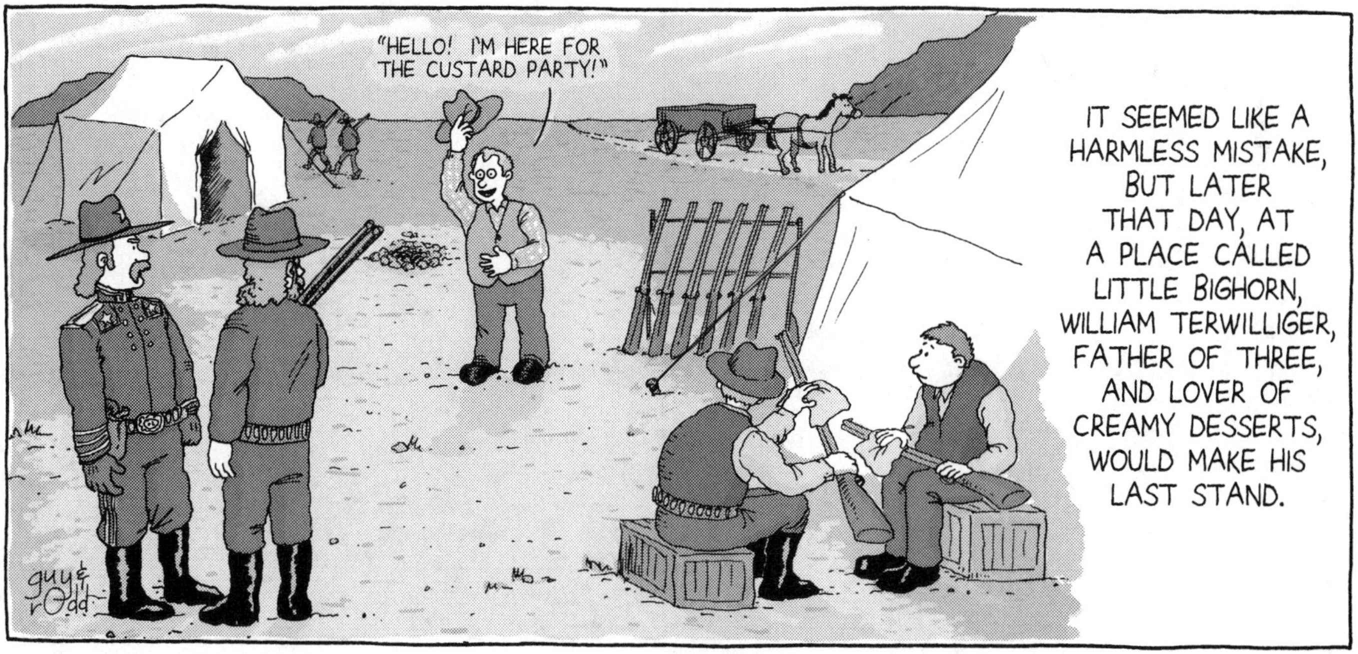
"HELLO! I'M HERE FOR THE CUSTARD PARTY!"

IT SEEMED LIKE A HARMLESS MISTAKE, BUT LATER THAT DAY, AT A PLACE CALLED LITTLE BIGHORN, WILLIAM TERWILLIGER, FATHER OF THREE, AND LOVER OF CREAMY DESSERTS, WOULD MAKE HIS LAST STAND.

"OKAY, YOU'RE STRANDED ON A DESERT ISLAND AND YOU CAN ONLY HAVE 5 MOVIES..."
guy & rOdd

LATER THAT NIGHT, TIM CREPT INTO ANDY'S CAVE AND COCONUTTED HIM TO DEATH.

"DID YOU EVER WONDER IF WHAT WE'RE DOING IS ANNOYING?"
guy & rOdd

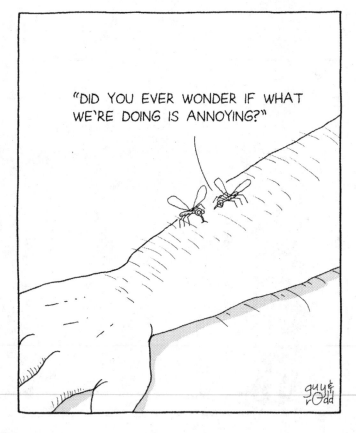

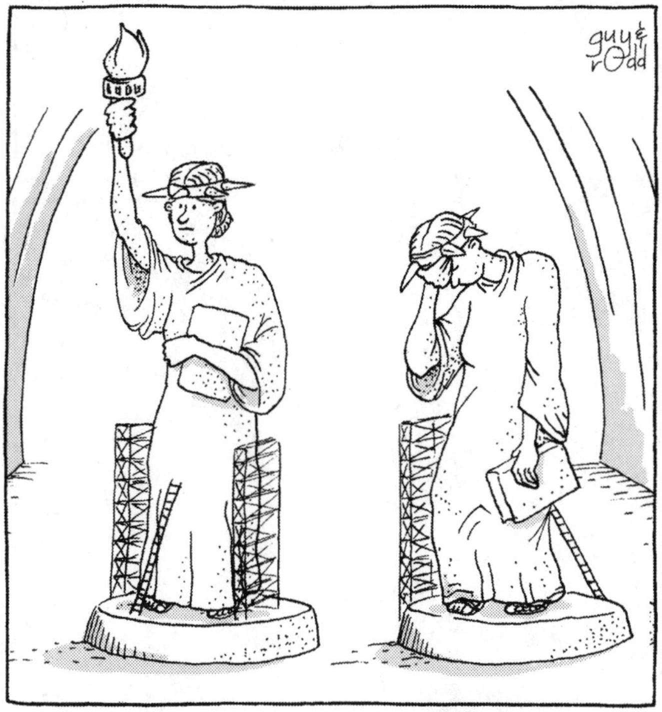
guy & rOdd

IN CASE THINGS HAD TURNED OUT DIFFERENTLY, THE FRENCH WERE READY WITH AN EQUALLY SPECTACULAR STATUE OF SHAME.

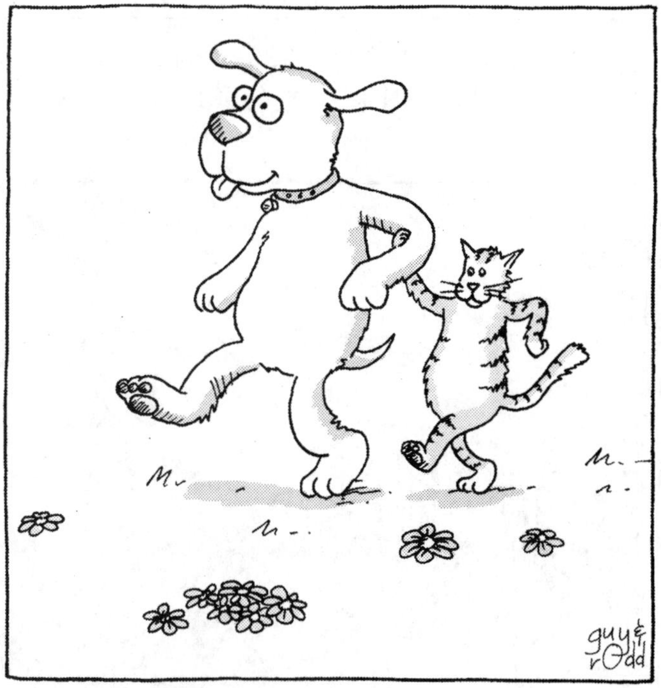
guy & rOdd

MOST PEOPLE DON'T KNOW THAT CATS AND DOGS USED TO BE BEST FRIENDS UNTIL SOME THOUGHTLESS CARTOONIST BEGAN STIRRING UP TROUBLE IN SEARCH OF EASY GAGS.

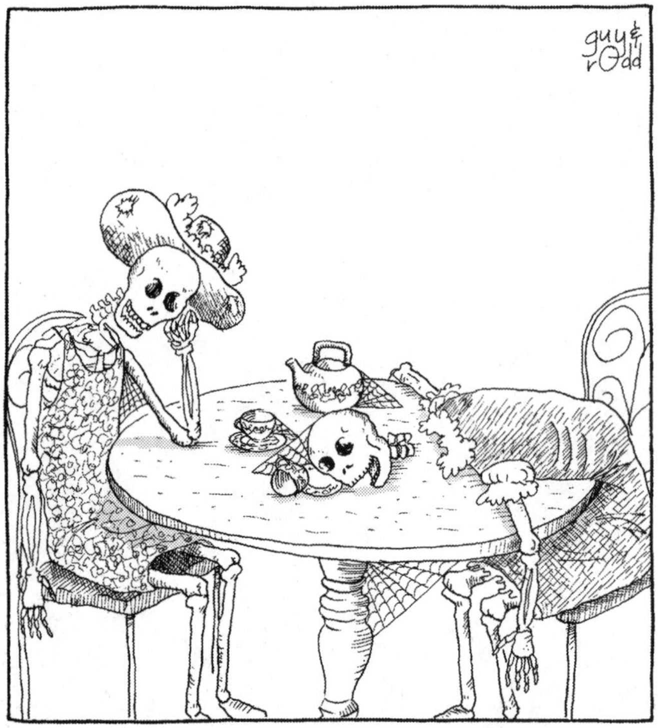

"AFTER YOU", SAID MISS MANNERS.
"OH, YOU FIRST" INSISTED MRS. ETIQUETTE.

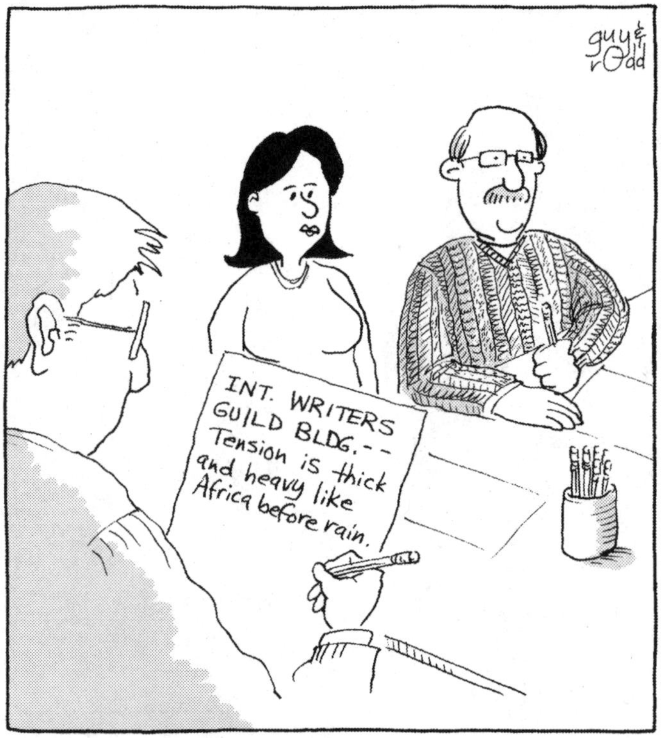
INT. WRITERS GUILD BLDG.-- Tension is thick and heavy like Africa before rain.

IN THE SCREENWRITERS GUILD, SECRETARY IS THE MOST COVETED POSITION.

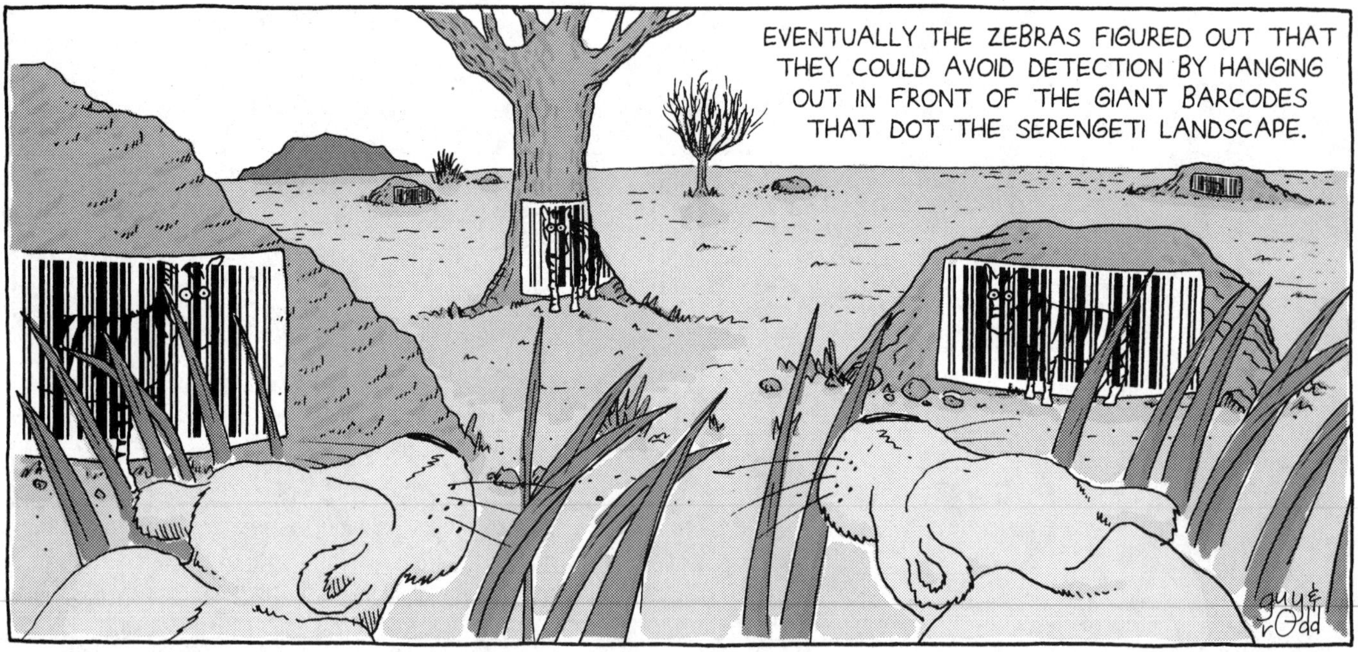

EVENTUALLY THE ZEBRAS FIGURED OUT THAT THEY COULD AVOID DETECTION BY HANGING OUT IN FRONT OF THE GIANT BARCODES THAT DOT THE SERENGETI LANDSCAPE.

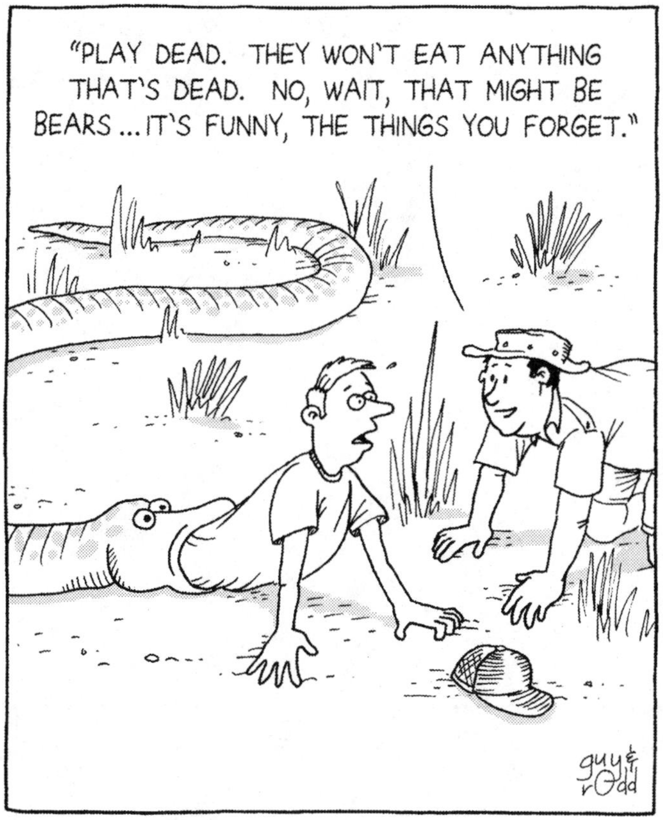
"PLAY DEAD. THEY WON'T EAT ANYTHING THAT'S DEAD. NO, WAIT, THAT MIGHT BE BEARS ... IT'S FUNNY, THE THINGS YOU FORGET."

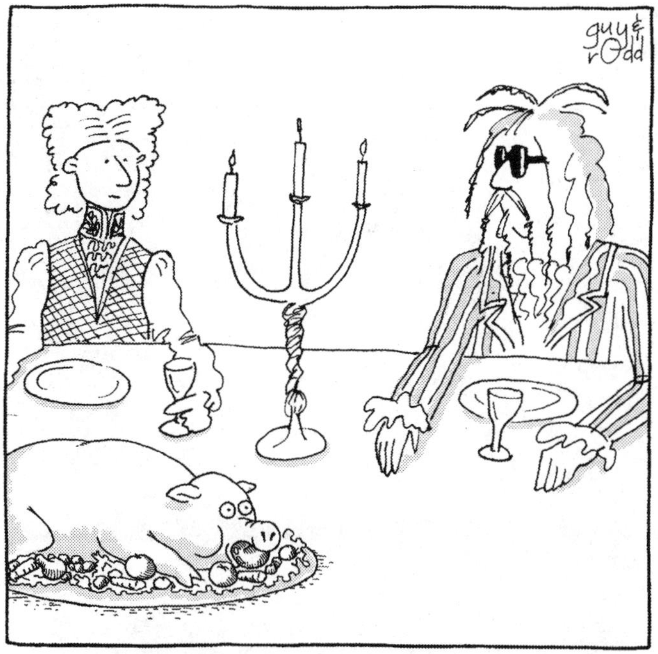

FOR YEARS HE HAD ENJOYED THE GOOD LIFE AT THE ROYAL COURT, UNTIL ONE DAY, PRINCE FREDERICK OF NORWAY POINTED OUT THAT THERE WAS, IN FACT, NO SUCH TITLE AS THE GRAND DUKE OF FUNKADELIA.

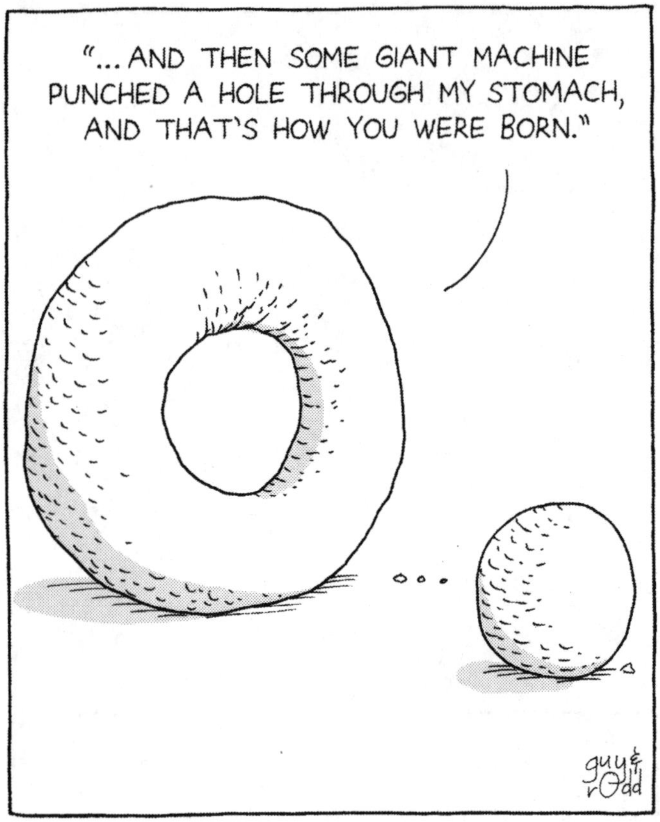
"... AND THEN SOME GIANT MACHINE PUNCHED A HOLE THROUGH MY STOMACH, AND THAT'S HOW YOU WERE BORN."
guy & rOdd

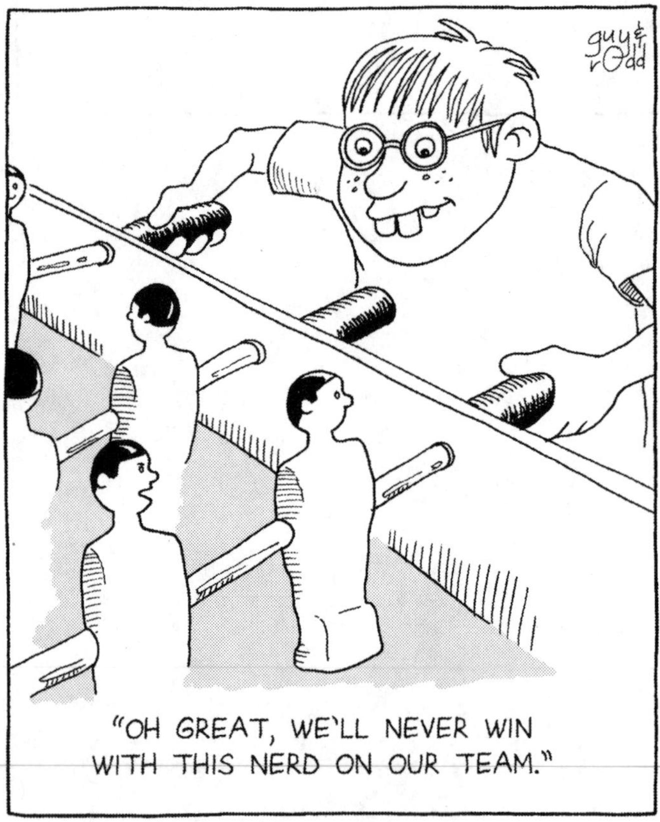
guy & rOdd
"OH GREAT, WE'LL NEVER WIN WITH THIS NERD ON OUR TEAM."

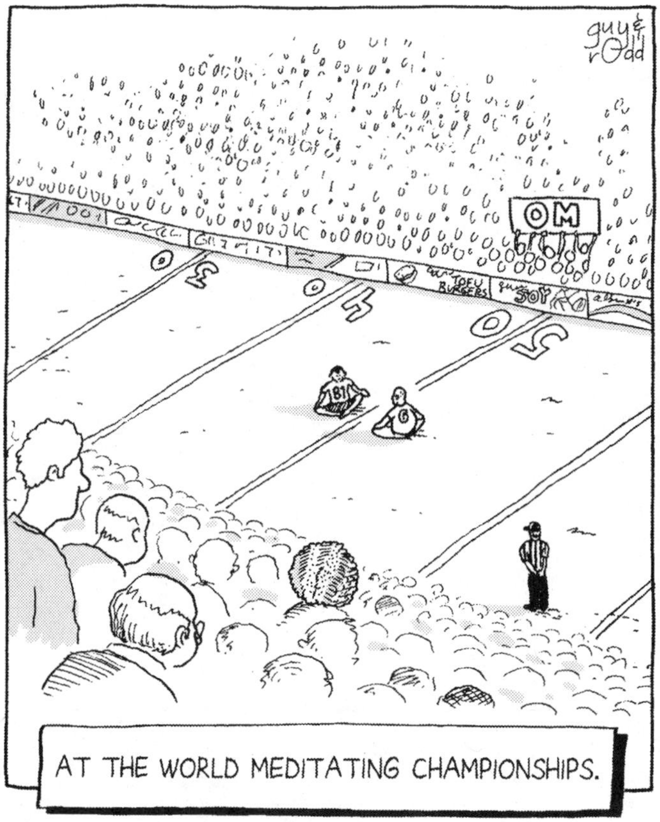
guy & rOdd
OM
TOFU BURGERS
SOY
AT THE WORLD MEDITATING CHAMPIONSHIPS.

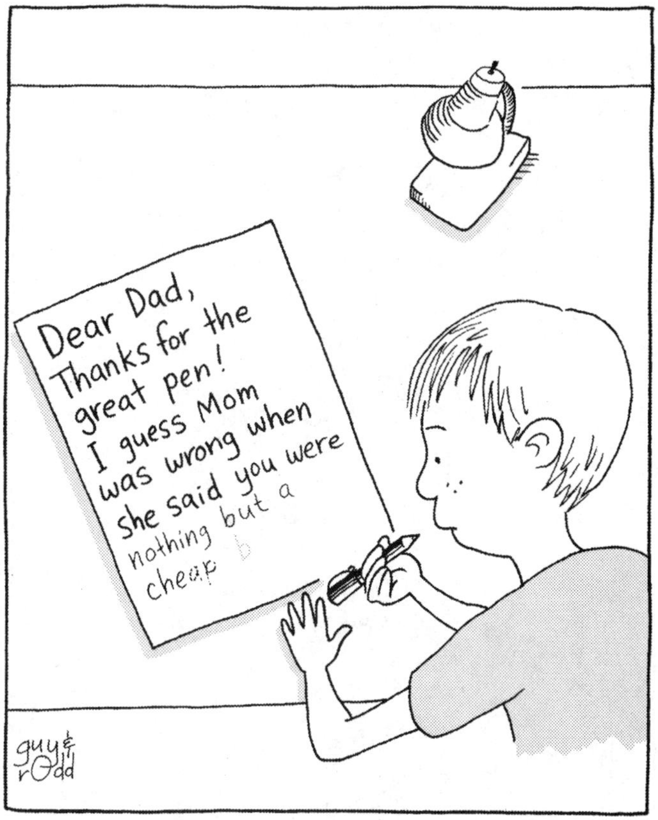
Dear Dad,
Thanks for the great pen!
I guess Mom was wrong when she said you were nothing but a cheap b
guy & rOdd

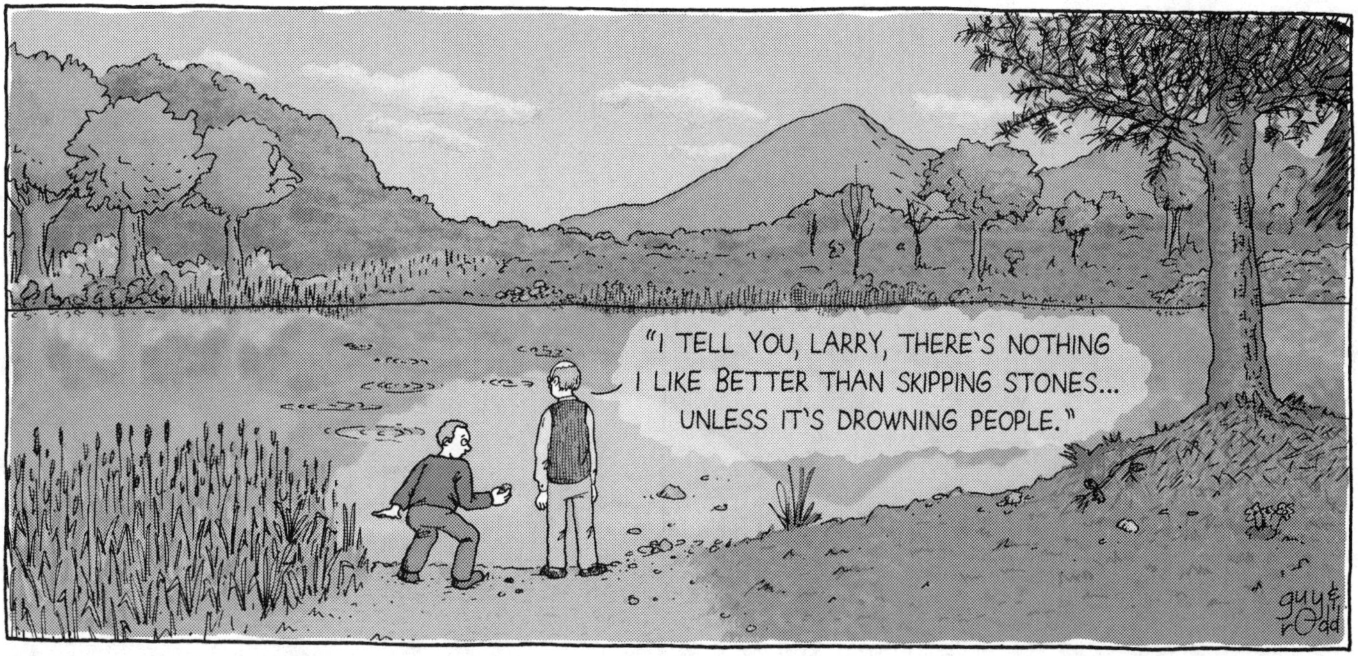
"I TELL YOU, LARRY, THERE'S NOTHING I LIKE BETTER THAN SKIPPING STONES... UNLESS IT'S DROWNING PEOPLE."
guy & rOdd

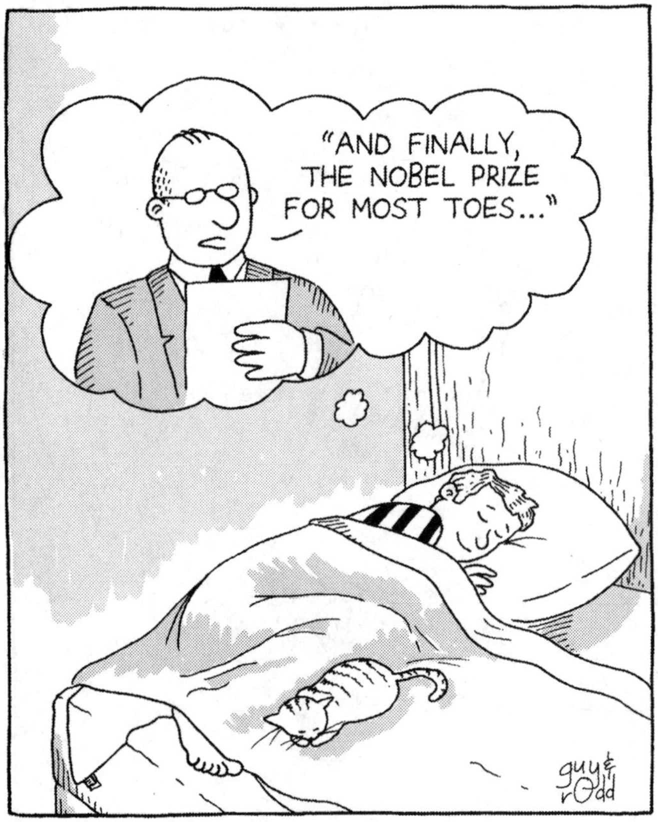
"AND FINALLY, THE NOBEL PRIZE FOR MOST TOES..."
guy & rOdd

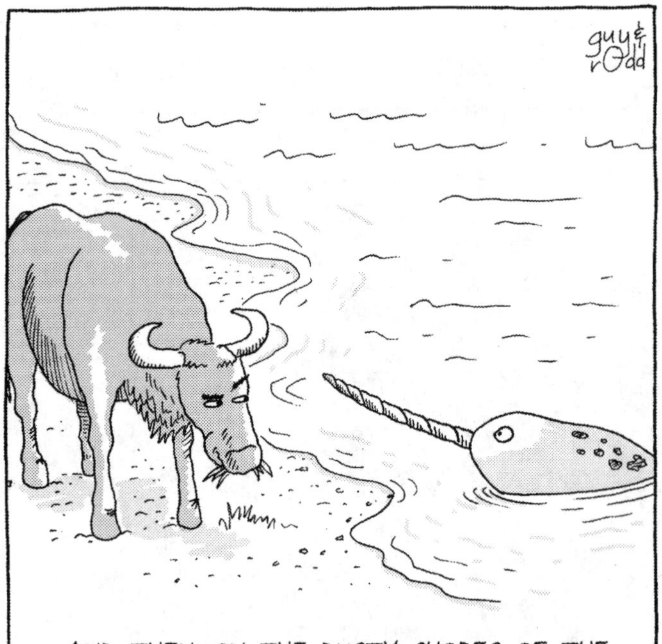
guy & rOdd

AND THEN, ON THE DUSTY SHORES OF THE GITCHE GUMEE, THE AGE OLD QUESTION OF WHO WOULD WIN A FIGHT BETWEEN A NARWHAL AND A WILDEBEEST WAS FINALLY ANSWERED.

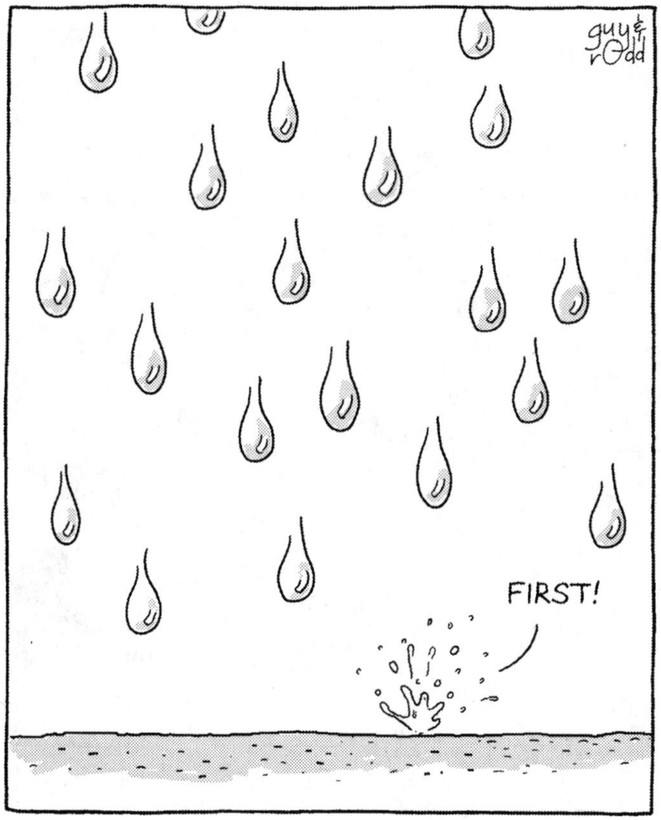
guy&
rOdd
FIRST!

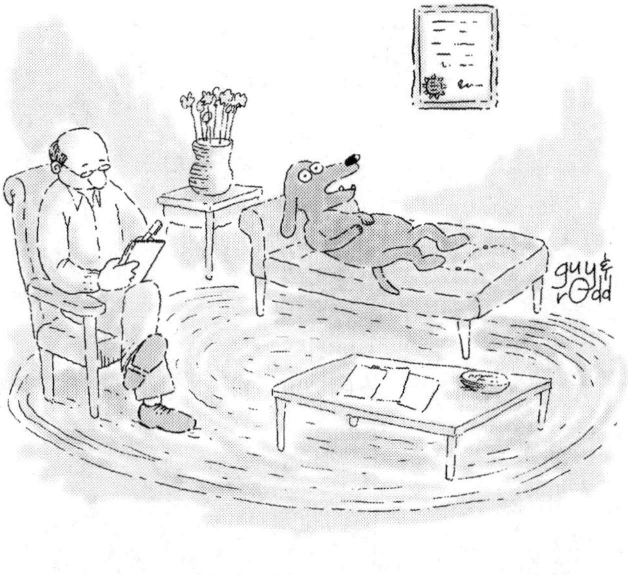
guy&
rOdd

"I can't escape it, Doc– that feeling that I'm stuck in some lame New Yorker cartoon."

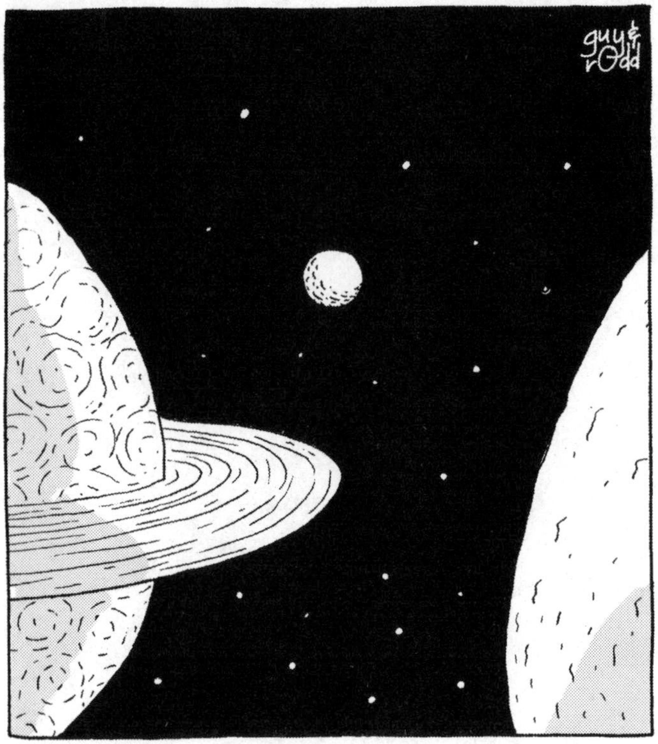

"LOOK AT HIM OUT THERE...SO COLD, SO DISTANT. WHY DO I ALWAYS FALL FOR THE BAD BOYS?"

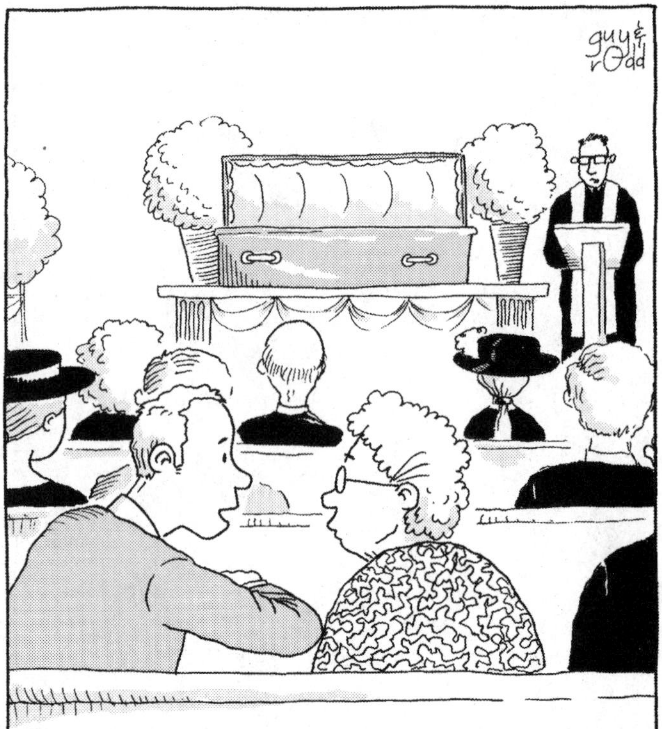

"THIS SUCKS. LET'S TRY AND START THE WAVE."

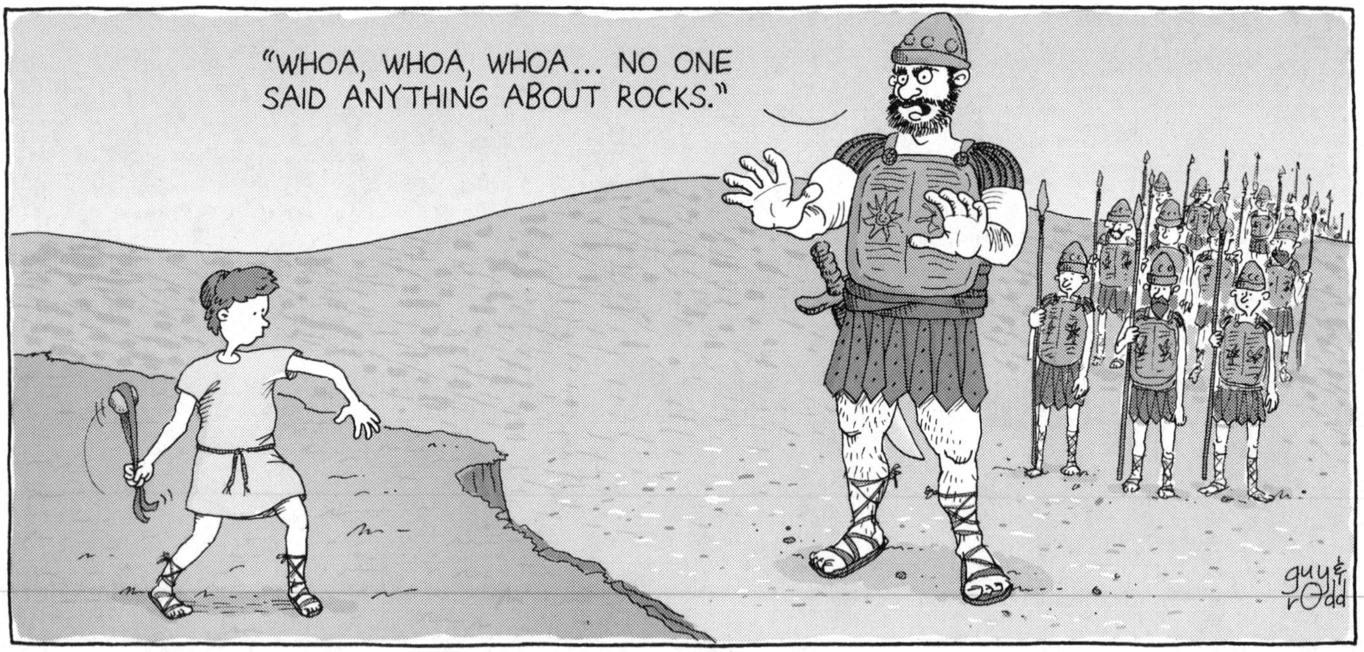

"WHOA, WHOA, WHOA... NO ONE SAID ANYTHING ABOUT ROCKS."

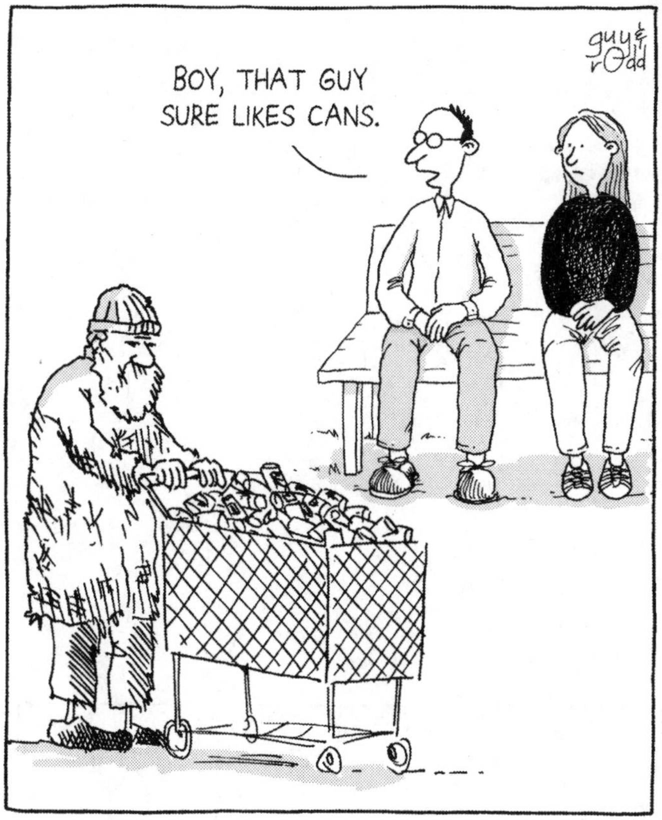
BOY, THAT GUY SURE LIKES CANS.
guy & rodd

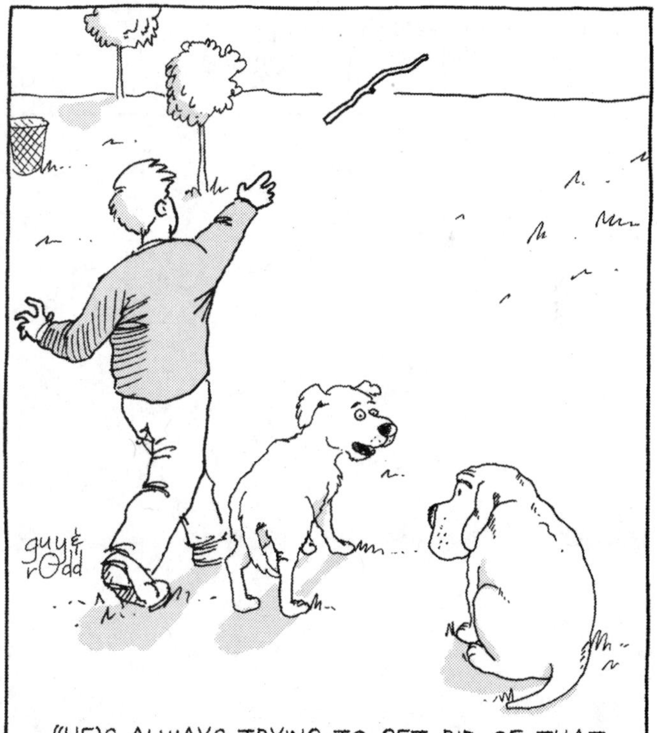
guy & rodd

"HE'S ALWAYS TRYING TO GET RID OF THAT STICK. I BRING IT BACK JUST TO TORTURE HIM."

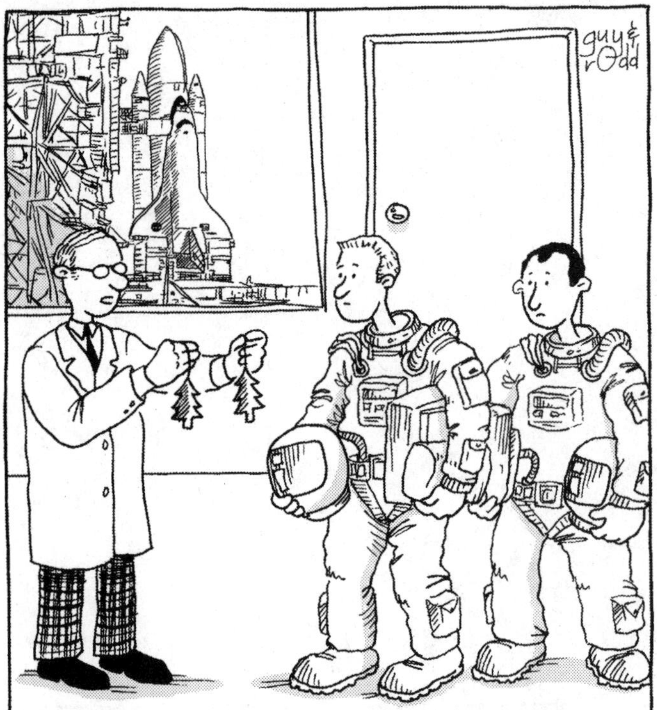

"...AND FINALLY, WOULD YOU LIKE WINTER PINE, OR POTPOURRI DELIGHT?"

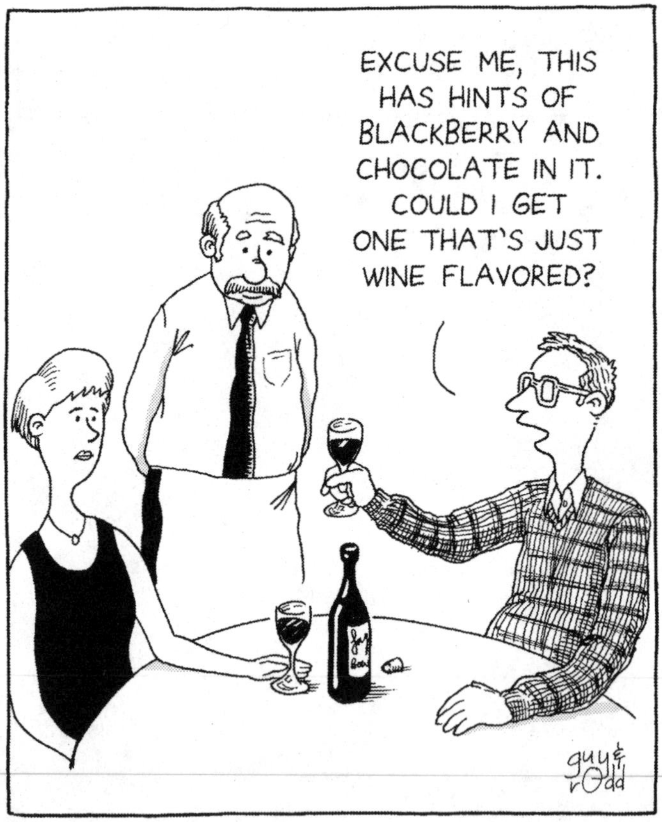
EXCUSE ME, THIS HAS HINTS OF BLACKBERRY AND CHOCOLATE IN IT. COULD I GET ONE THAT'S JUST WINE FLAVORED?

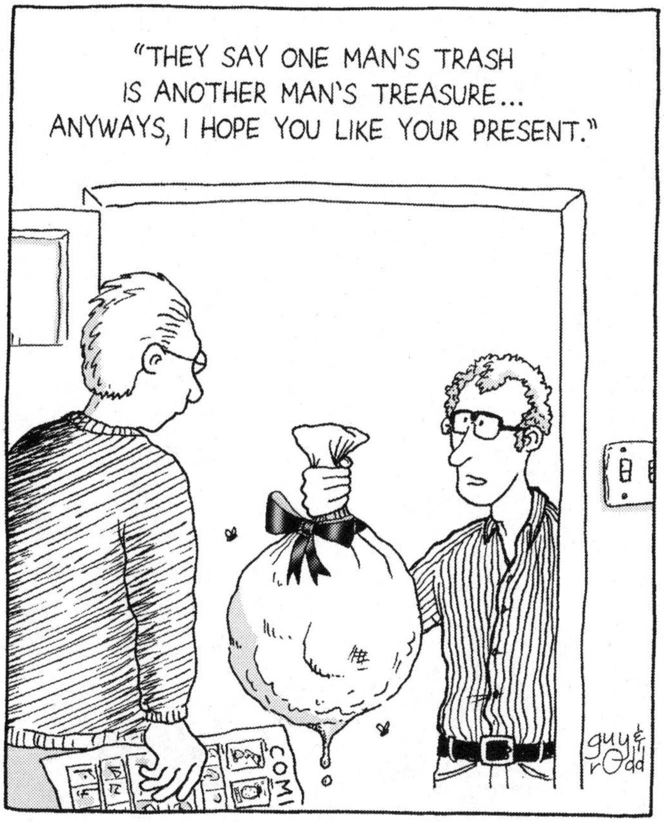
"THEY SAY ONE MAN'S TRASH
IS ANOTHER MAN'S TREASURE...
ANYWAYS, I HOPE YOU LIKE YOUR PRESENT."
COMI
guy & rodd

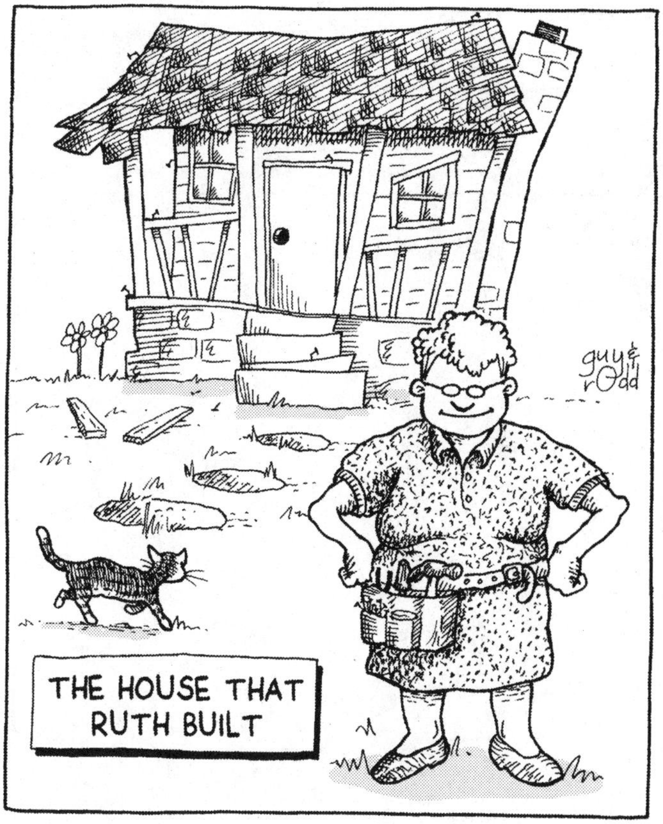
THE HOUSE THAT
RUTH BUILT
guy & rodd

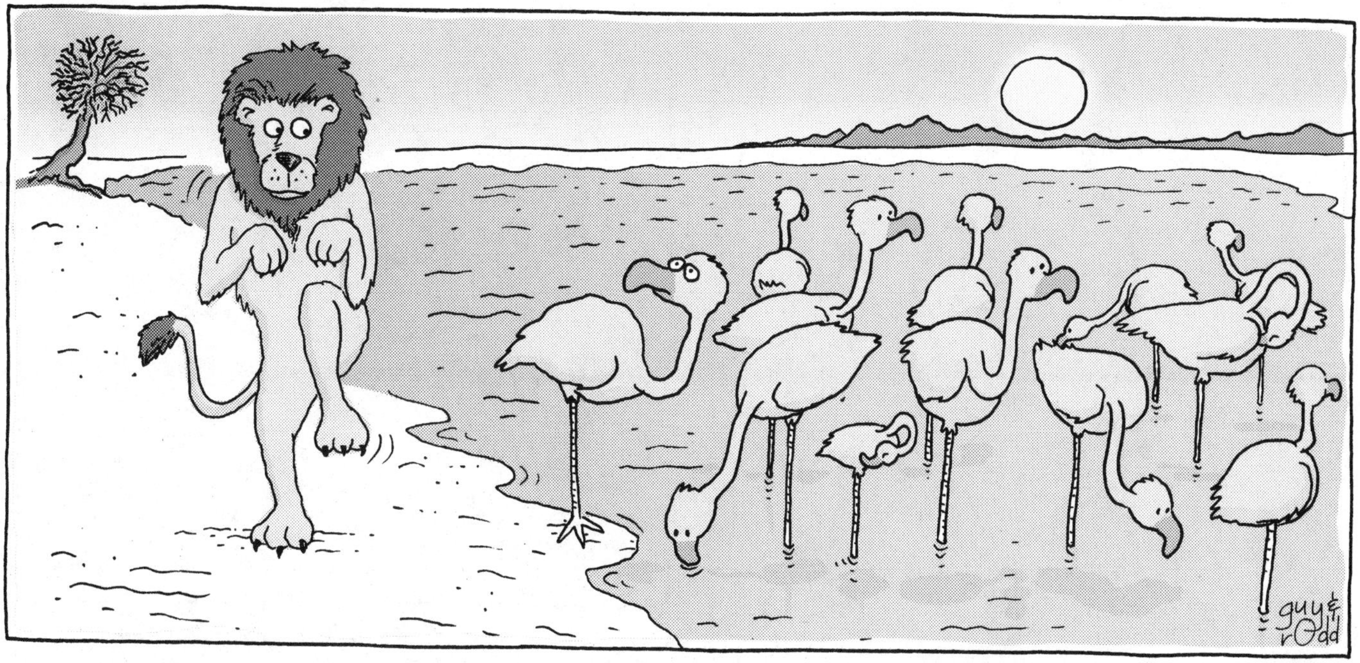
guy & rodd

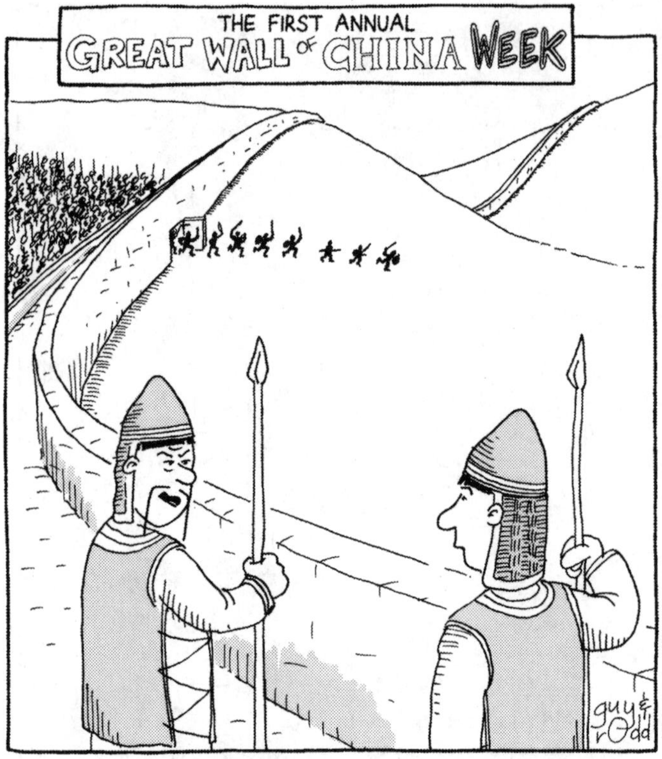
THE FIRST ANNUAL
GREAT WALL of CHINA WEEK
guy & rOdd

"WAY TO GO, CHANG. NOT SUCH A GREAT WALL IF YOU FORGET TO LOCK THE DOOR."

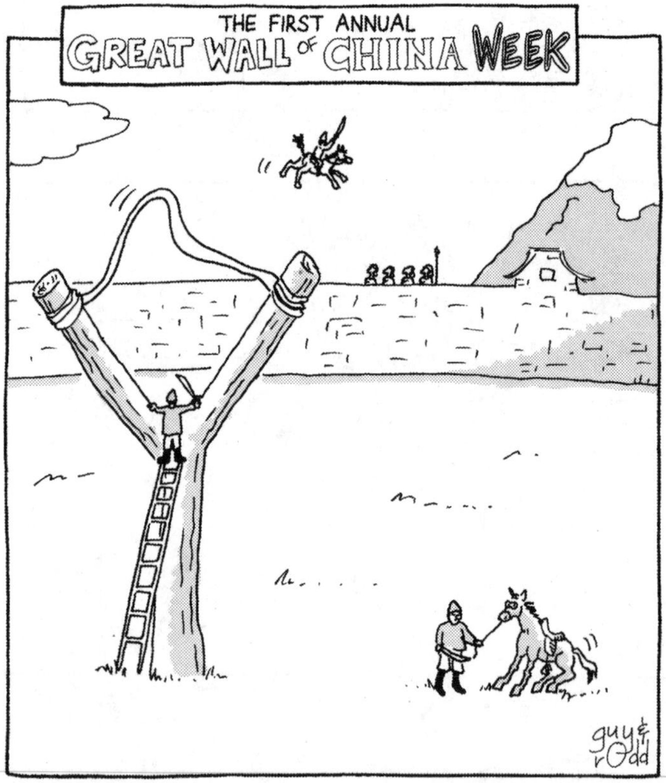
THE FIRST ANNUAL
GREAT WALL of CHINA WEEK
guy & rOdd

THE GREAT SLINGSHOT OF MONGOLIA

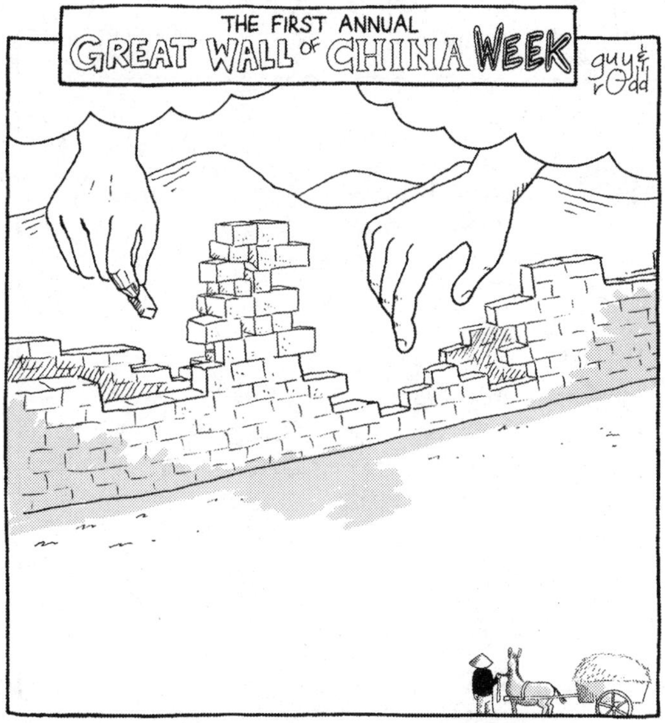
THE FIRST ANNUAL
GREAT WALL OF CHINA WEEK
guy & rOdd

SOMETIMES, WHEN THEY WERE BORED, THE GODS WOULD PLAY JENGA® WITH THE CUTE LITTLE WALL THAT THE HUMANS MADE.

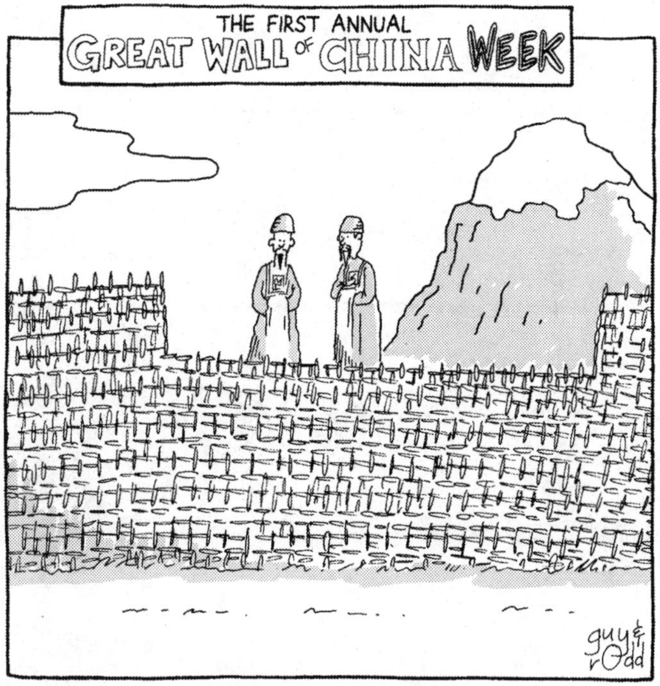
THE FIRST ANNUAL
GREAT WALL OF CHINA WEEK
guy & rOdd

MOST PEOPLE DON'T KNOW THAT THE GREAT WALL WAS ORIGINALLY BUILT OUT OF POPSICLE STICKS. OF COURSE, BACK THEN IT WAS JUST CALLED "THE WALL".

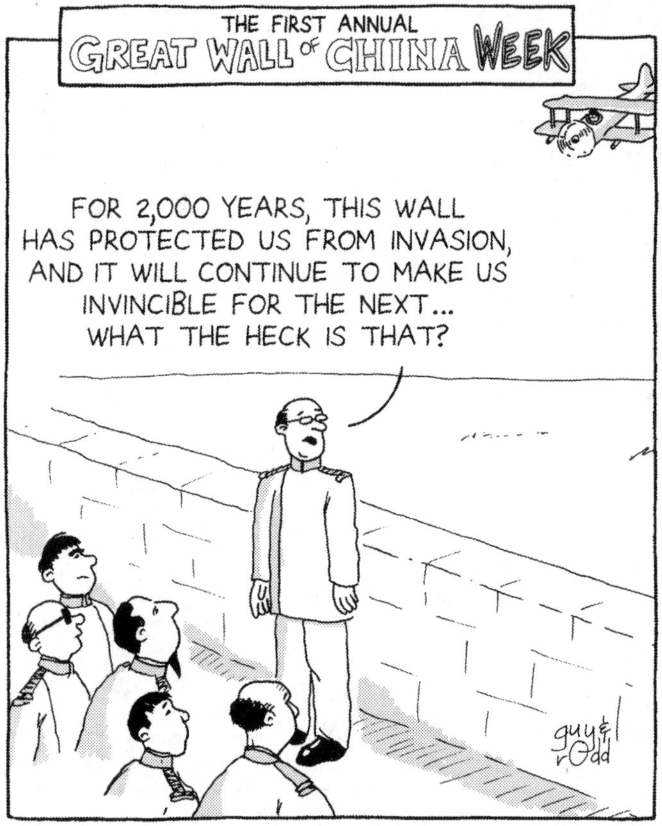
THE FIRST ANNUAL
GREAT WALL OF CHINA WEEK
FOR 2,000 YEARS, THIS WALL HAS PROTECTED US FROM INVASION, AND IT WILL CONTINUE TO MAKE US INVINCIBLE FOR THE NEXT... WHAT THE HECK IS THAT?
guy & rOdd

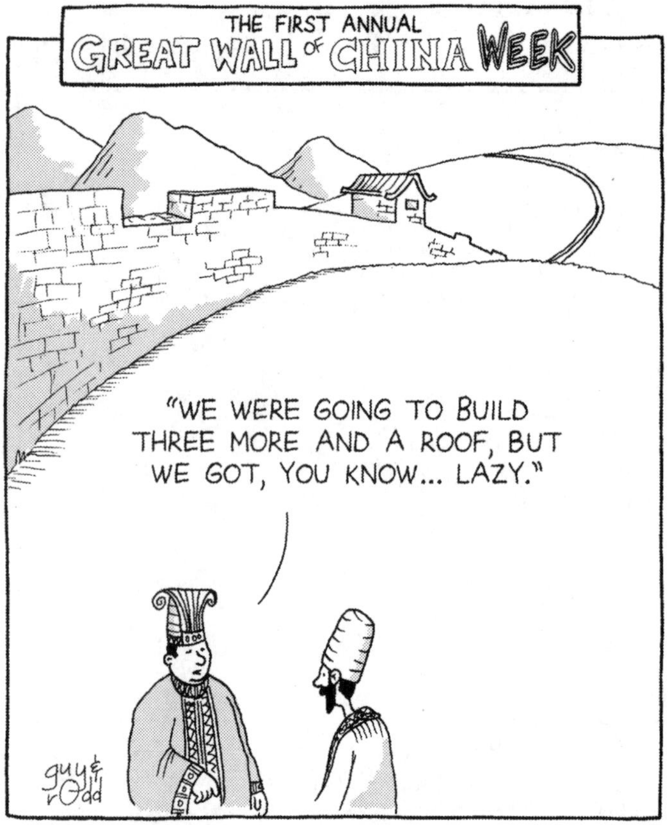
THE FIRST ANNUAL
GREAT WALL OF CHINA WEEK
"WE WERE GOING TO BUILD THREE MORE AND A ROOF, BUT WE GOT, YOU KNOW... LAZY."
guy & rOdd

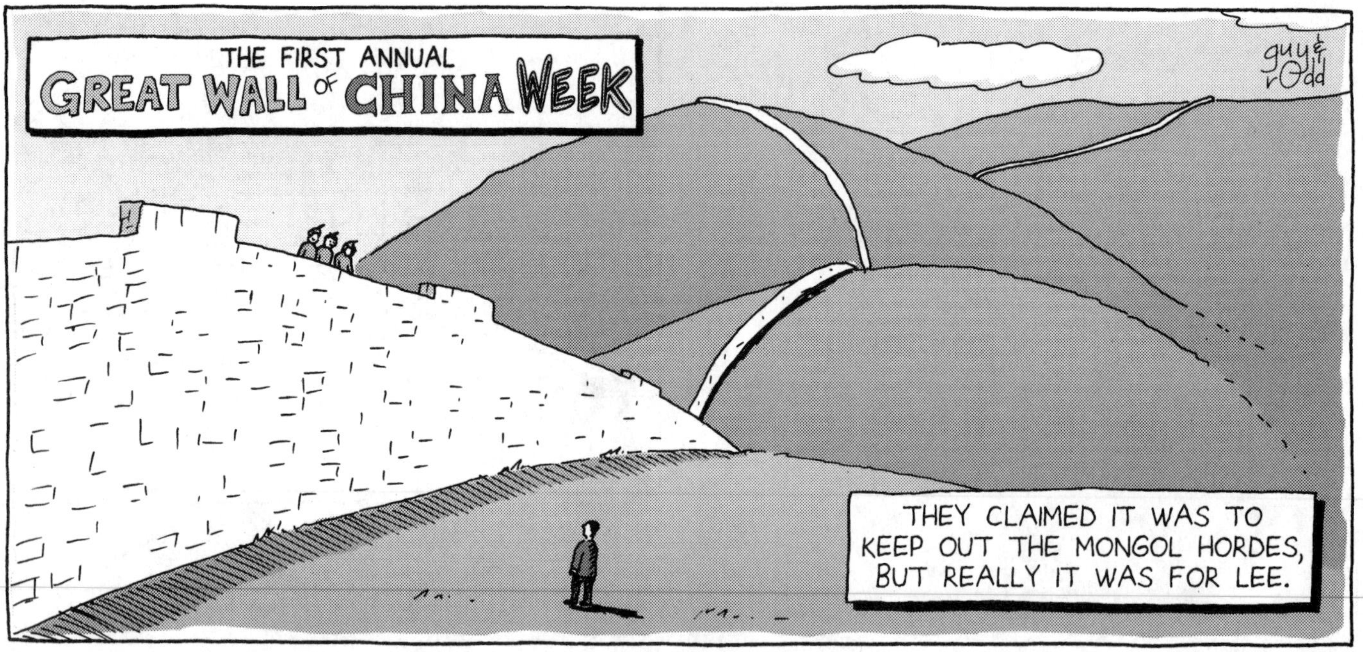
THE FIRST ANNUAL
GREAT WALL OF CHINA WEEK
guy & rOdd
THEY CLAIMED IT WAS TO KEEP OUT THE MONGOL HORDES, BUT REALLY IT WAS FOR LEE.

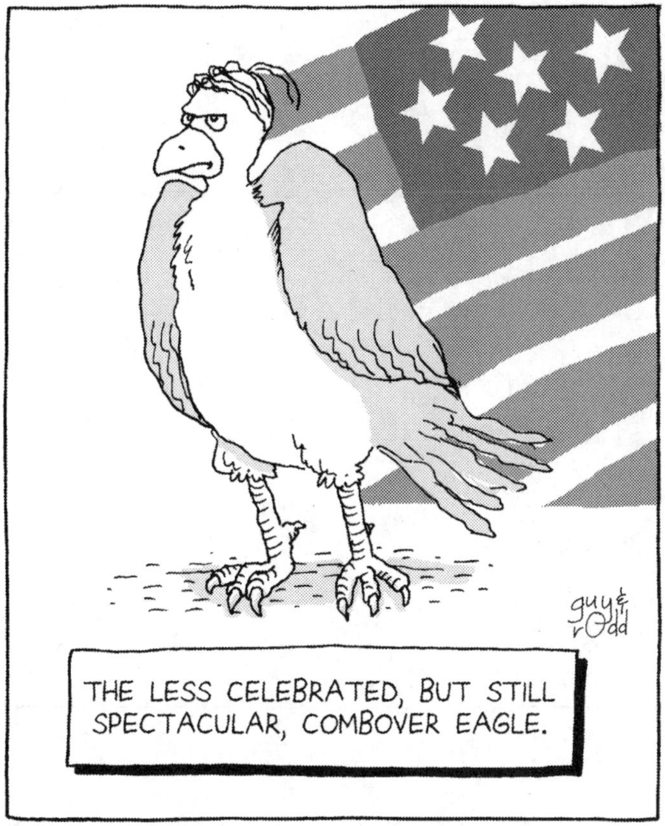
guy & rodd

THE LESS CELEBRATED, BUT STILL SPECTACULAR, COMBOVER EAGLE.

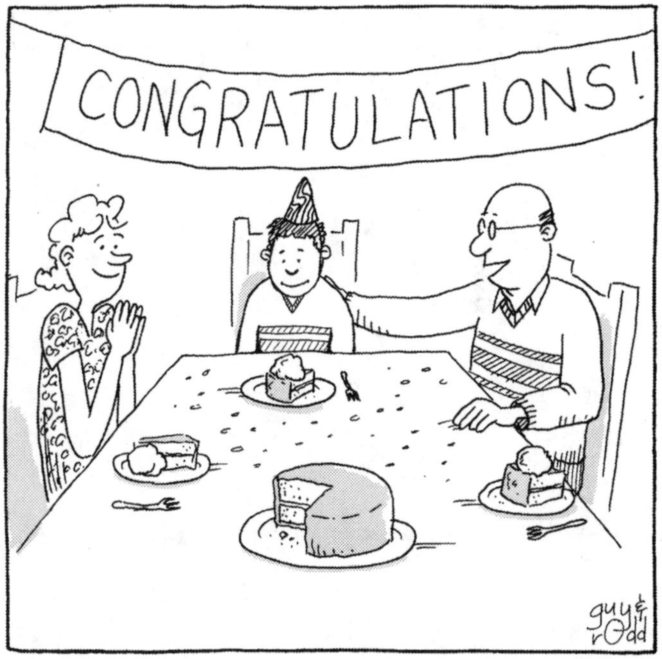
CONGRATULATIONS!
guy & rodd

THE CAKE WAS GREAT AND THE ICE CREAM WAS DELICIOUS, BUT DEEP DOWN INSIDE, HE KNEW THAT SOME DAY HIS PARENTS WOULD DISCOVER THAT "F" WASN'T FOR FANTASTIC, AND THEN NONE OF IT WOULD BE WORTH IT.

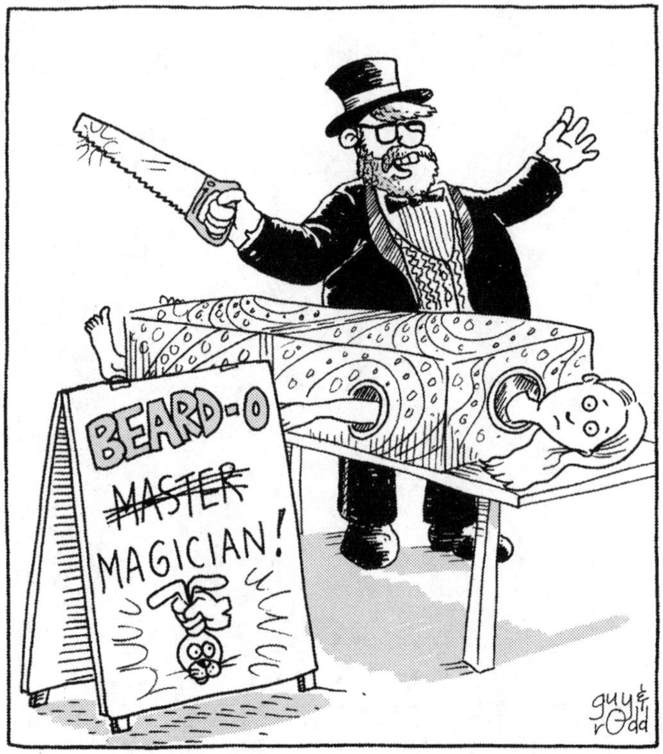
BEARD-O
MASTER
MAGICIAN!
guy & rOdd

SUDDENLY, BECKY NOTICED SOMETHING WHICH GAVE HER PAUSE.

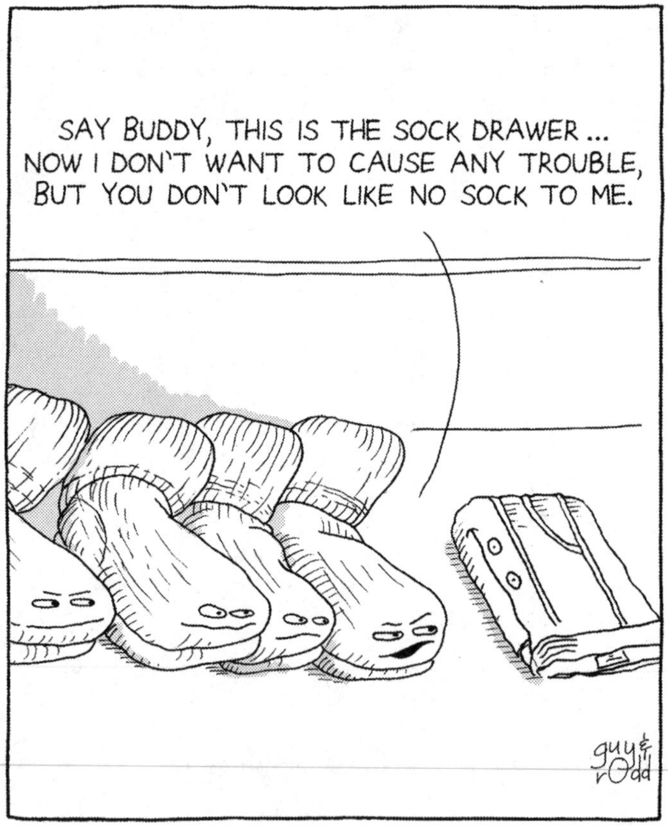
SAY BUDDY, THIS IS THE SOCK DRAWER ... NOW I DON'T WANT TO CAUSE ANY TROUBLE, BUT YOU DON'T LOOK LIKE NO SOCK TO ME.
guy & rOdd

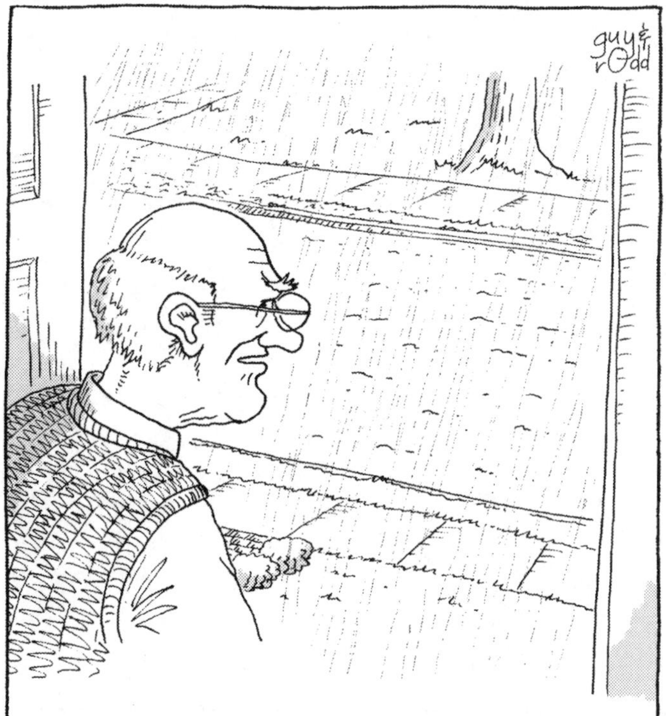

"DANG IT, I JUST WASHED THIS STREET. BOY, EVERY TIME..."

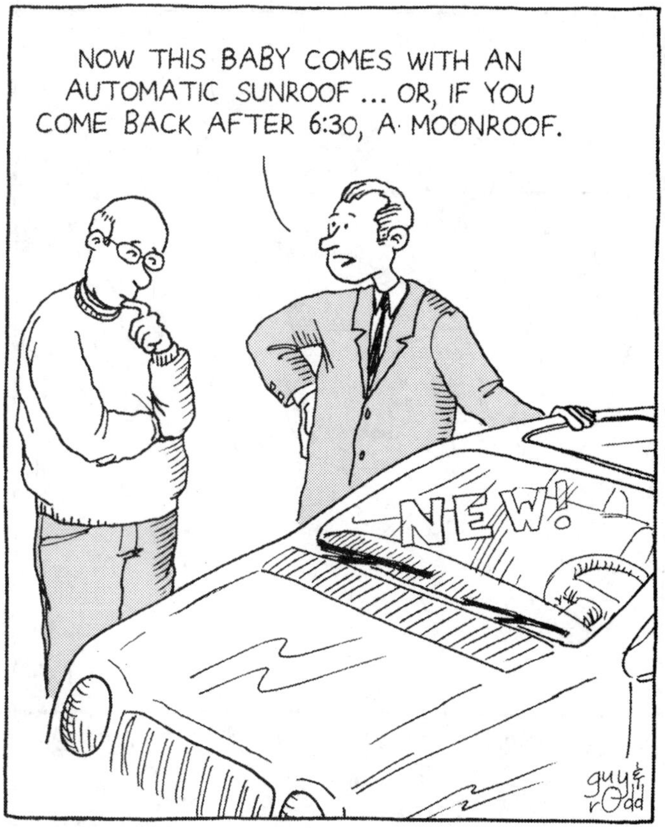
NOW THIS BABY COMES WITH AN AUTOMATIC SUNROOF ... OR, IF YOU COME BACK AFTER 6:30, A MOONROOF.
NEW!

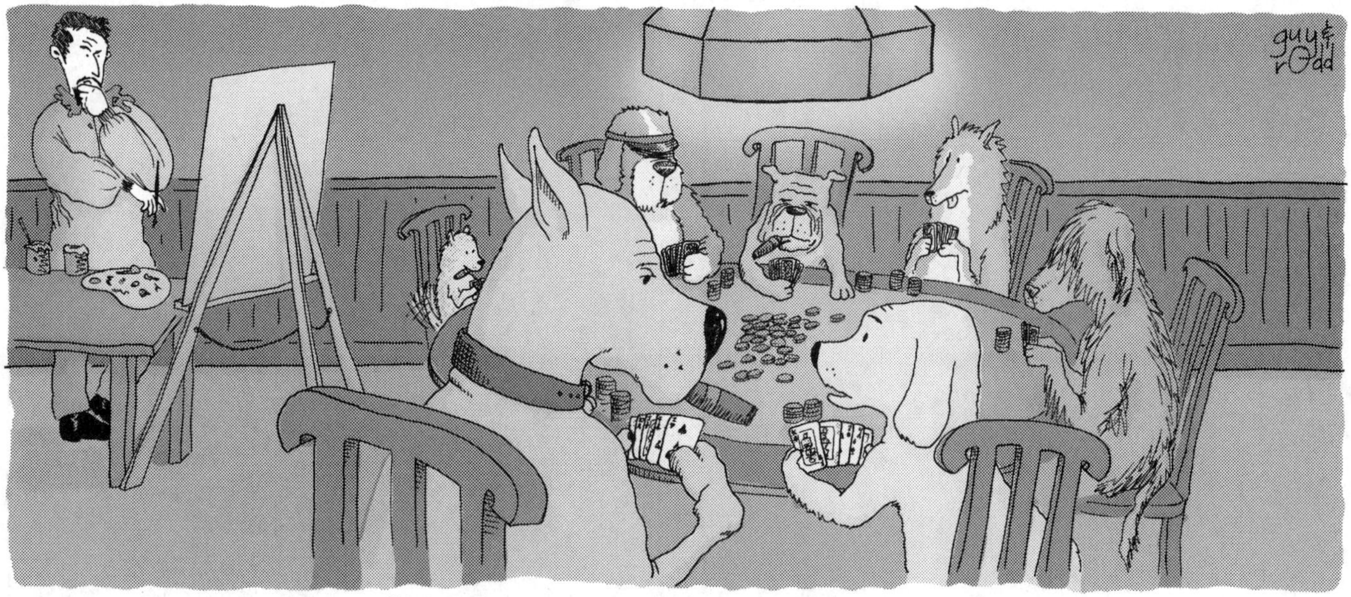

"PSST! I HAVE NO IDEA WHAT I'M DOING."

UNBEKNOWNST TO MOST HUMANS, THE TRUE
KING OF THE JUNGLE ISN'T A LION ...
IT'S A CLICKING BEETLE, NAMED AL.

"AND ANOTHER THING, HE THINKS 11:11:11 IS A
COOLER TIME THAN 12:34:56. I MEAN 11:11:11...
COULD HE BE ANY MORE TRITE?"

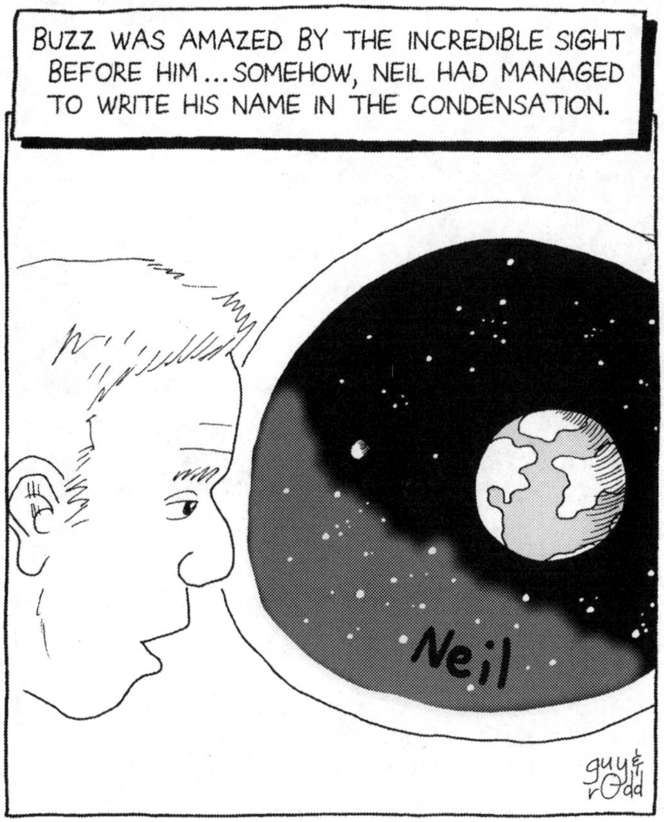
BUZZ WAS AMAZED BY THE INCREDIBLE SIGHT BEFORE HIM...SOMEHOW, NEIL HAD MANAGED TO WRITE HIS NAME IN THE CONDENSATION.
Neil
guy & rOdd

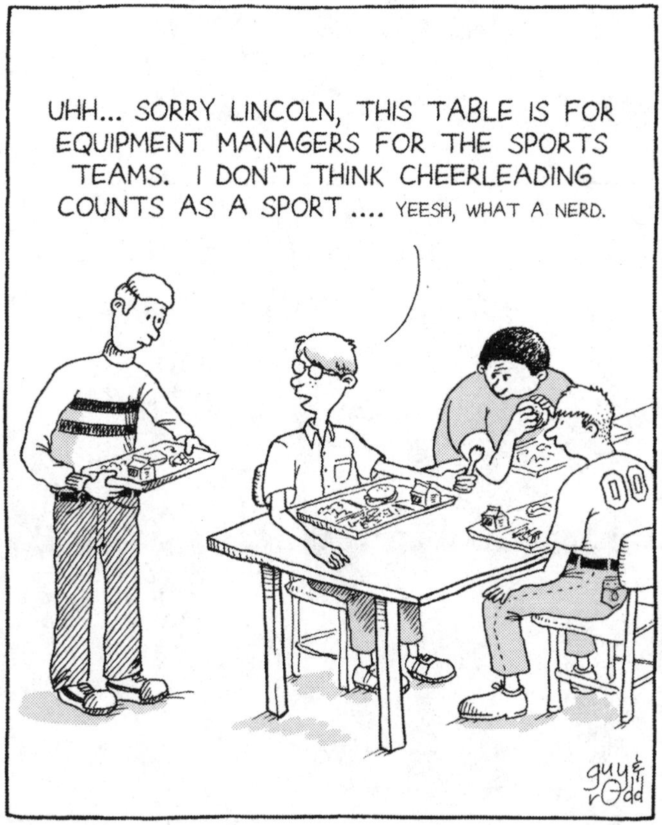
UHH... SORRY LINCOLN, THIS TABLE IS FOR EQUIPMENT MANAGERS FOR THE SPORTS TEAMS. I DON'T THINK CHEERLEADING COUNTS AS A SPORT .... YEESH, WHAT A NERD.
00
guy & rOdd

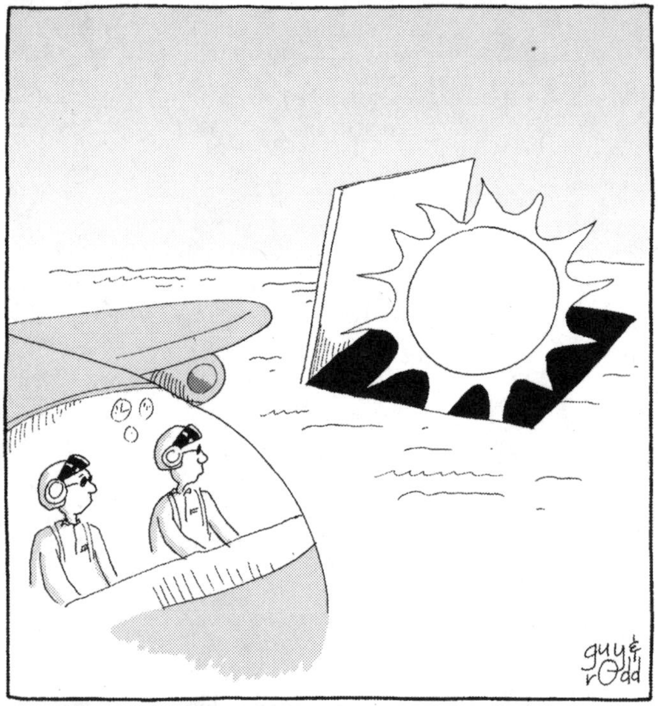
guy & rOdd

WHILE DOING ROUTINE RECON OVER THE PACIFIC OCEAN, LIEUTENANTS CROMWELL AND OLSEN MAKE A STARTLING DISCOVERY.

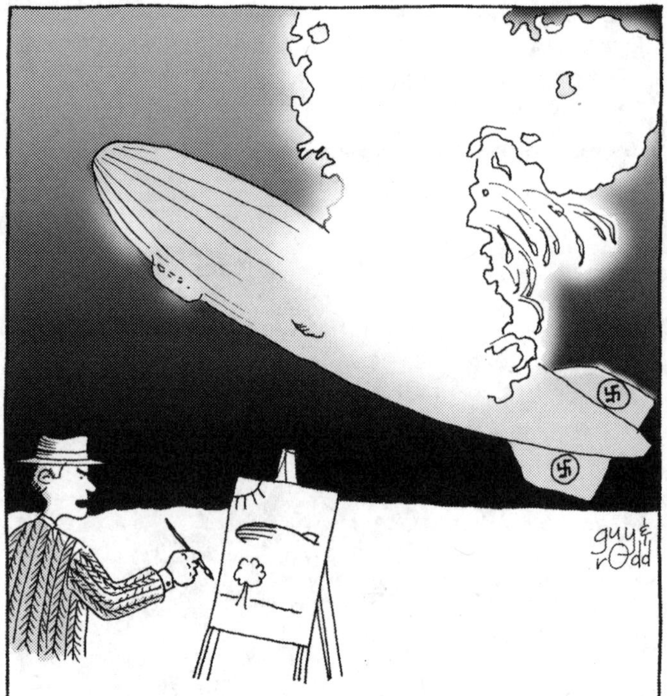
guy & rOdd

"OH JEEZ, I GOTTA BE THE SINGLE UNLUCKIEST GUY IN THE ENTIRE WORLD."

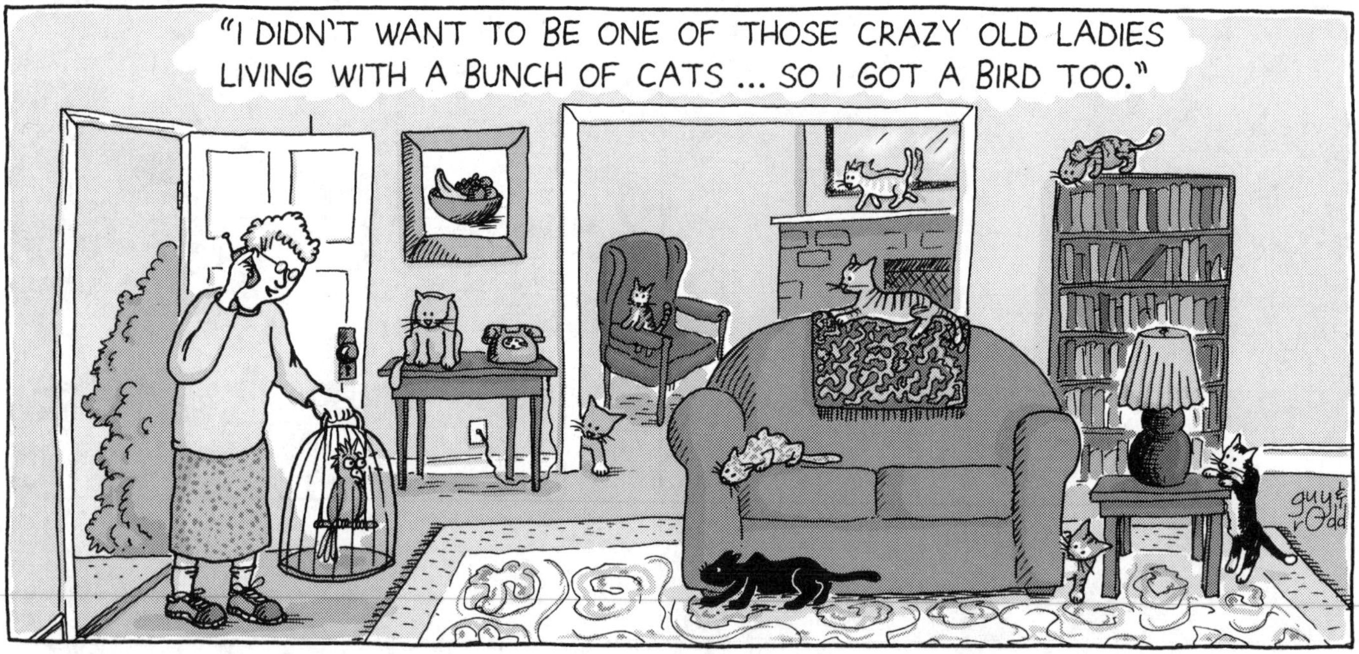
"I DIDN'T WANT TO BE ONE OF THOSE CRAZY OLD LADIES LIVING WITH A BUNCH OF CATS ... SO I GOT A BIRD TOO."
guy & rOdd

"MERLE, DO YOU THINK WE SOUND STUPID WHEN WE SAY 'AARGH'? I MEAN, IT'S NOT REALLY A WORD, IS IT?"

BEFORE WE DO THIS, I JUST WANT TO SAY SOMETHING: I REALLY ADMIRE YOUR HAT... ALWAYS HAVE.

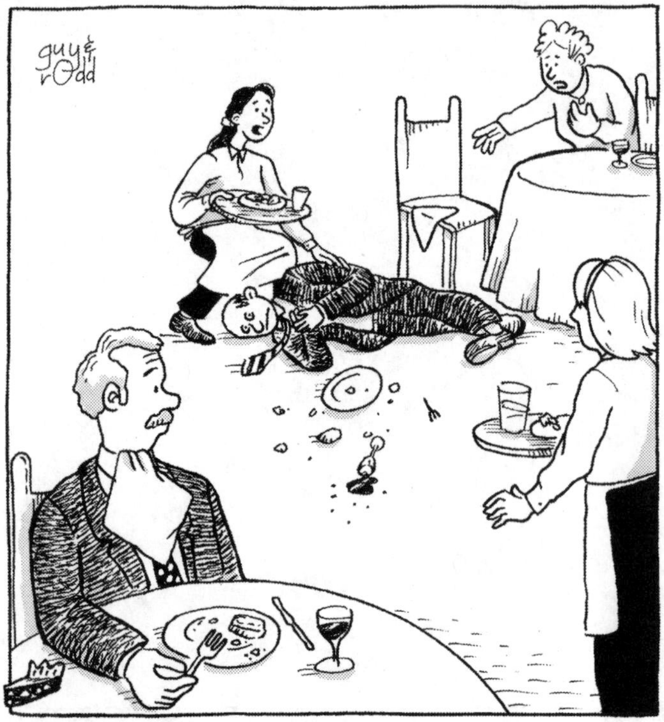
guy & rOdd

LARRY FROZE, UNSURE OF WHAT TO DO. YES, HE WAS A DOCTOR, BUT ON THE OTHER HAND, THIS WASN'T TECHNICALLY A HOUSE.

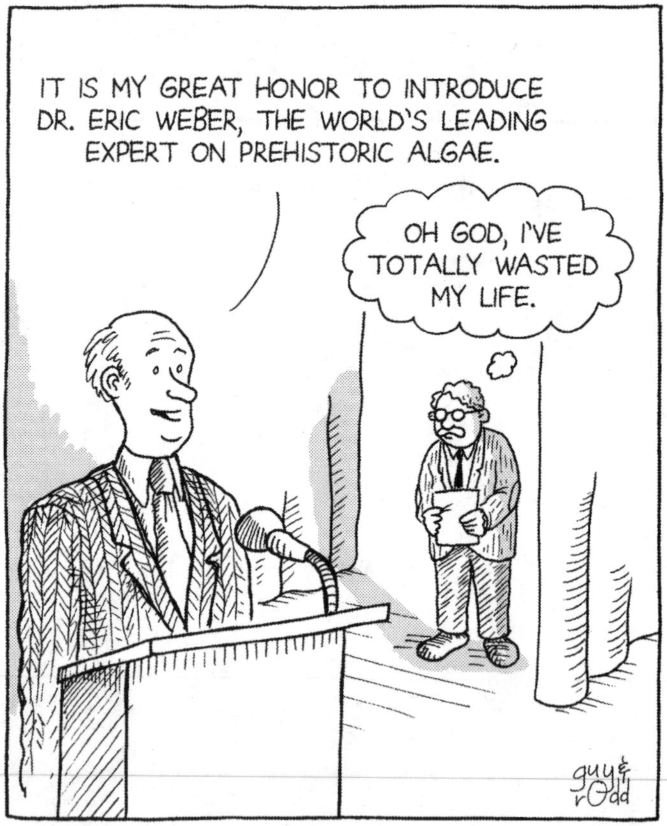
IT IS MY GREAT HONOR TO INTRODUCE DR. ERIC WEBER, THE WORLD'S LEADING EXPERT ON PREHISTORIC ALGAE.
OH GOD, I'VE TOTALLY WASTED MY LIFE.
guy & rOdd

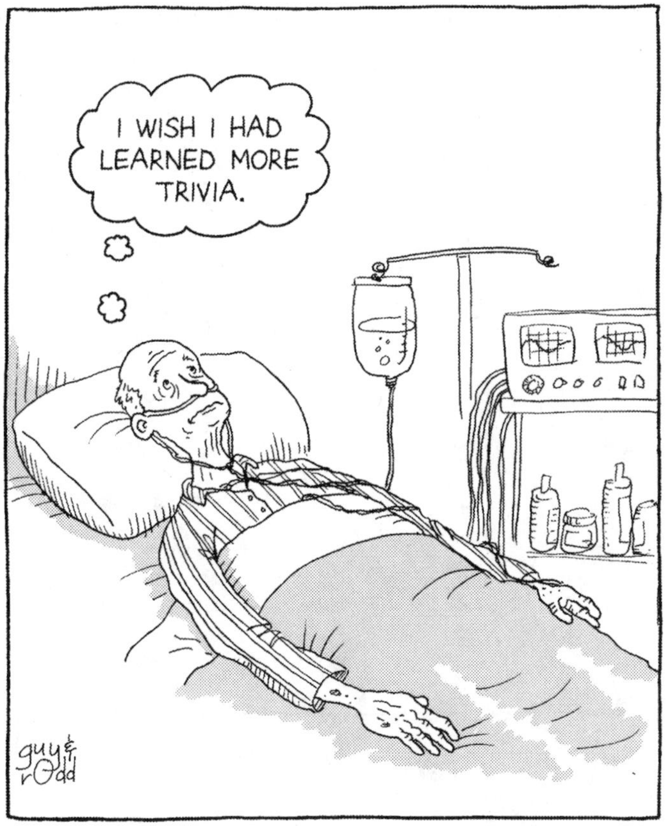
I WISH I HAD LEARNED MORE TRIVIA.
guy & rOdd

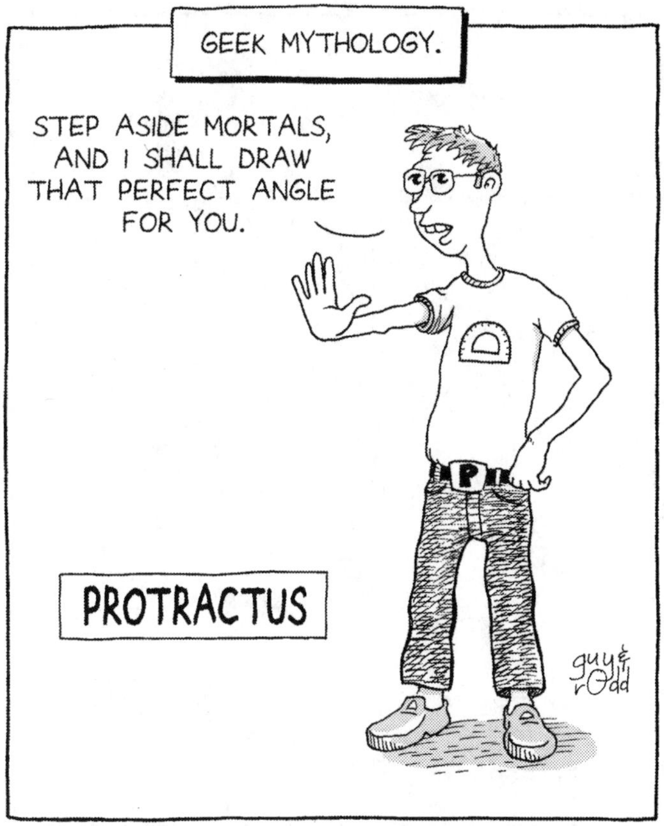
GEEK MYTHOLOGY.
STEP ASIDE MORTALS, AND I SHALL DRAW THAT PERFECT ANGLE FOR YOU.
PROTRACTUS
guy & rOdd

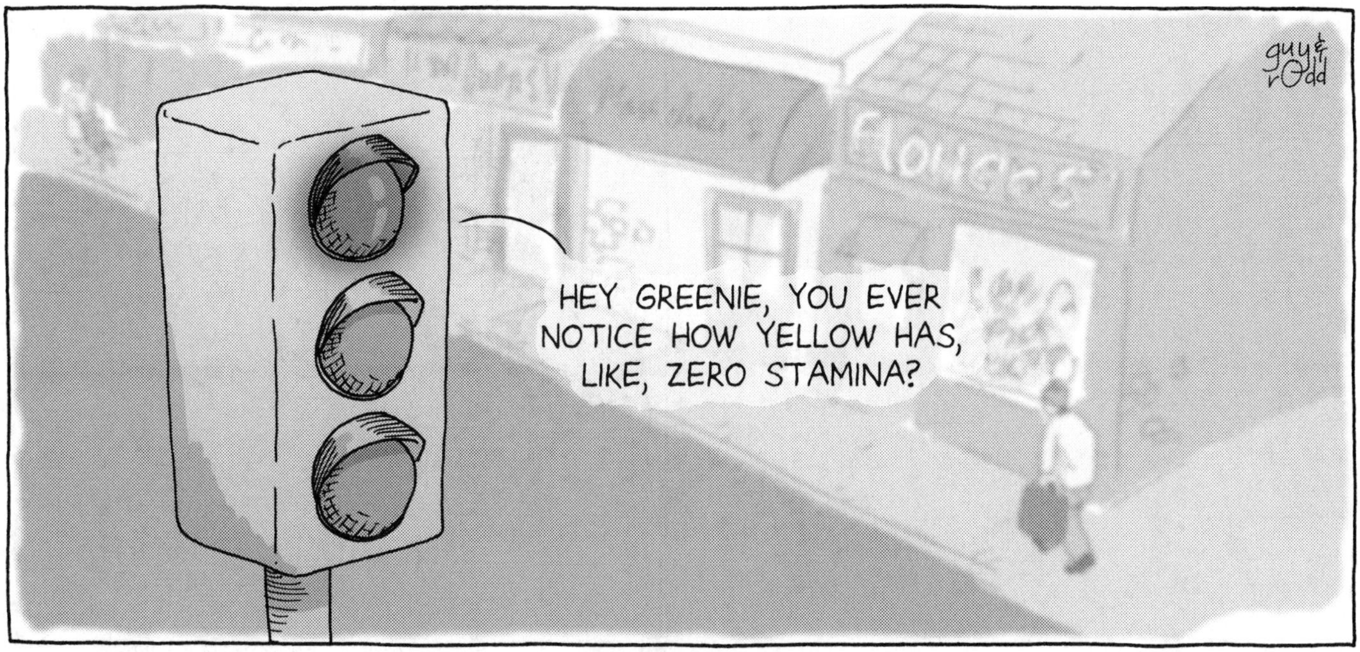
HEY GREENIE, YOU EVER NOTICE HOW YELLOW HAS, LIKE, ZERO STAMINA?
guy & rOdd

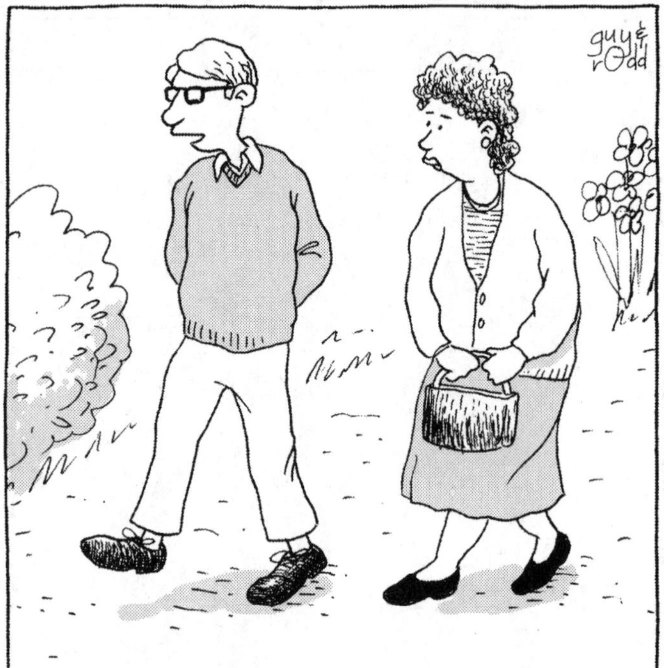

"BY THE WAY, I USUALLY SNEEZE IN TWOS. SO THAT'S ANOTHER INTERESTING THING ABOUT ME."

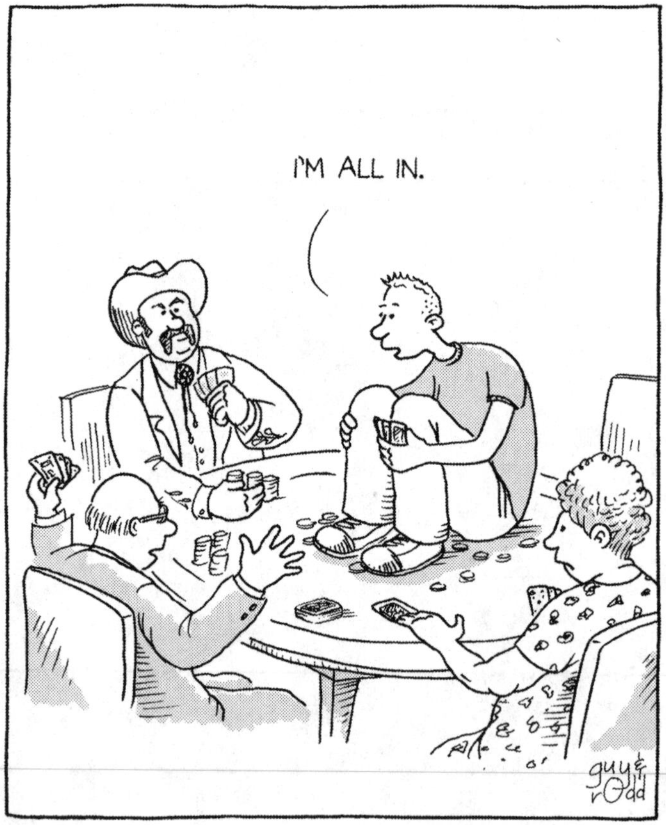
I'M ALL IN.

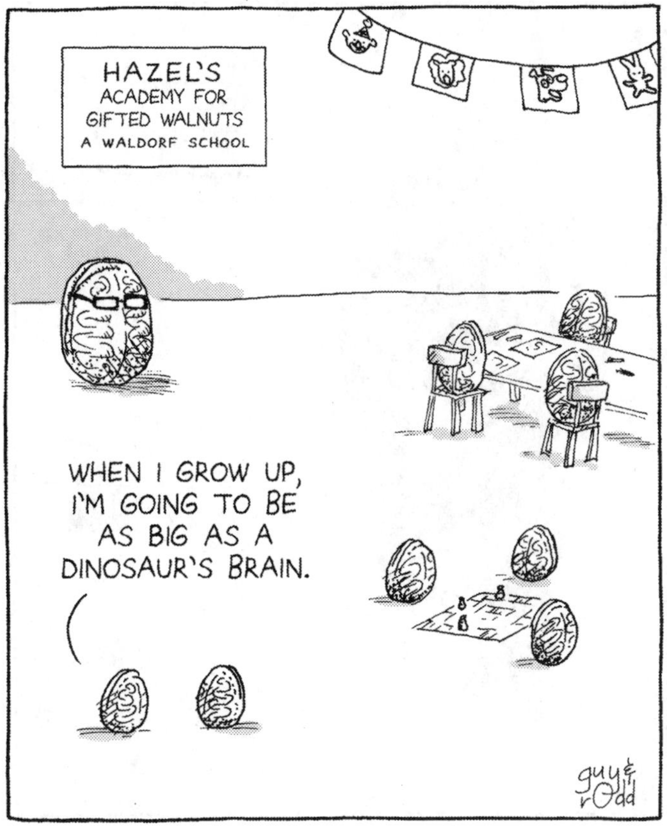
HAZEL'S
ACADEMY FOR
GIFTED WALNUTS
A WALDORF SCHOOL
WHEN I GROW UP, I'M GOING TO BE AS BIG AS A DINOSAUR'S BRAIN.
guy & rOdd

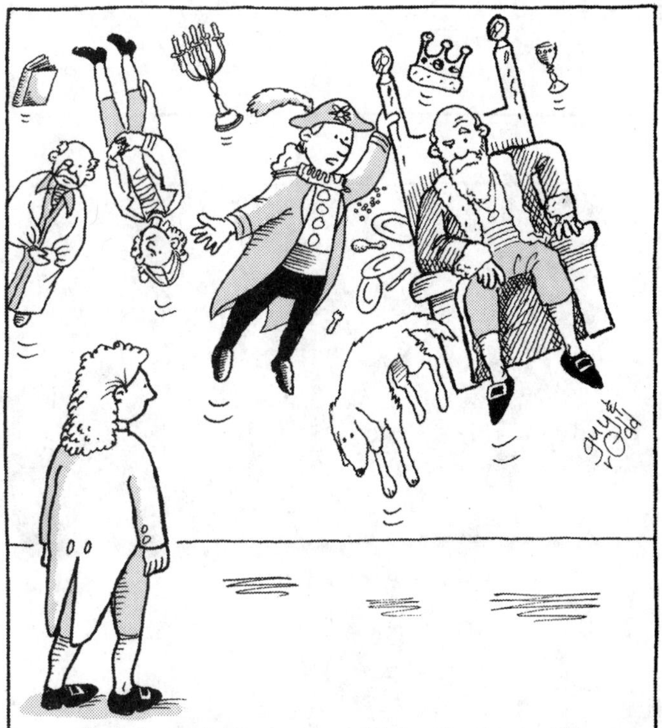
guy & rOdd

"MAY I PRESENT SIR ISAAC NEWTON. HE CLAIMS TO HAVE DISCOVERED SOMETHING BIG."

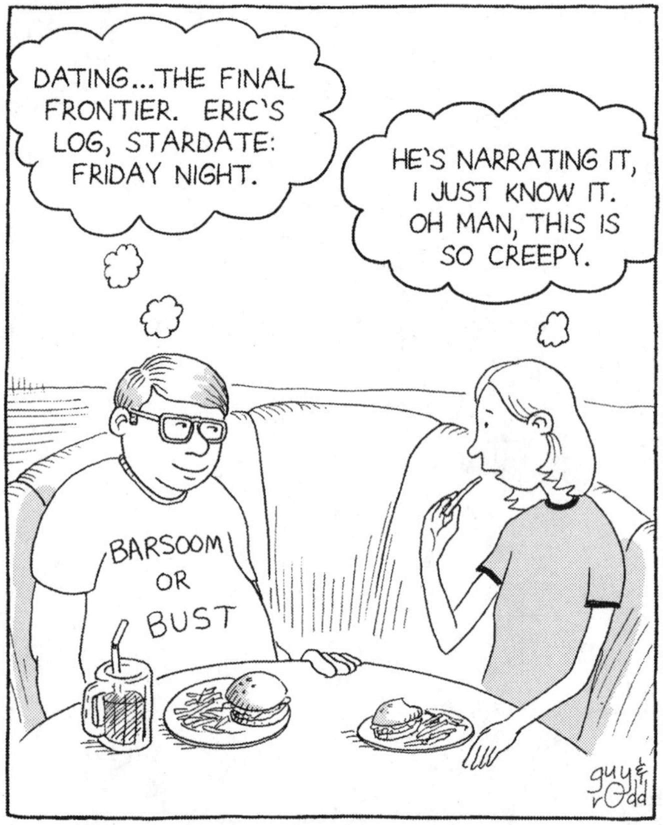
DATING...THE FINAL FRONTIER. ERIC'S LOG, STARDATE: FRIDAY NIGHT.
HE'S NARRATING IT, I JUST KNOW IT. OH MAN, THIS IS SO CREEPY.
BARSOOM OR BUST
guy & rOdd

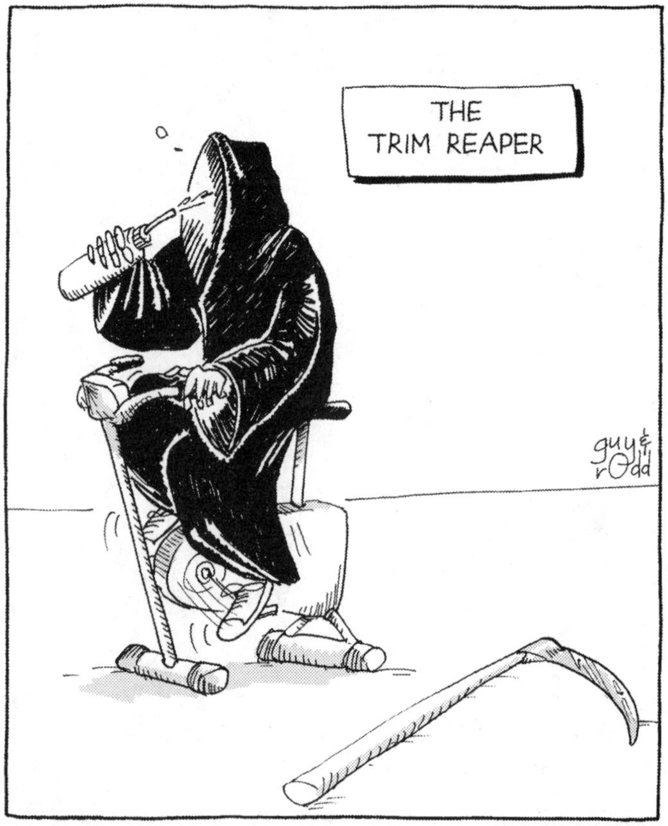
THE TRIM REAPER
guy & rOdd

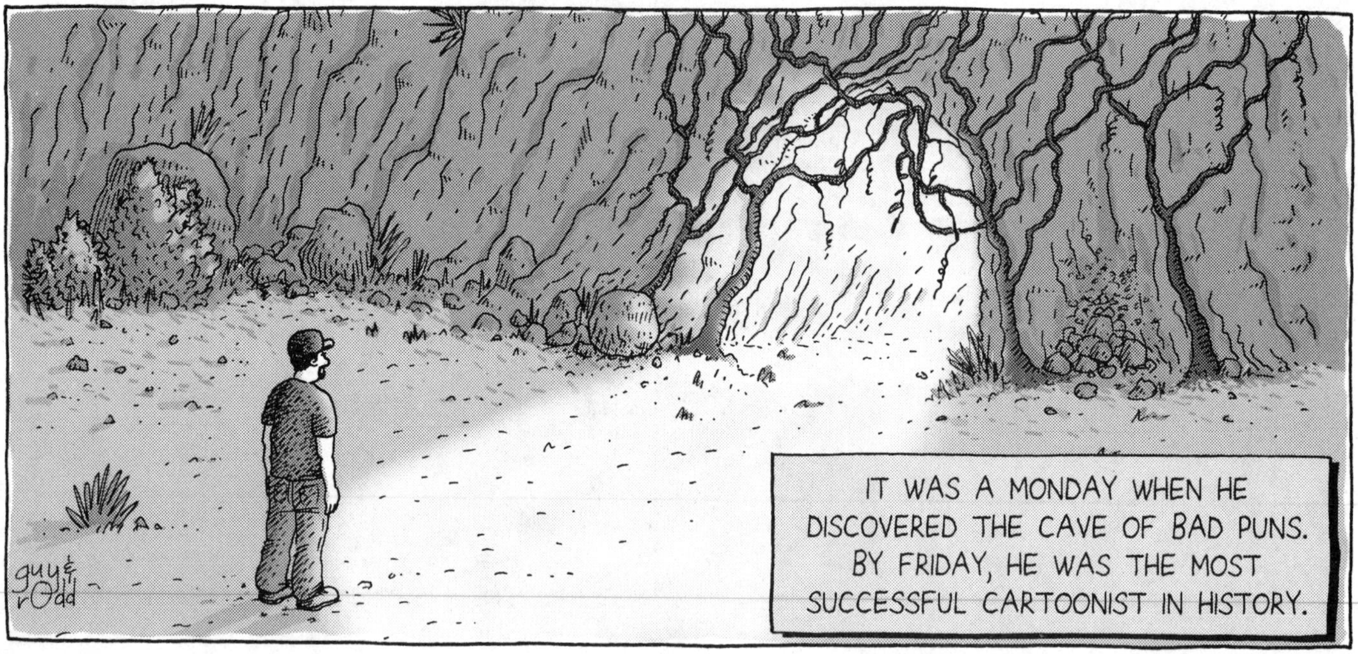
IT WAS A MONDAY WHEN HE DISCOVERED THE CAVE OF BAD PUNS. BY FRIDAY, HE WAS THE MOST SUCCESSFUL CARTOONIST IN HISTORY.
guy & rOdd

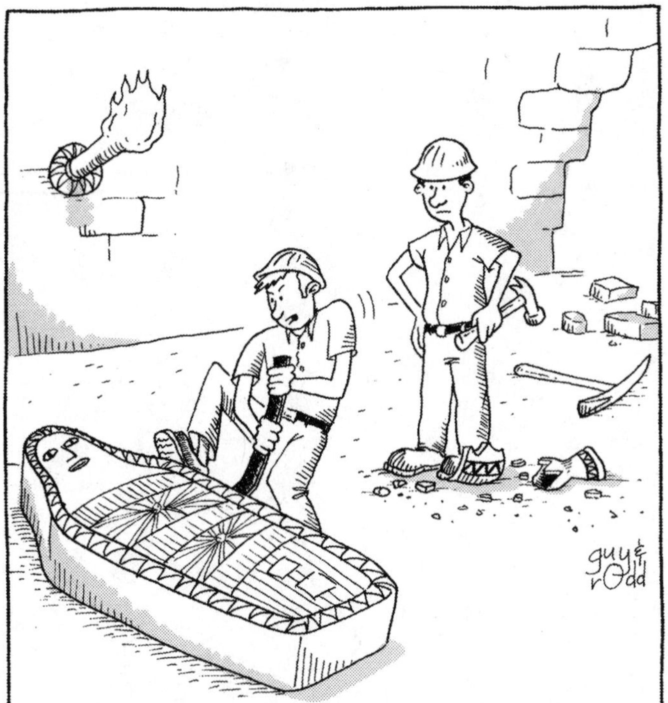
guy & rOdd

"ALL I'M SAYING IS, YOU KNOW I MADE THAT SANDWICH FOR MYSELF... I JUST THINK SOME THINGS ARE SACRED, EARL."

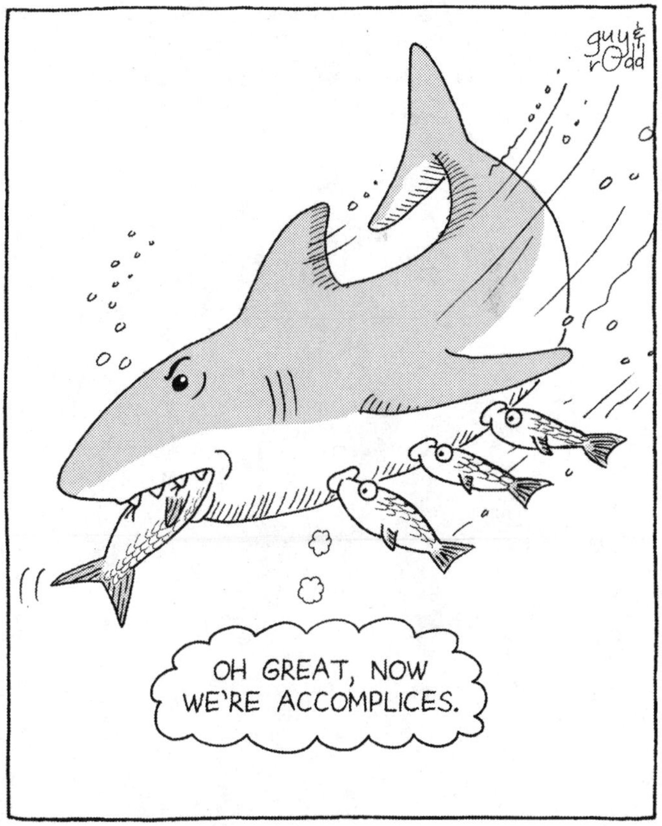
guy & rOdd
OH GREAT, NOW WE'RE ACCOMPLICES.

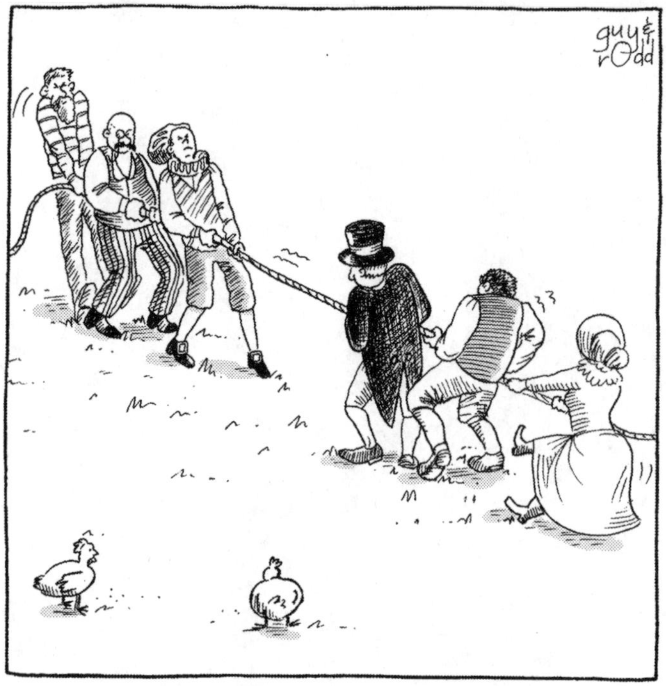
guy & rOdd

MOST PEOPLE DON'T KNOW THAT TUG-O-WAR GOT ITS START IN THE LATE 1600'S WHEN, FOR A BRIEF PERIOD OF TIME, ROPE WAS CONSIDERED LEGAL TENDER.

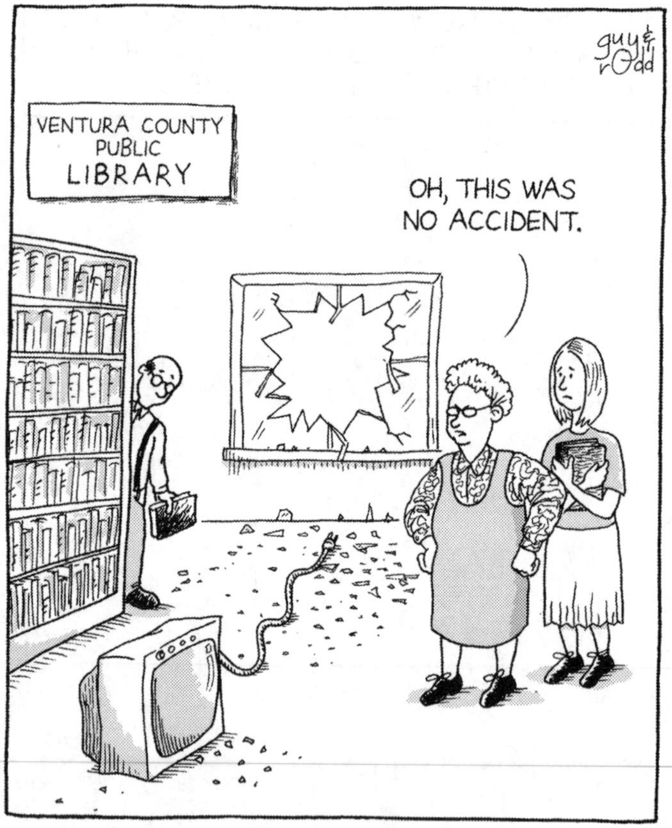
guy & rOdd
VENTURA COUNTY PUBLIC LIBRARY
OH, THIS WAS NO ACCIDENT.

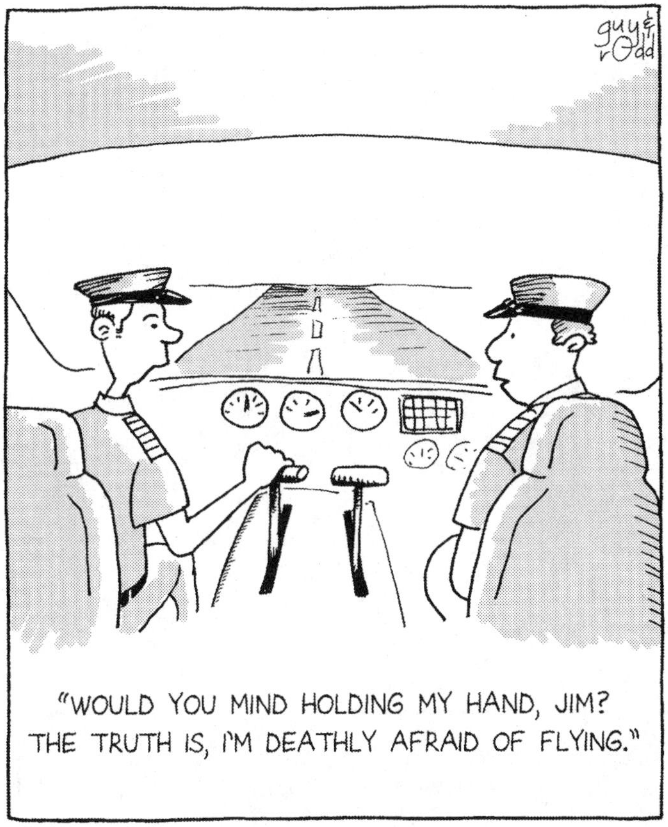
guy & rodd

"WOULD YOU MIND HOLDING MY HAND, JIM? THE TRUTH IS, I'M DEATHLY AFRAID OF FLYING."

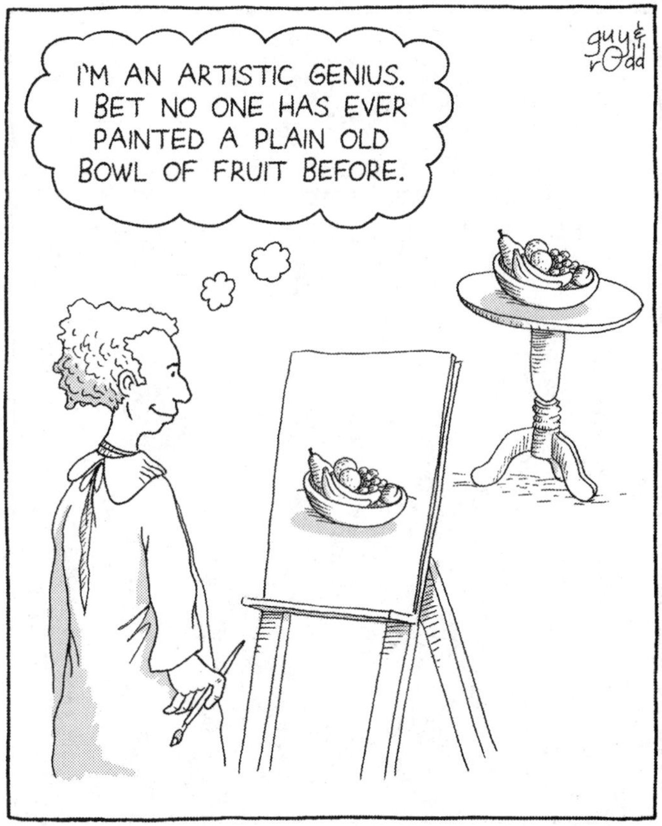
guy & rodd
I'M AN ARTISTIC GENIUS. I BET NO ONE HAS EVER PAINTED A PLAIN OLD BOWL OF FRUIT BEFORE.

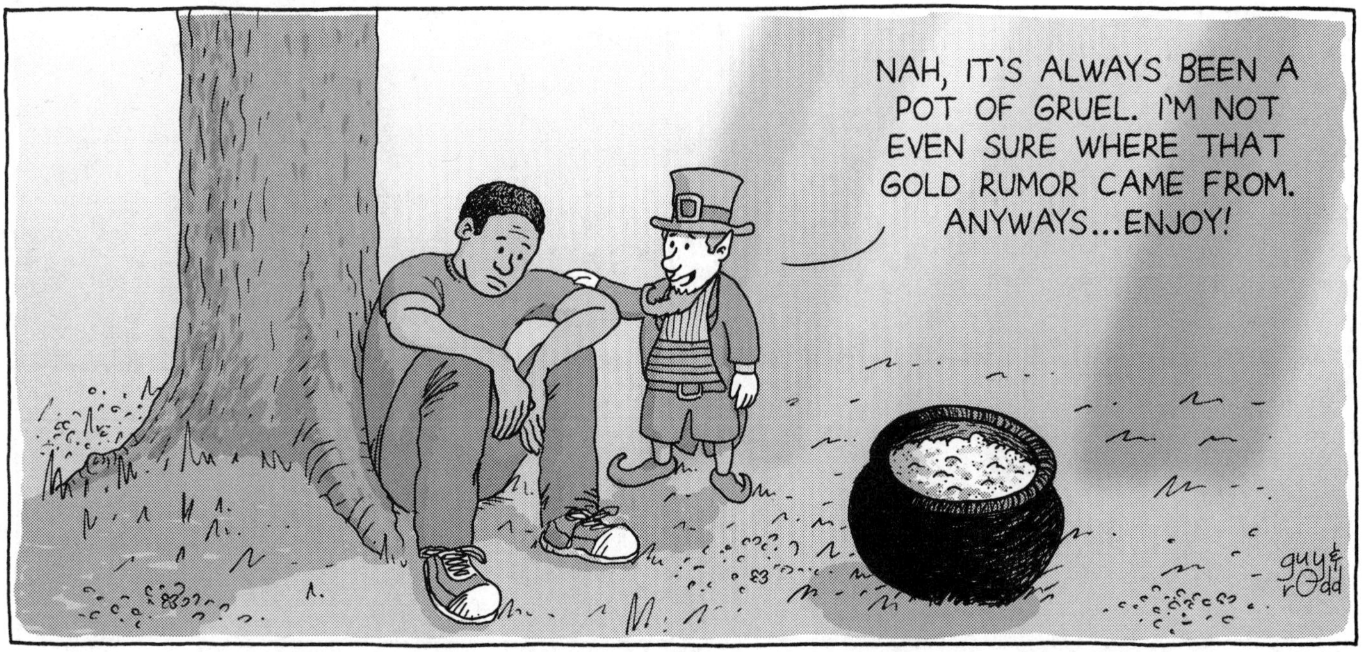
NAH, IT'S ALWAYS BEEN A POT OF GRUEL. I'M NOT EVEN SURE WHERE THAT GOLD RUMOR CAME FROM. ANYWAYS...ENJOY!
guy & rodd

THIS MAN'S GOING INTO ANAPHYLACTIC SHOCK. I NEED 10 CC'S OF BICARBONATE DIOXIDE STAT! OH WHAT THE HECK, MAKE IT 11.
guy & rOdd

HELLO, IS THIS THE GOVERNMENT? YES, I WAS JUST WONDERING... IS THE LAMBADA STILL FORBIDDEN?
guy & rOdd

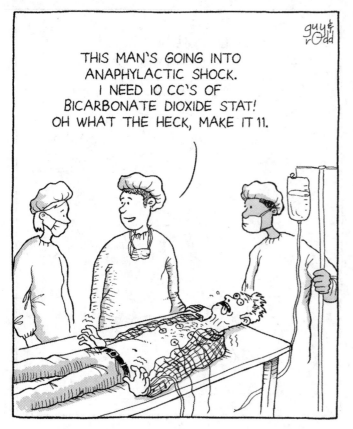

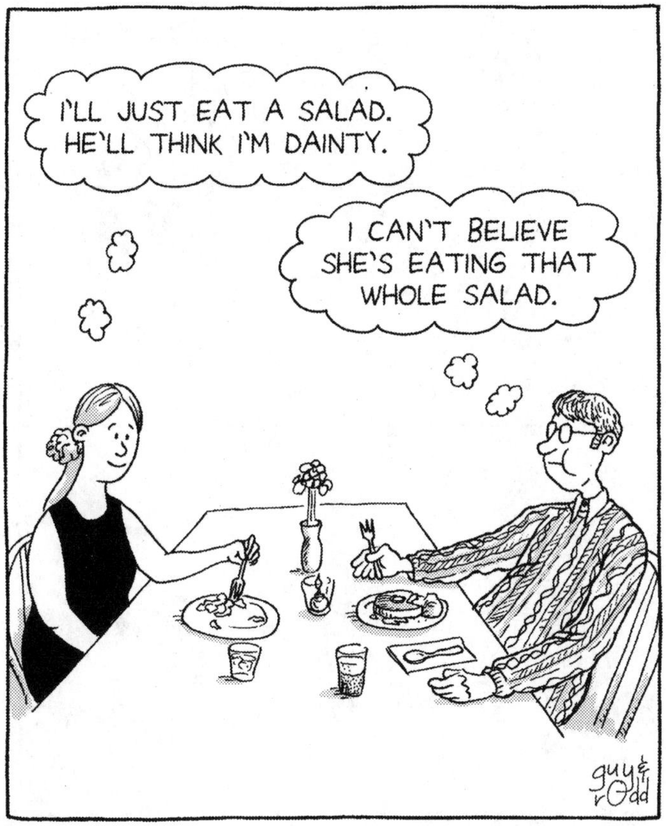
I'LL JUST EAT A SALAD. HE'LL THINK I'M DAINTY.
I CAN'T BELIEVE SHE'S EATING THAT WHOLE SALAD.
guy & rOdd

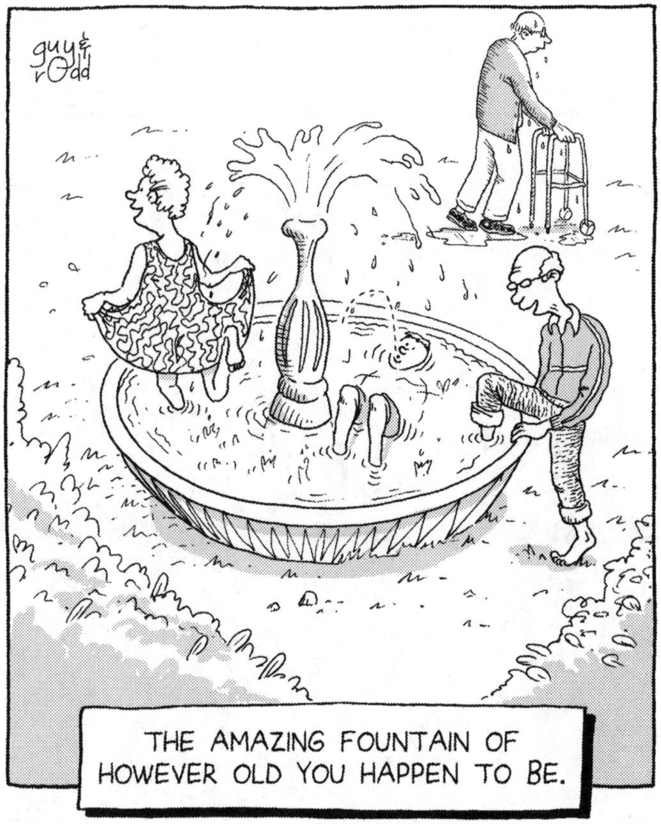
guy & rOdd
THE AMAZING FOUNTAIN OF HOWEVER OLD YOU HAPPEN TO BE.

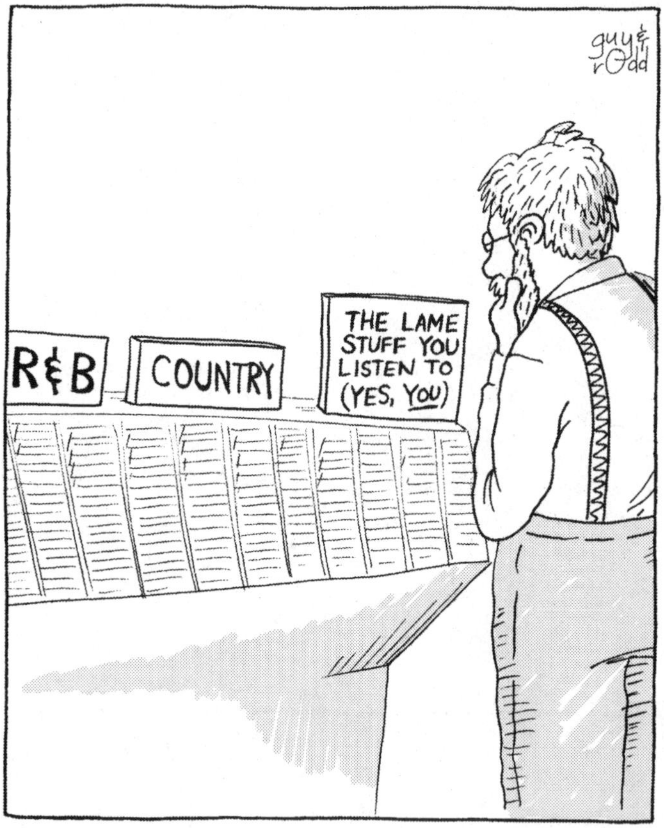
guy & rOdd
R&B
COUNTRY
THE LAME STUFF YOU LISTEN TO (YES, YOU)

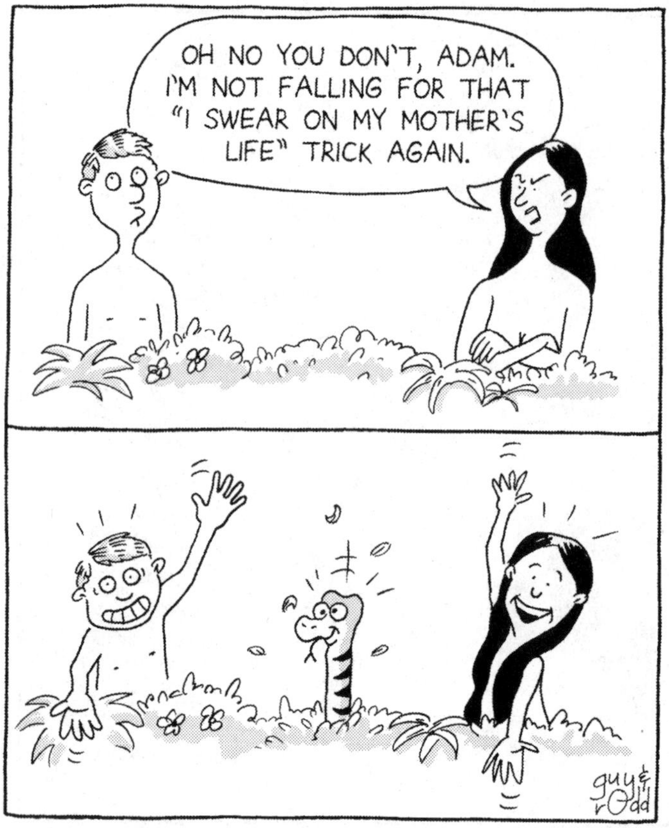
OH NO YOU DON'T, ADAM. I'M NOT FALLING FOR THAT "I SWEAR ON MY MOTHER'S LIFE" TRICK AGAIN.
guy & rOdd

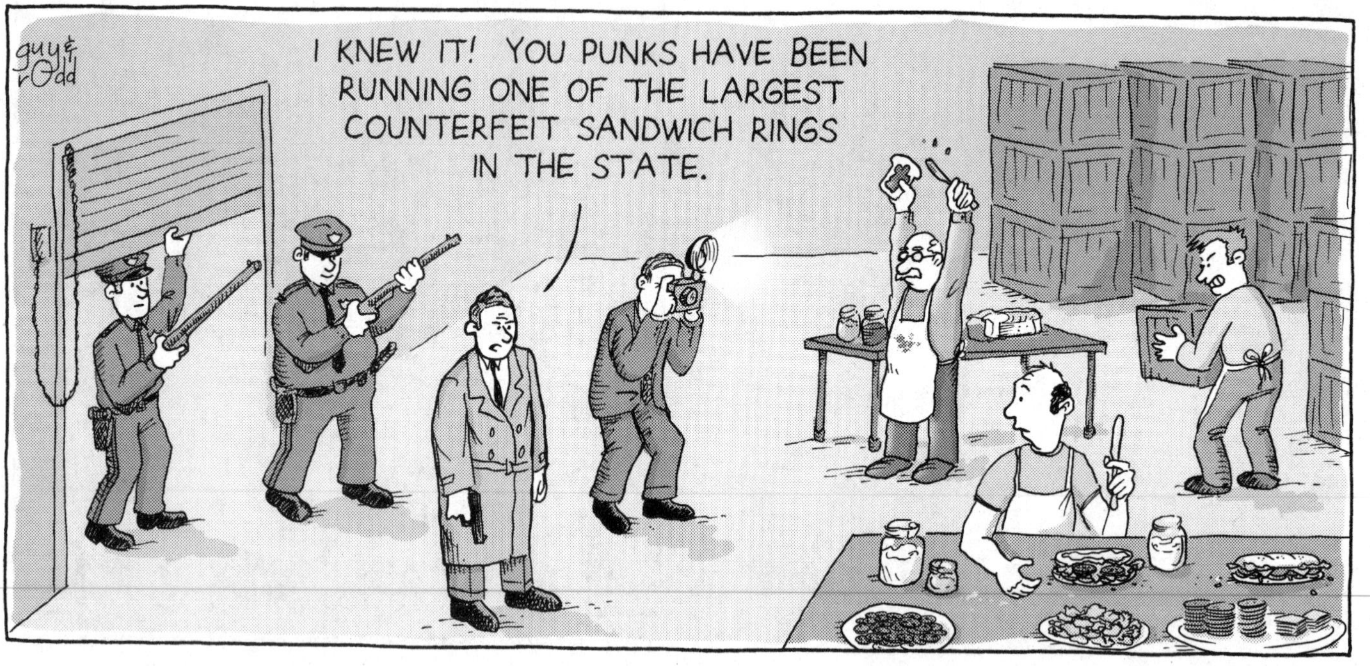
guy & rOdd
I KNEW IT! YOU PUNKS HAVE BEEN RUNNING ONE OF THE LARGEST COUNTERFEIT SANDWICH RINGS IN THE STATE.

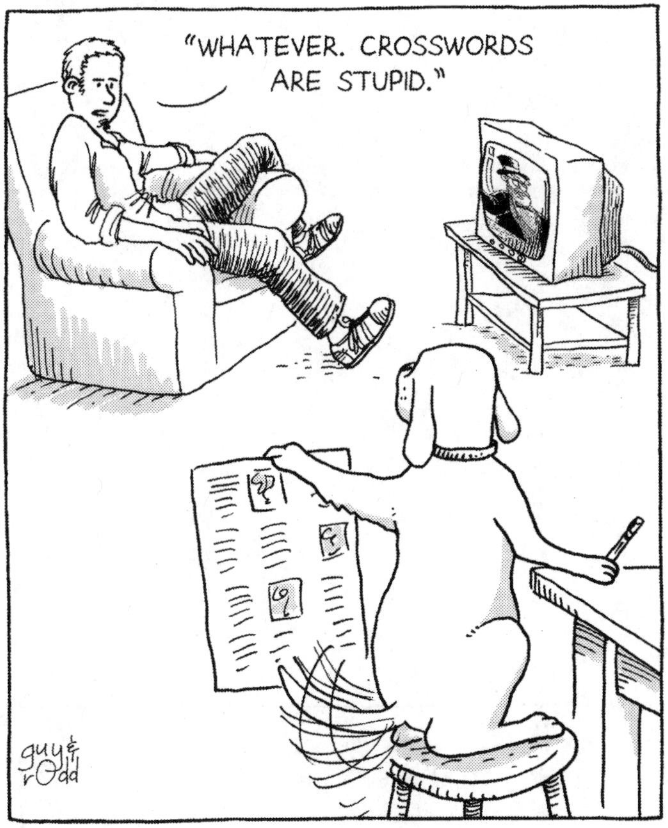
"WHATEVER. CROSSWORDS ARE STUPID."

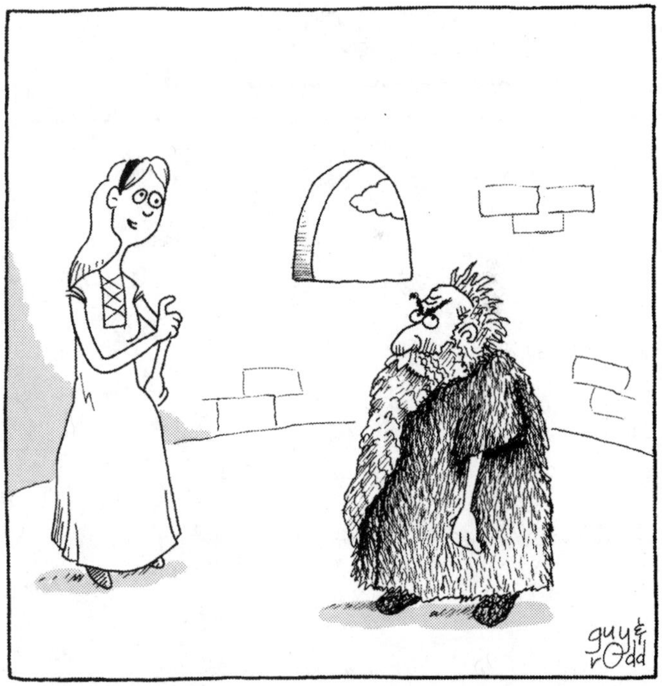

HIS NAME WAS ACTUALLY LARRY, BUT BY THE TIME SHE STARTED GUESSING RANDOM NONSENSE LIKE "RUMPELSTILTSKIN" HE GOT BORED AND TOLD HER SHE WAS RIGHT.

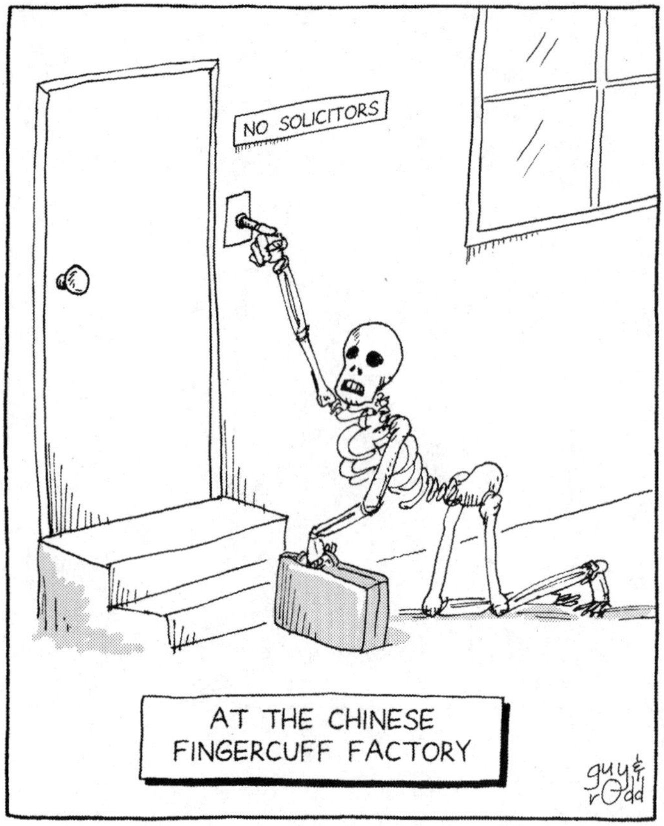
NO SOLICITORS

AT THE CHINESE FINGERCUFF FACTORY

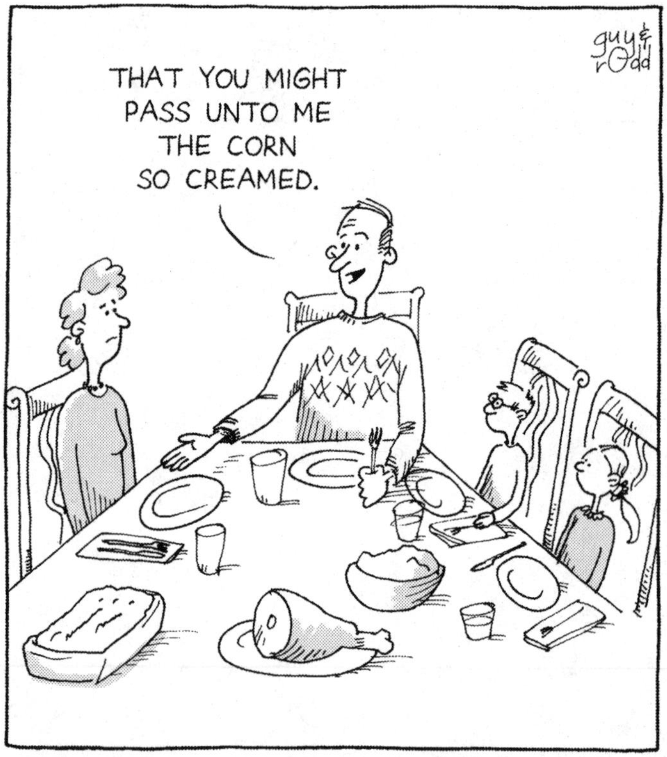
THAT YOU MIGHT PASS UNTO ME THE CORN SO CREAMED.

THAT NIGHT, NEIL THOMAS DECLARED HIMSELF THE POET LAUREATE OF 1673 SHEFFIELD LANE.

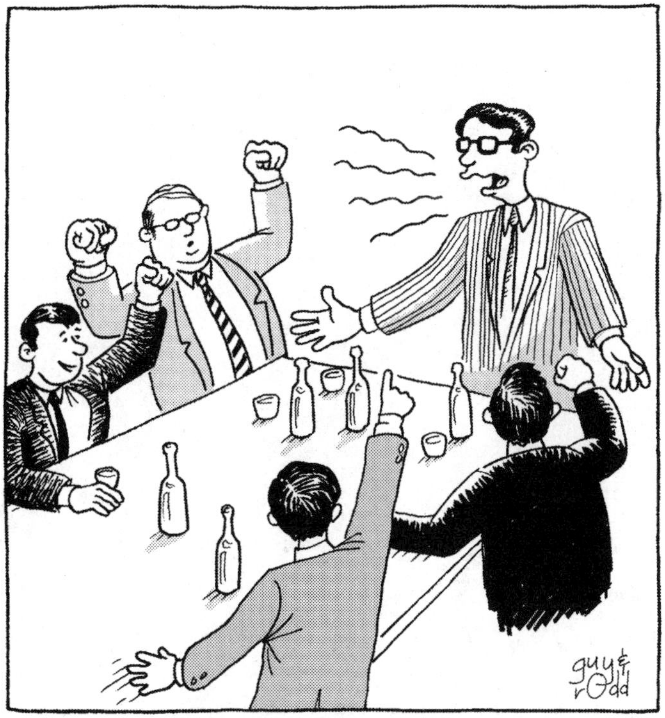

BECAUSE IT CONTAINS THOUSANDS OF INDIVIDUAL CHARACTERS, BURPING THE ALPHABET IN JAPAN IS TRULY A GLORIOUS ACHIEVEMENT.

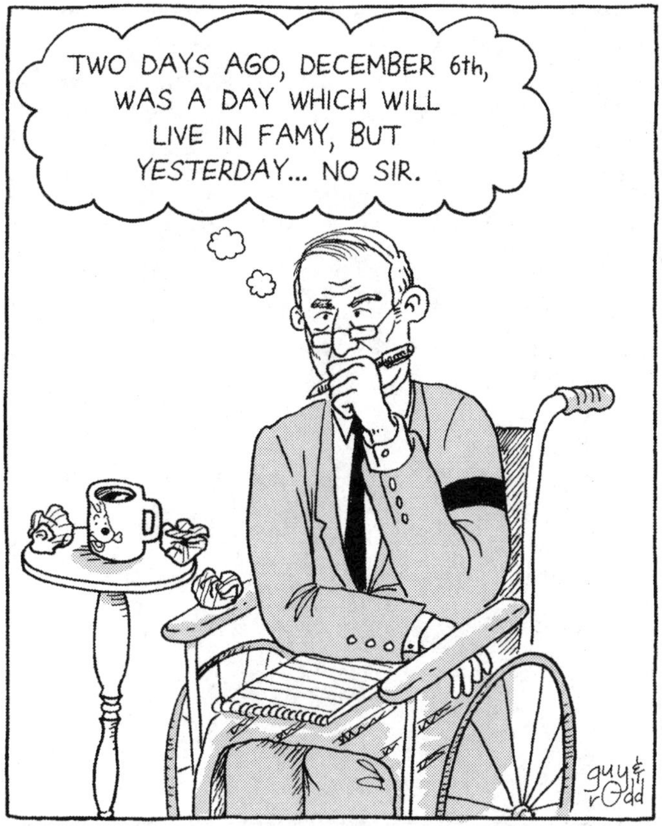
TWO DAYS AGO, DECEMBER 6th, WAS A DAY WHICH WILL LIVE IN FAMY, BUT YESTERDAY... NO SIR.

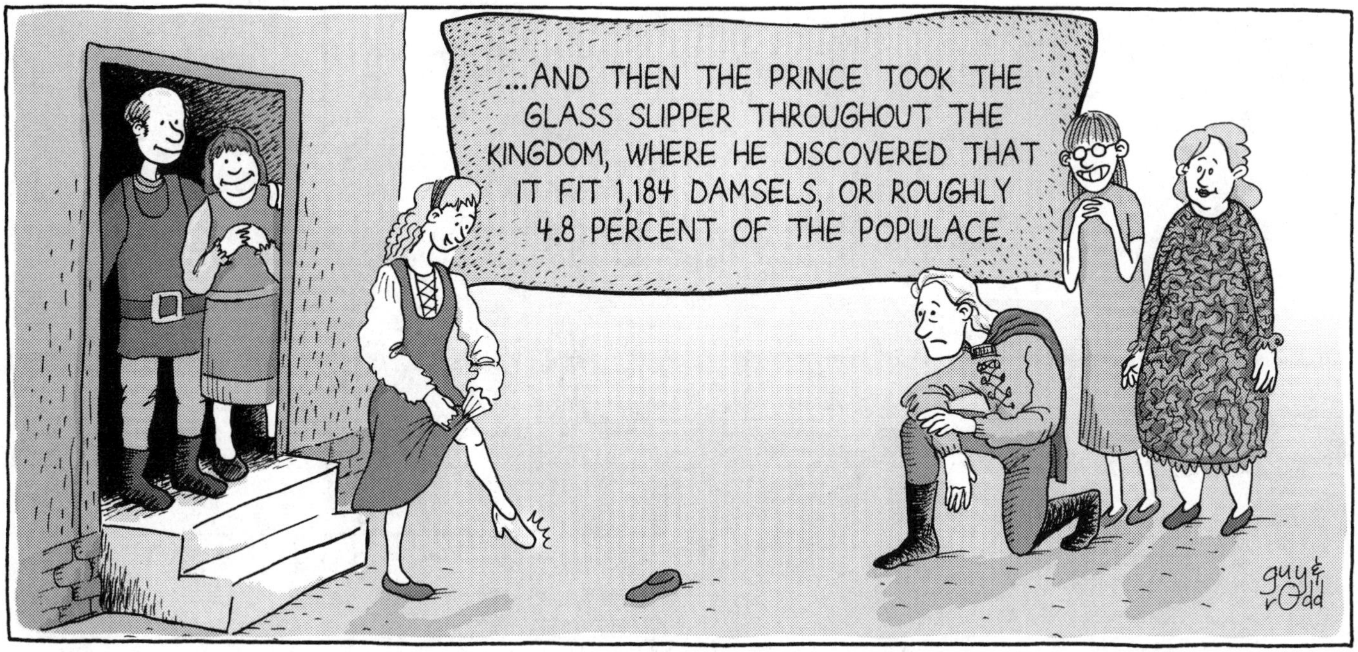
...AND THEN THE PRINCE TOOK THE GLASS SLIPPER THROUGHOUT THE KINGDOM, WHERE HE DISCOVERED THAT IT FIT 1,184 DAMSELS, OR ROUGHLY 4.8 PERCENT OF THE POPULACE.

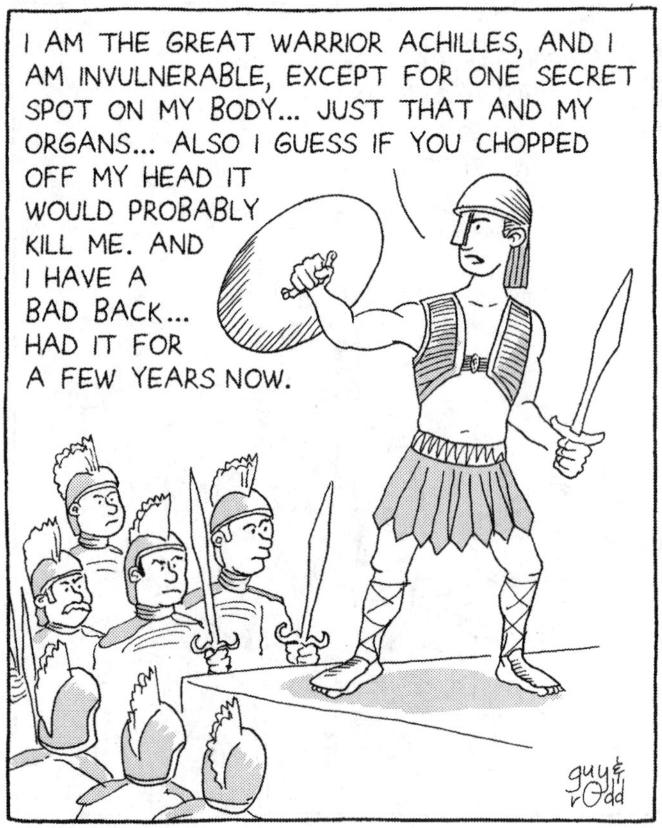
I AM THE GREAT WARRIOR ACHILLES, AND I AM INVULNERABLE, EXCEPT FOR ONE SECRET SPOT ON MY BODY... JUST THAT AND MY ORGANS... ALSO I GUESS IF YOU CHOPPED OFF MY HEAD IT WOULD PROBABLY KILL ME. AND I HAVE A BAD BACK... HAD IT FOR A FEW YEARS NOW.

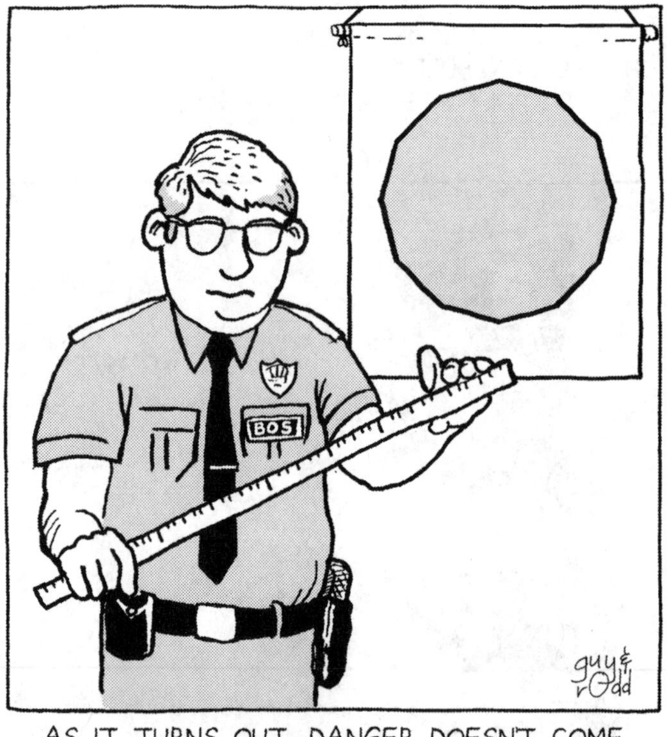

AS IT TURNS OUT, DANGER DOESN'T COME IN ALL SHAPES AND SIZES...THE EXCEPTIONS BEING THE DODECAGON AND 3 FEET 7 INCHES.

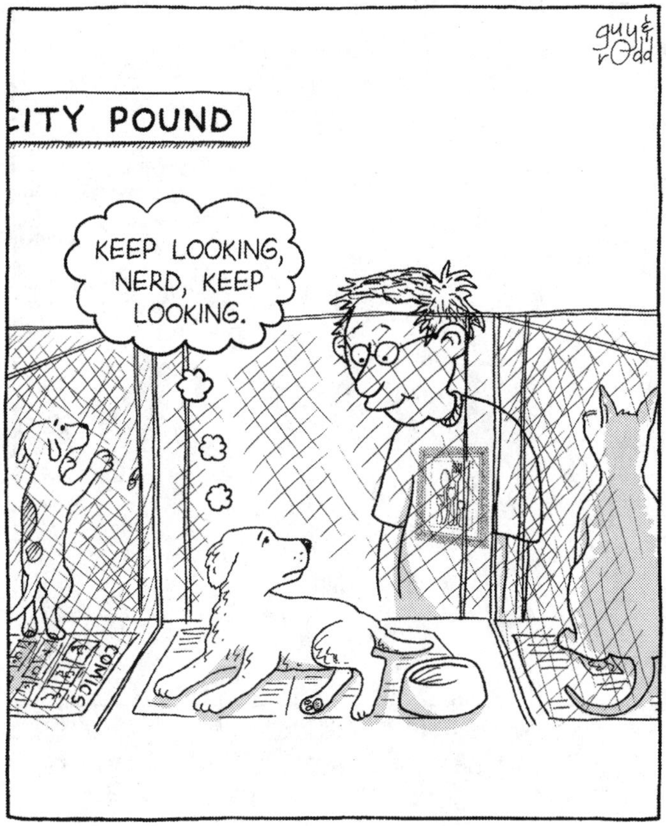
CITY POUND
KEEP LOOKING, NERD, KEEP LOOKING.
COMICS

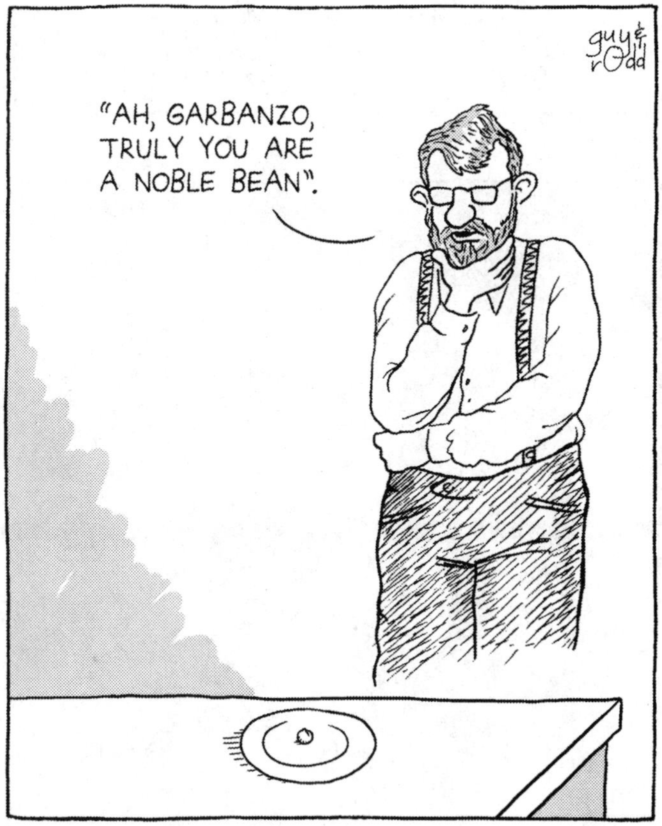
"AH, GARBANZO, TRULY YOU ARE A NOBLE BEAN".

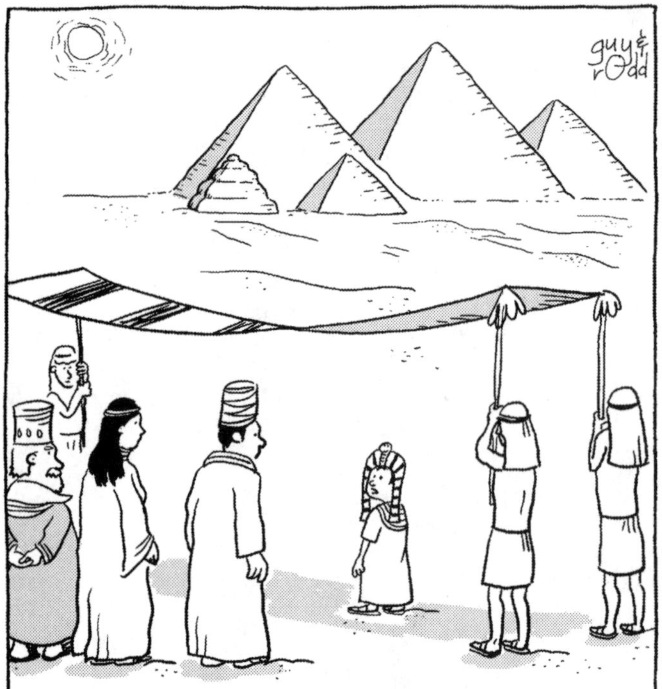

"I'M THINKING SOMETHING A LITTLE MORE MODEST... SAY, WHATEVER 1,000 SLAVES CAN DO IN 50 YEARS."

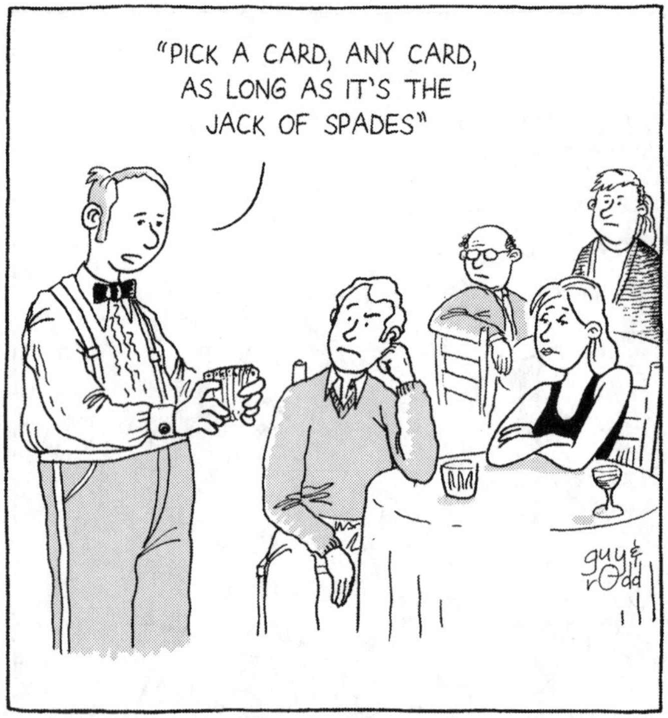
"PICK A CARD, ANY CARD, AS LONG AS IT'S THE JACK OF SPADES"

AND WITH THAT, THE SIMPLE MALAISE THAT HAD BEEN BUBBLING UP FOR MONTHS OFFICIALLY BECAME A GENERAL MALAISE.

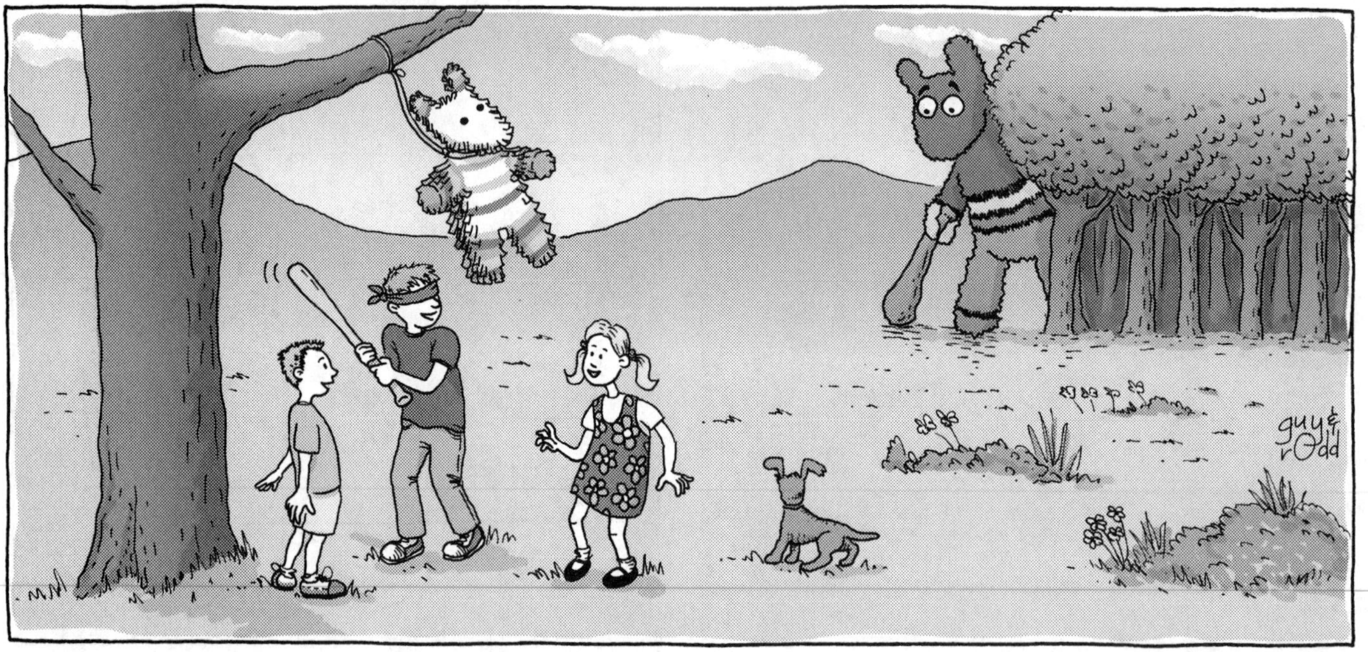

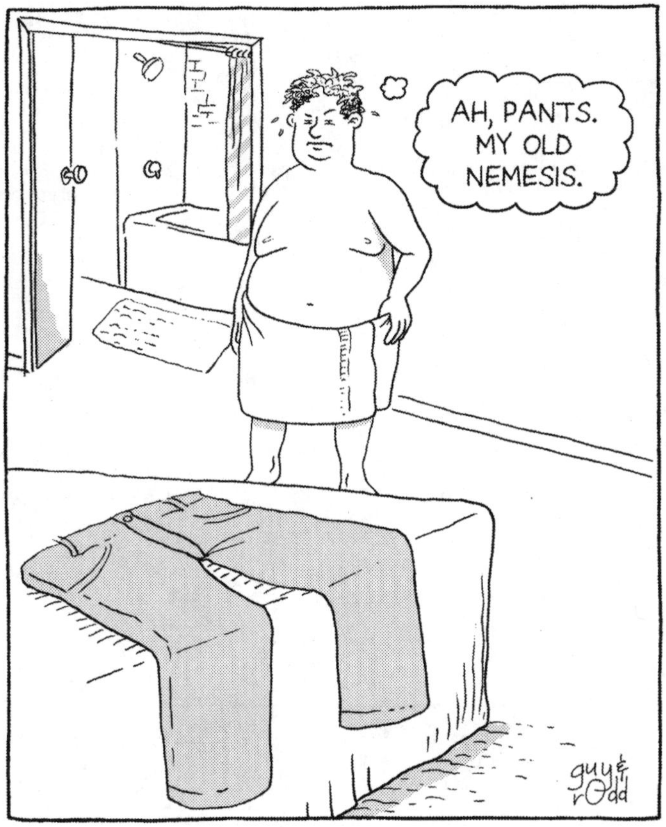
AH, PANTS. MY OLD NEMESIS.
guy & rOdd

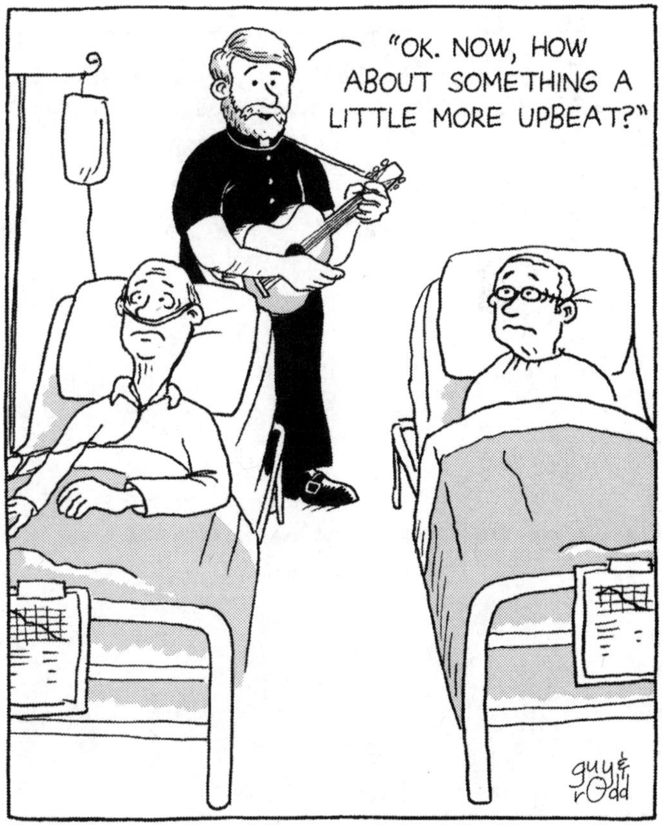
"OK. NOW, HOW ABOUT SOMETHING A LITTLE MORE UPBEAT?"
guy & rOdd

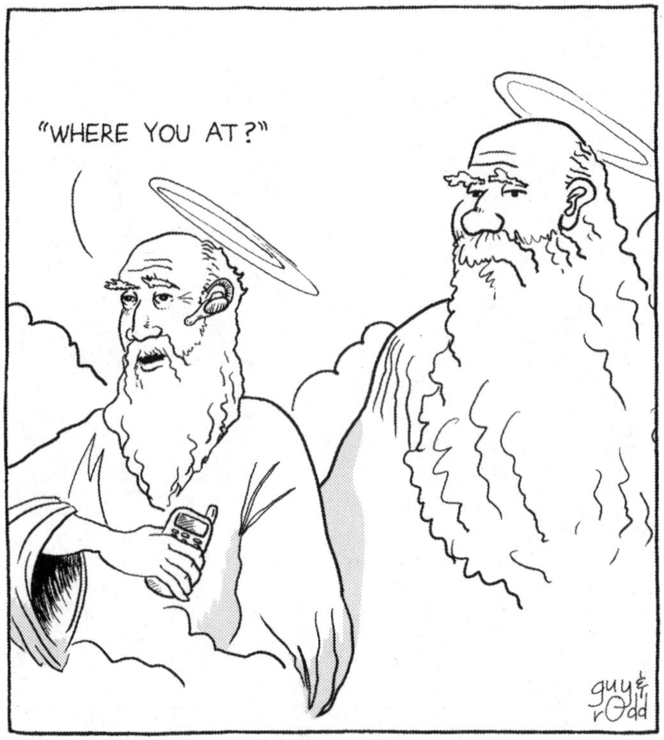
"WHERE YOU AT?"

SUDDENLY, GOD WONDERED IF SAINT ANDREW HAD A COOLER CELL PHONE THAN HIM.

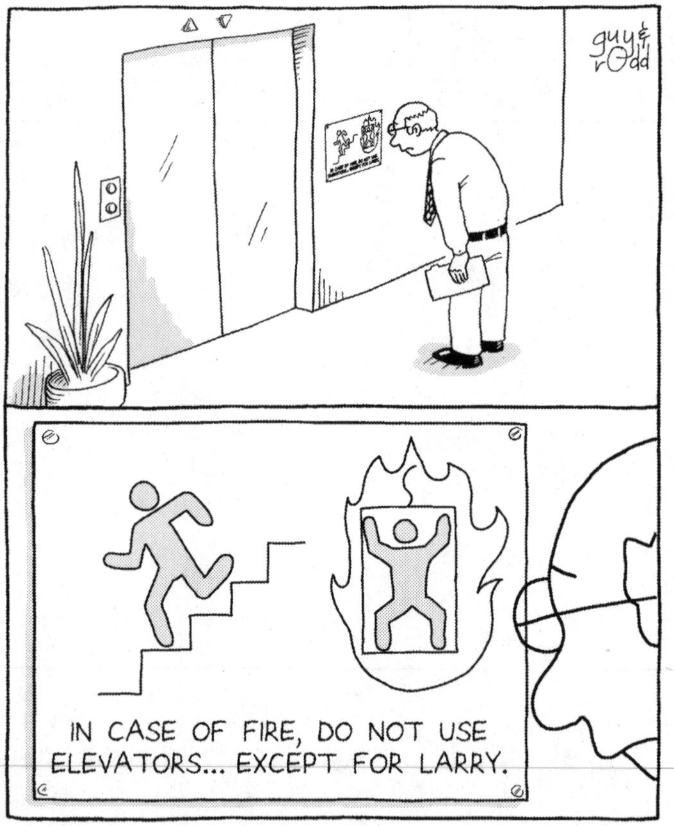
IN CASE OF FIRE, DO NOT USE
ELEVATORS... EXCEPT FOR LARRY.

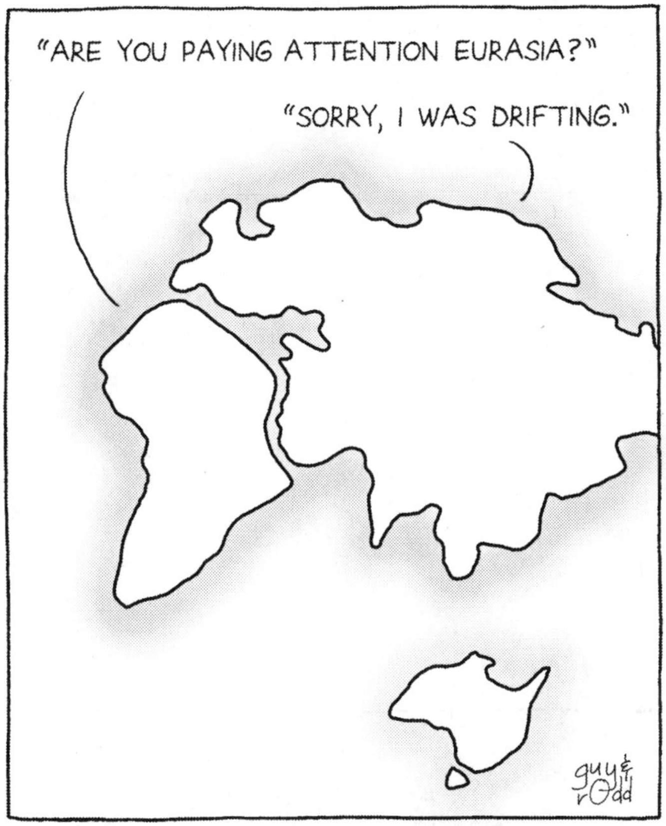
"ARE YOU PAYING ATTENTION EURASIA?"
"SORRY, I WAS DRIFTING."
guy & rodd

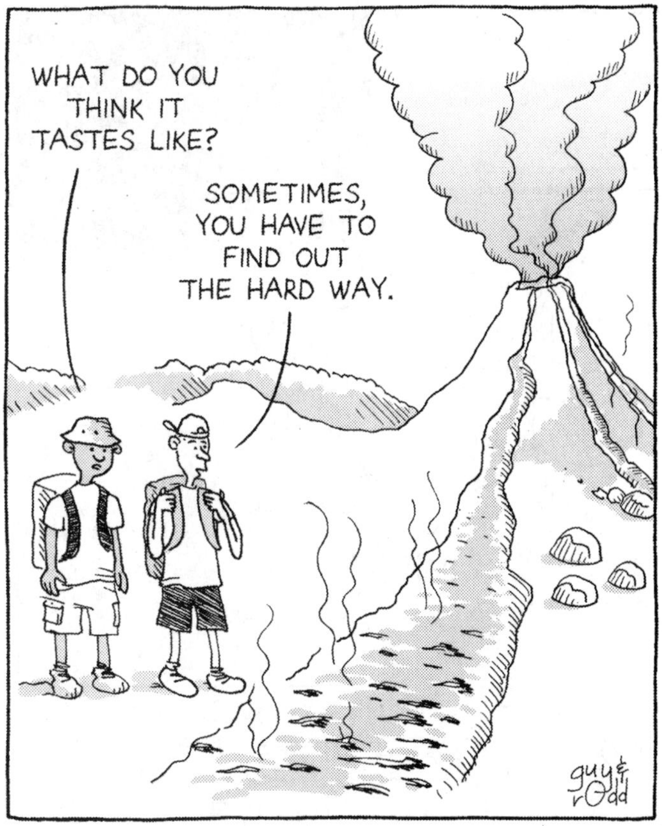
WHAT DO YOU THINK IT TASTES LIKE?
SOMETIMES, YOU HAVE TO FIND OUT THE HARD WAY.
guy & rodd

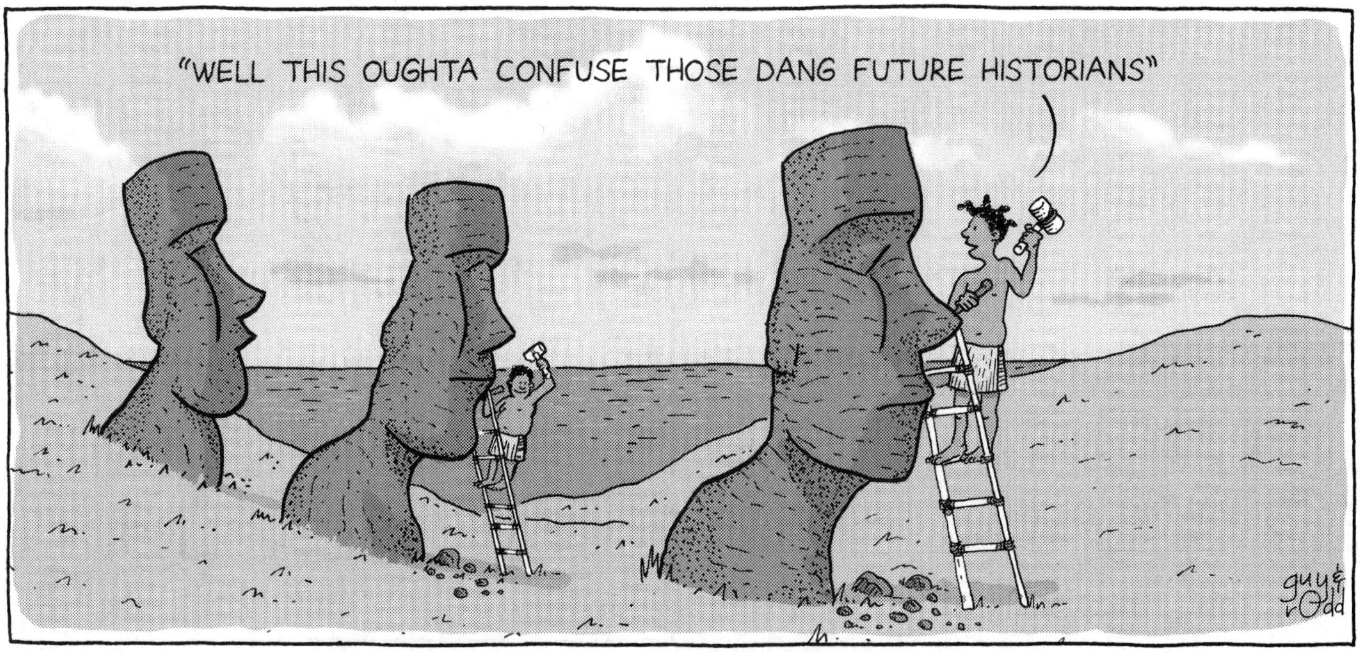
"WELL THIS OUGHTA CONFUSE THOSE DANG FUTURE HISTORIANS"
guy & rodd

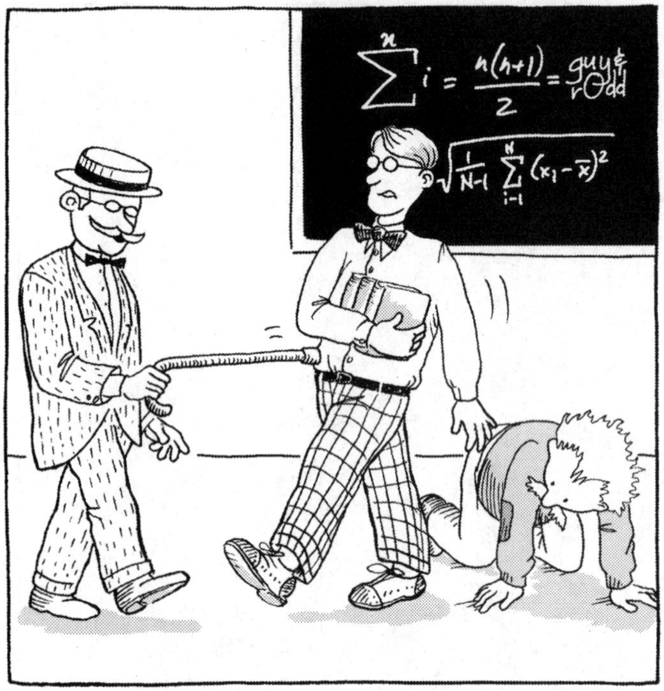
$\sum^{n} i = \frac{n(n+1)}{2} =$ guy & rOdd
$\sqrt{\frac{1}{N-1} \sum_{i=1}^{N} (x_i - \bar{x})^2}$

MOST PEOPLE DON'T KNOW THAT
IN ADDITION TO THE THEORY OF RELATIVITY,
EINSTEIN WAS ALSO THE INVENTOR OF
THE "KNEEL AND PUSH".

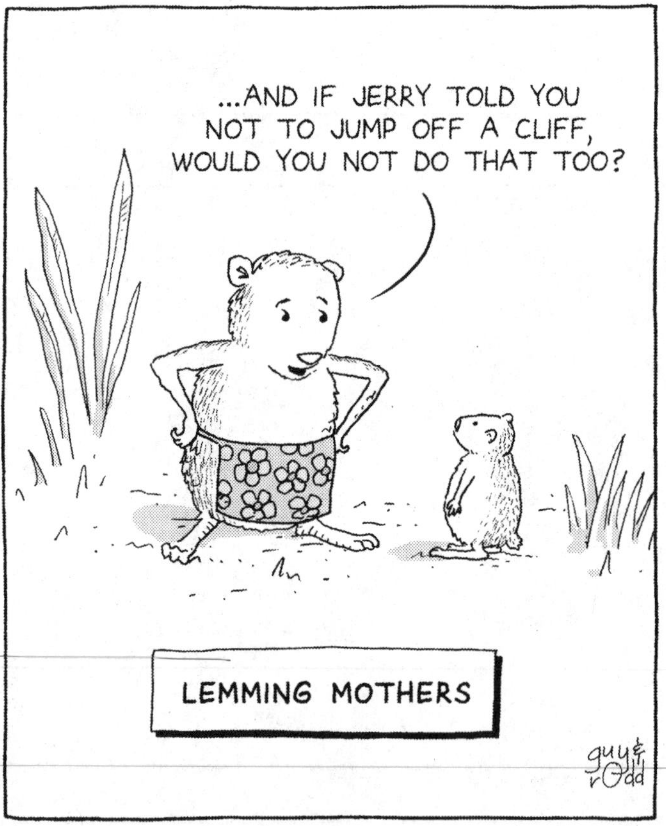
...AND IF JERRY TOLD YOU
NOT TO JUMP OFF A CLIFF,
WOULD YOU NOT DO THAT TOO?
LEMMING MOTHERS
guy & rOdd

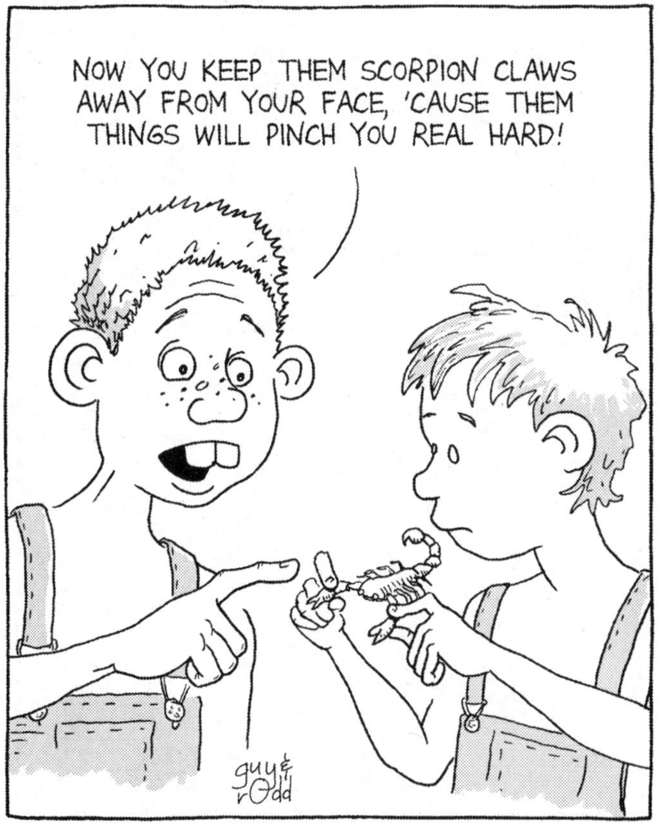
NOW YOU KEEP THEM SCORPION CLAWS AWAY FROM YOUR FACE, 'CAUSE THEM THINGS WILL PINCH YOU REAL HARD!
guy & rOdd

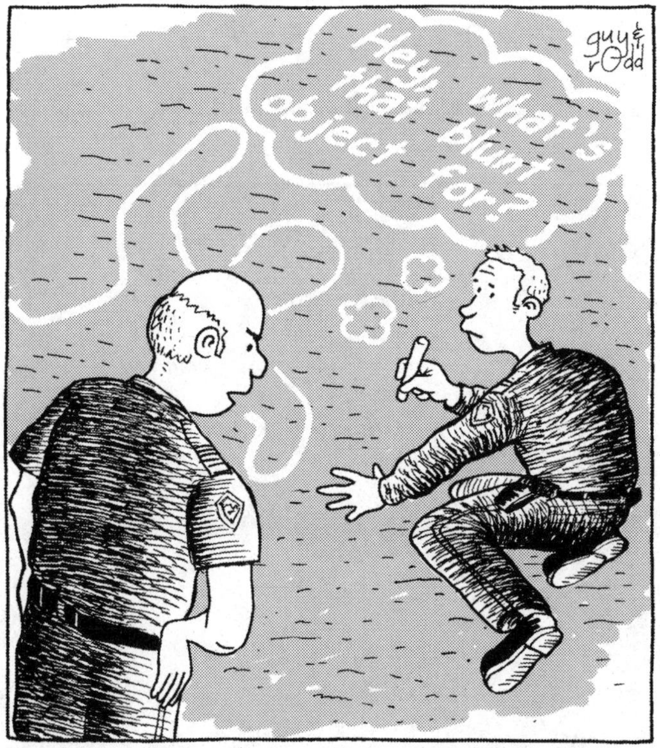
Hey, what's that blunt object for?
guy & rOdd

"SOLOMON, WHAT DID I TELL YOU ABOUT GIVING THE CHALK OUTLINES THOUGHT BUBBLES!?"

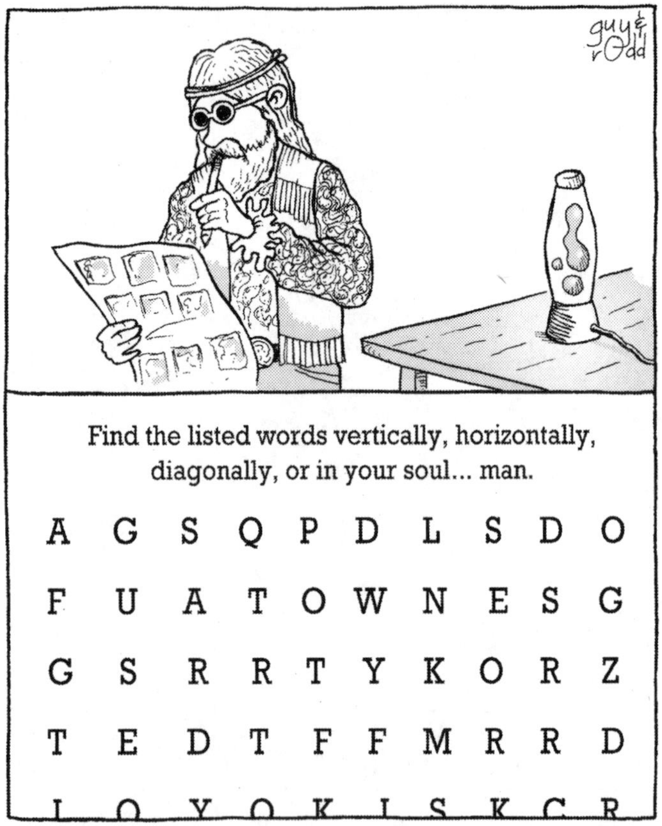
guy & rodd
Find the listed words vertically, horizontally, diagonally, or in your soul... man.
A G S Q P D L S D O
F U A T O W N E S G
G S R R T Y K O R Z
T E D T F F M R R D

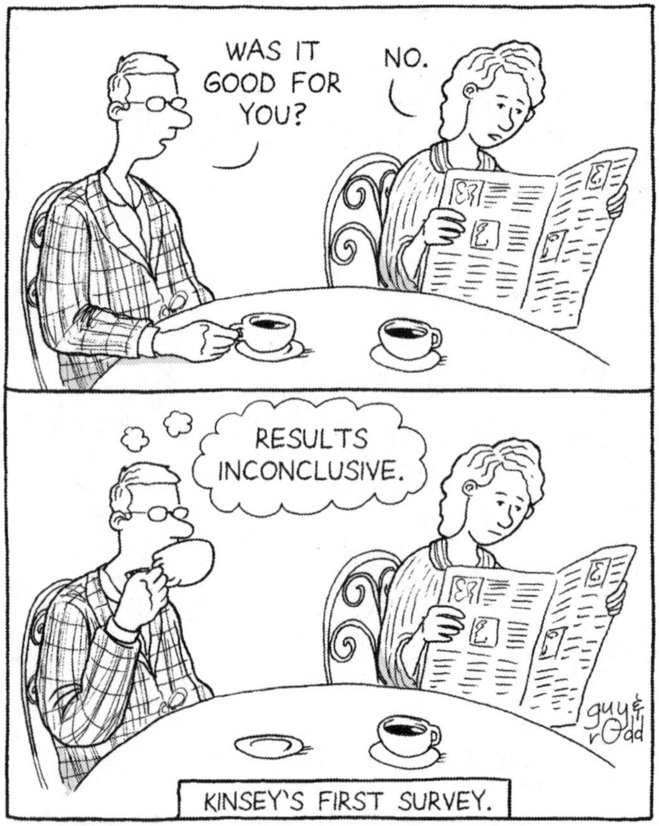
WAS IT GOOD FOR YOU?
NO.
RESULTS INCONCLUSIVE.
guy & rodd
KINSEY'S FIRST SURVEY.

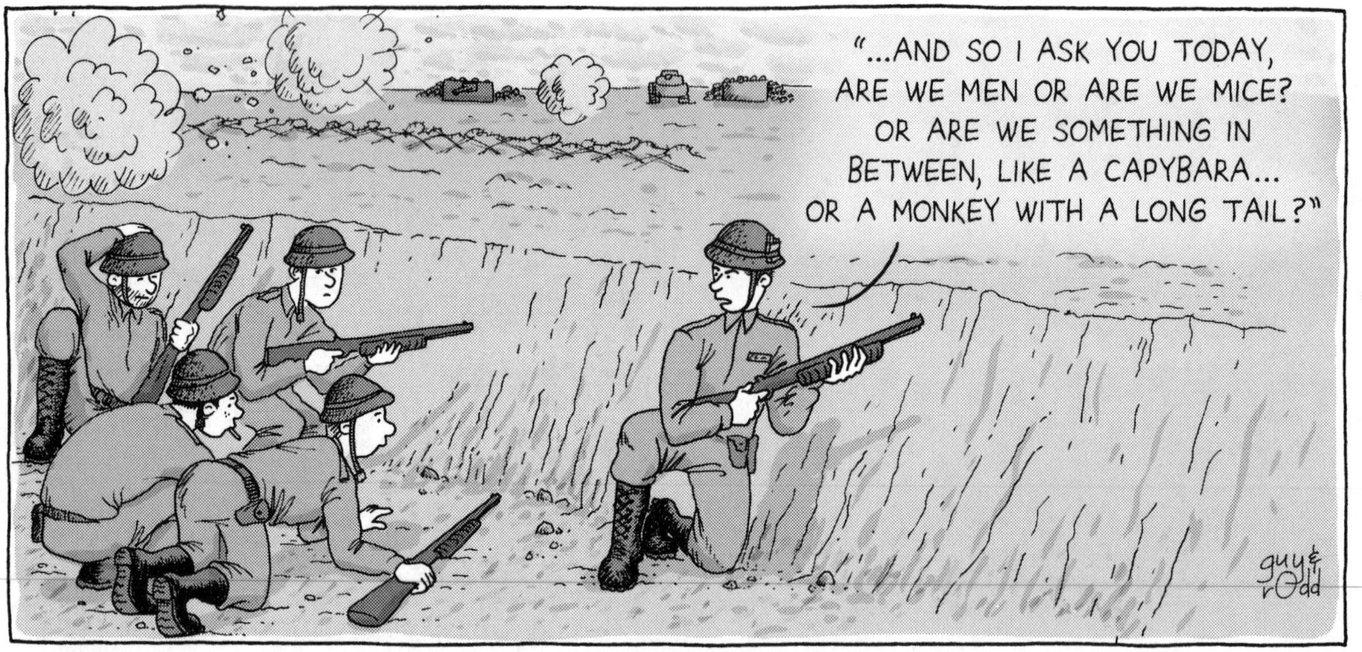
"...AND SO I ASK YOU TODAY, ARE WE MEN OR ARE WE MICE? OR ARE WE SOMETHING IN BETWEEN, LIKE A CAPYBARA... OR A MONKEY WITH A LONG TAIL?"
guy & rodd

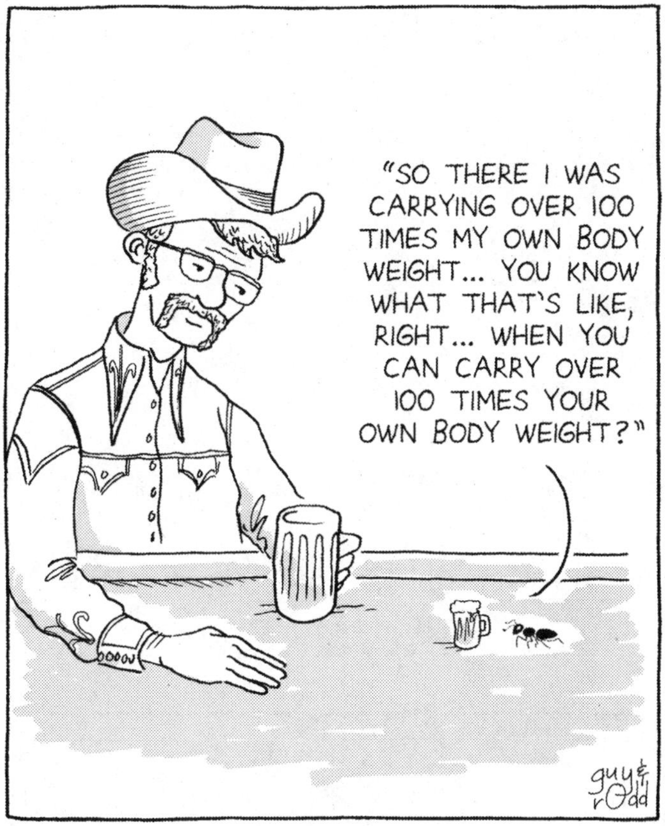
"SO THERE I WAS CARRYING OVER 100 TIMES MY OWN BODY WEIGHT... YOU KNOW WHAT THAT'S LIKE, RIGHT... WHEN YOU CAN CARRY OVER 100 TIMES YOUR OWN BODY WEIGHT?"
guy & rOdd

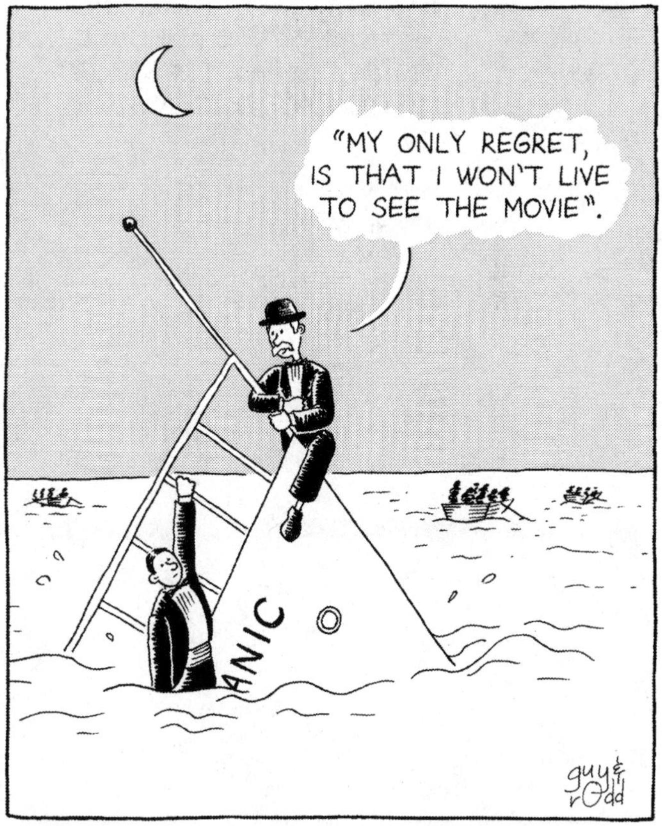
"MY ONLY REGRET, IS THAT I WON'T LIVE TO SEE THE MOVIE".
ANIC
guy & rOdd

AND THEN, ON A BEAUTIFUL SPRING DAY IN 2003, WITH THE SCENT OF RHODODENDRUMS FILLING THE AIR, ADAM HINDS BECAME THE FIRST, AND STILL ONLY, PERSON TO ACTUALLY USE ZAPF DINGBATS.

HOUSED DEEP WITHIN THE BOWELS OF THE MOTION PICTURE ASSOCIATION OF AMERICA IS A MAN NAMED WALLACE McENTYRE, AND HE, AND HE ALONE, UNDERSTANDS WHAT MAY AND MAY NOT BE APPROPRIATE FOR CHILDREN UNDER THIRTEEN.

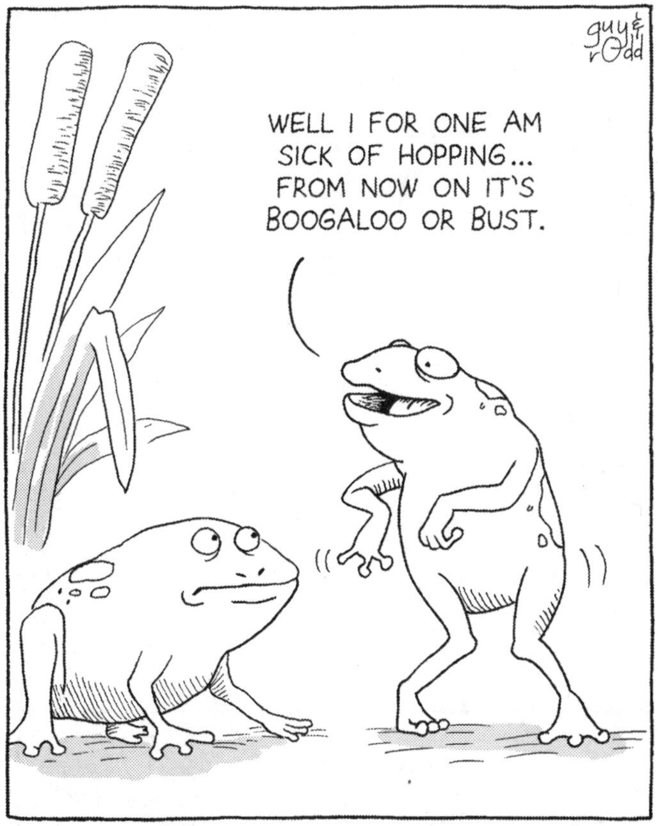
guy & rOdd
WELL I FOR ONE AM SICK OF HOPPING... FROM NOW ON IT'S BOOGALOO OR BUST.

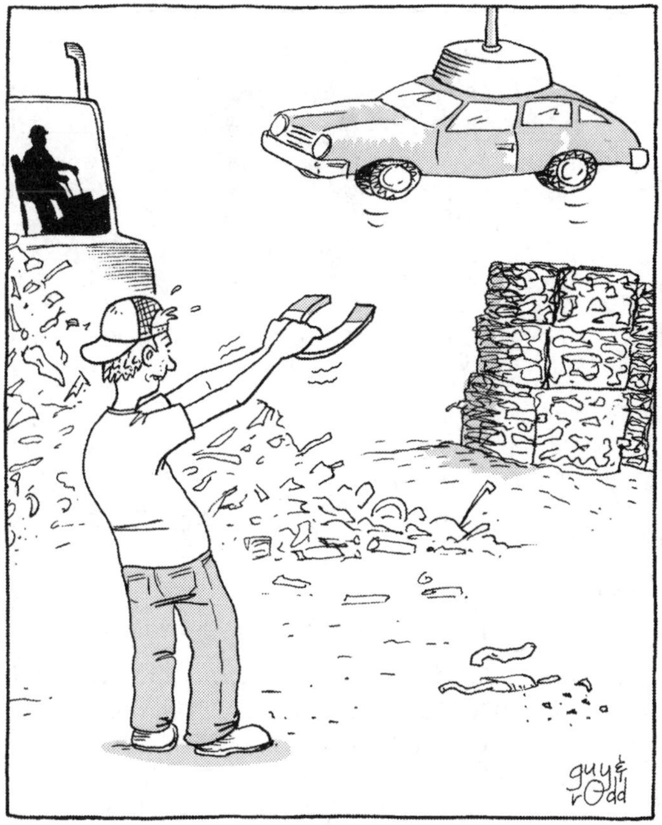
guy & rOdd

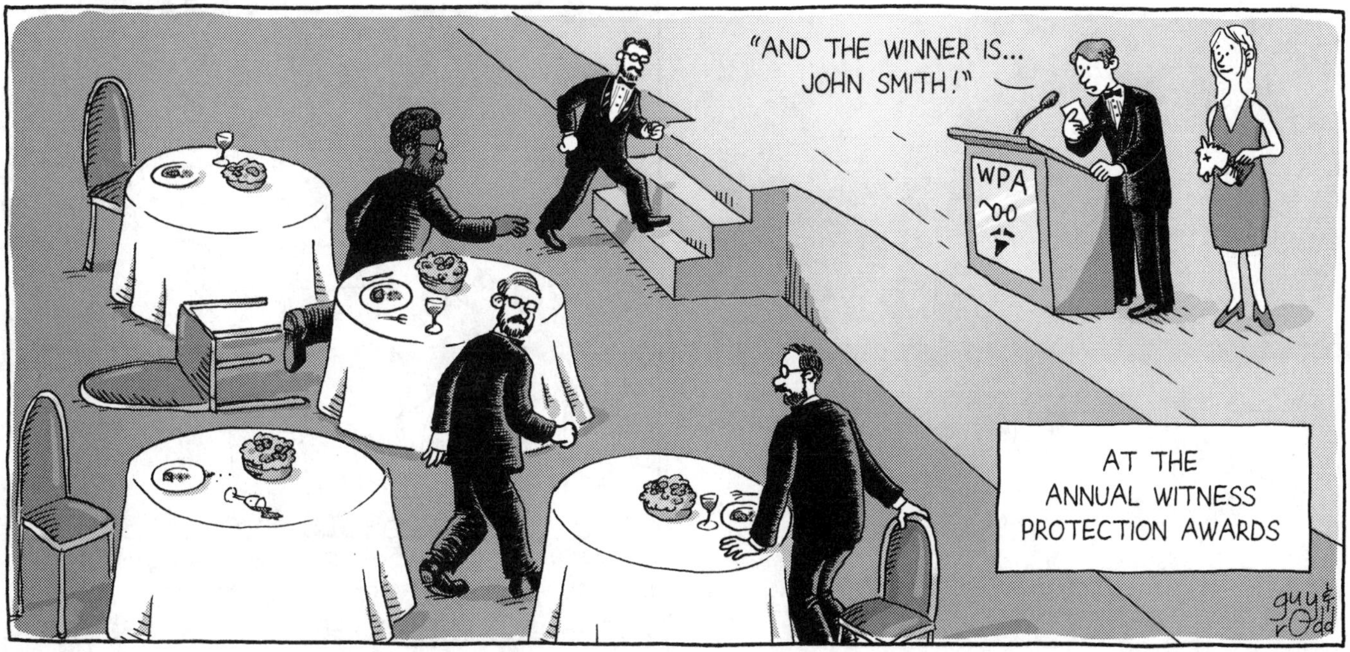
"AND THE WINNER IS... JOHN SMITH!"
WPA
AT THE ANNUAL WITNESS PROTECTION AWARDS
guy & rOdd

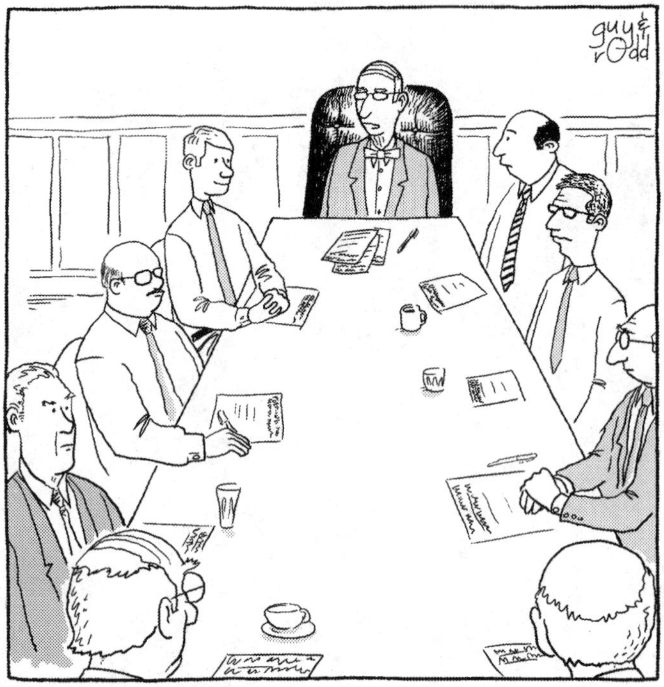
guy & rodd

"ABRAMOWITZ AND LOWENSTEIN, YOU'VE CERTAINLY EARNED THIS, BUT UNFORTUNATELY WE DON'T HAVE ENOUGH ROOM ON THE LETTERHEAD... SMITH, CONGRATULATIONS!"

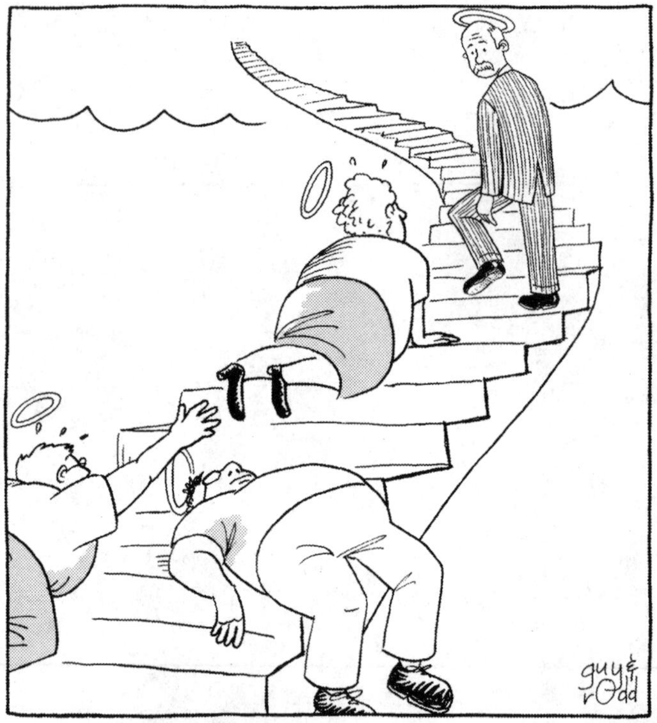
guy & rodd

EVERYONE'S HEARD OF THE STAIRWAY TO HEAVEN, BUT MOST PEOPLE DON'T KNOW IT WAS ACTUALLY BUILT TO KEEP THE FATTIES OUT.

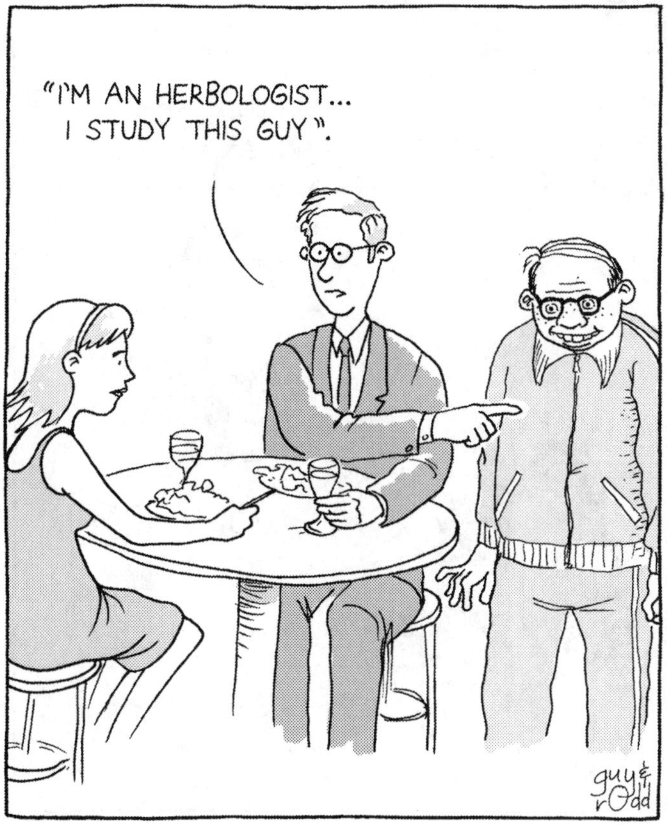
"I'M AN HERBOLOGIST...
I STUDY THIS GUY".
guy & rodd

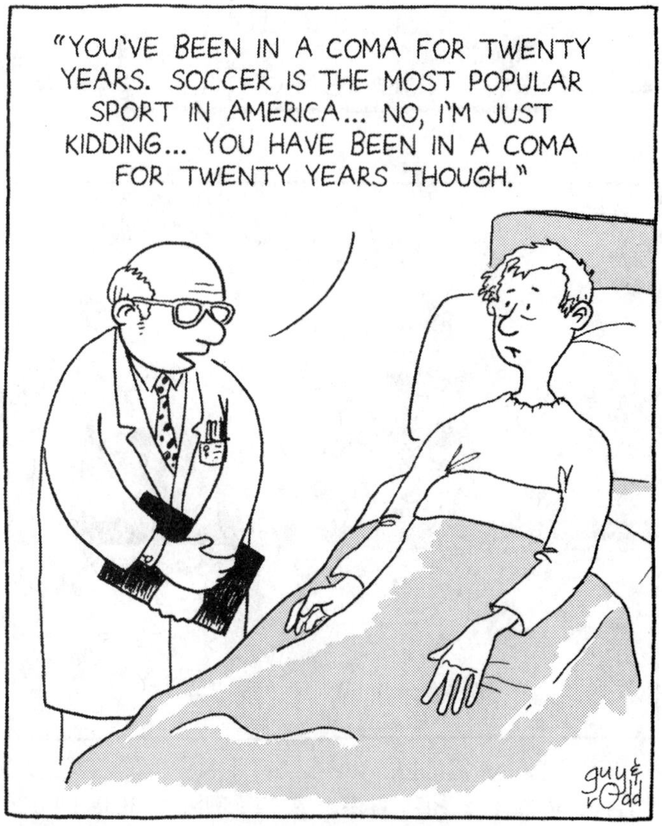
"YOU'VE BEEN IN A COMA FOR TWENTY YEARS. SOCCER IS THE MOST POPULAR SPORT IN AMERICA... NO, I'M JUST KIDDING... YOU HAVE BEEN IN A COMA FOR TWENTY YEARS THOUGH."
guy & rodd

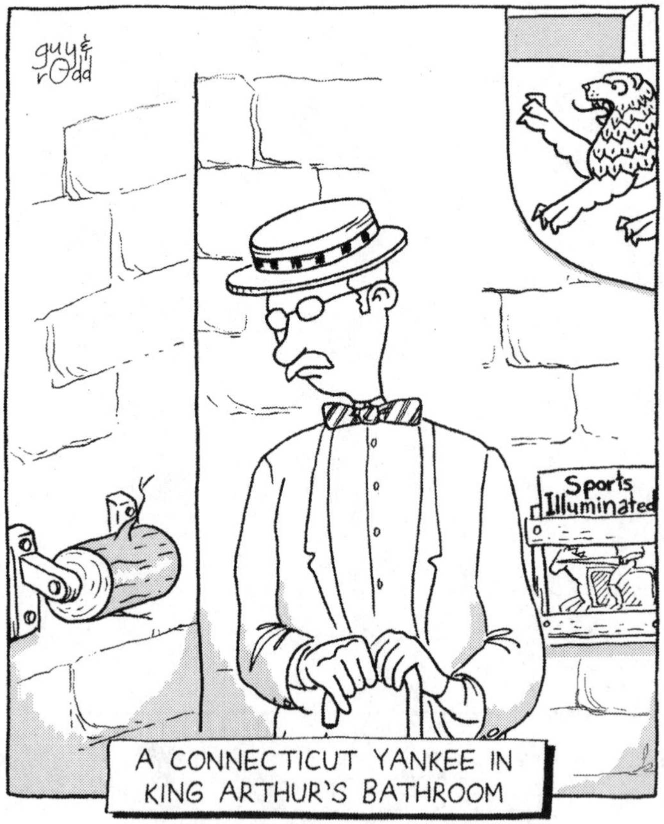
guy & rOdd
Sports Illuminated

A CONNECTICUT YANKEE IN KING ARTHUR'S BATHROOM

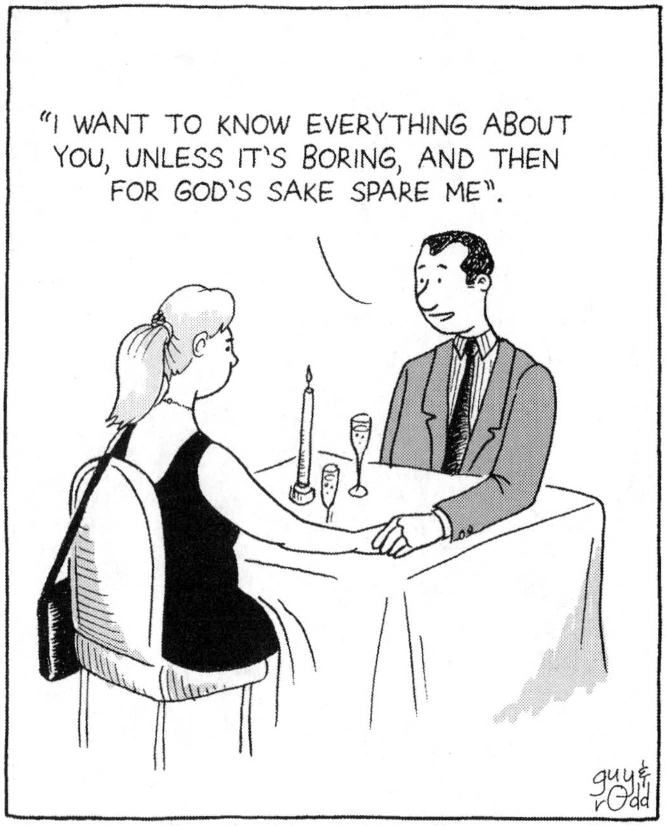
guy & rOdd

"I WANT TO KNOW EVERYTHING ABOUT YOU, UNLESS IT'S BORING, AND THEN FOR GOD'S SAKE SPARE ME".

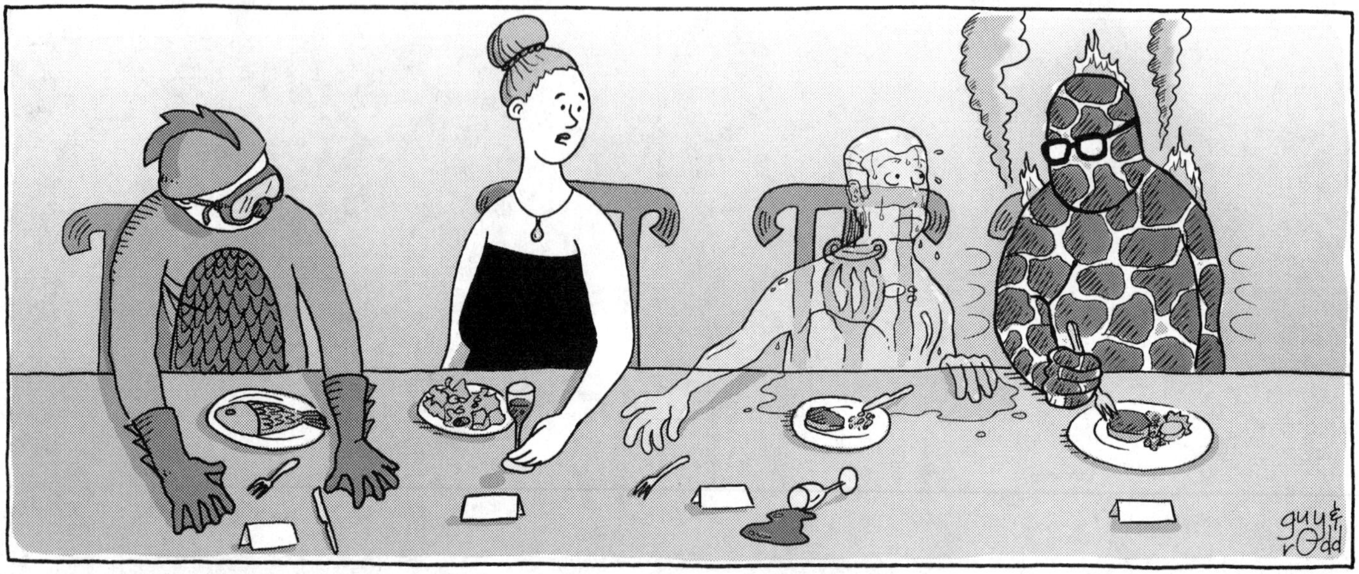
guy & rOdd

CAPTAIN ICICLE WAS SITTING NEXT TO DOCTOR MAGMA, AND MS. AQUAMAN SWORE THIS WOULD BE THE LAST TIME HER HUSBAND HANDLED THE SEATING ARRANGEMENTS.

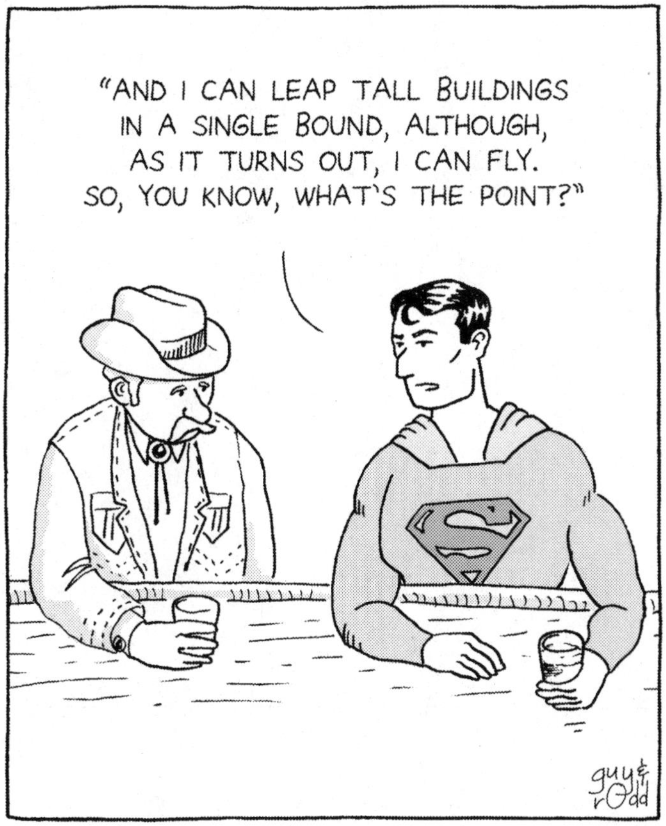
"AND I CAN LEAP TALL BUILDINGS IN A SINGLE BOUND, ALTHOUGH, AS IT TURNS OUT, I CAN FLY. SO, YOU KNOW, WHAT'S THE POINT?"
guy & rOdd

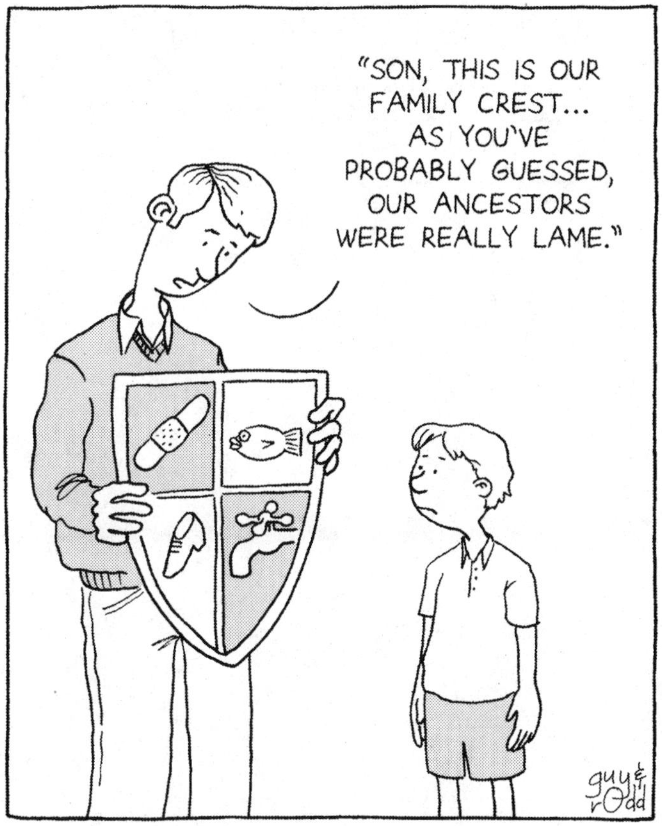
"SON, THIS IS OUR FAMILY CREST... AS YOU'VE PROBABLY GUESSED, OUR ANCESTORS WERE REALLY LAME."
guy & rOdd

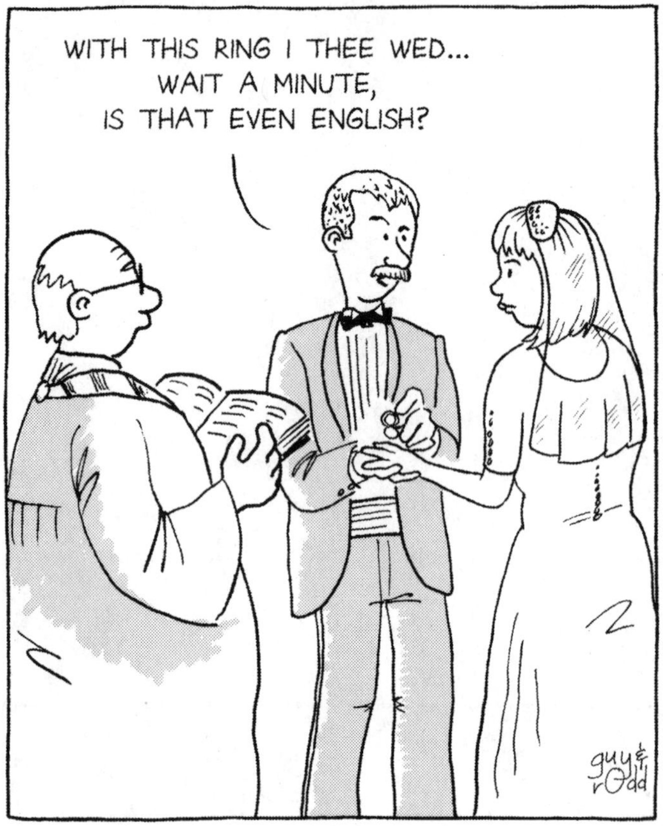
WITH THIS RING I THEE WED... WAIT A MINUTE, IS THAT EVEN ENGLISH?
guy & rOdd

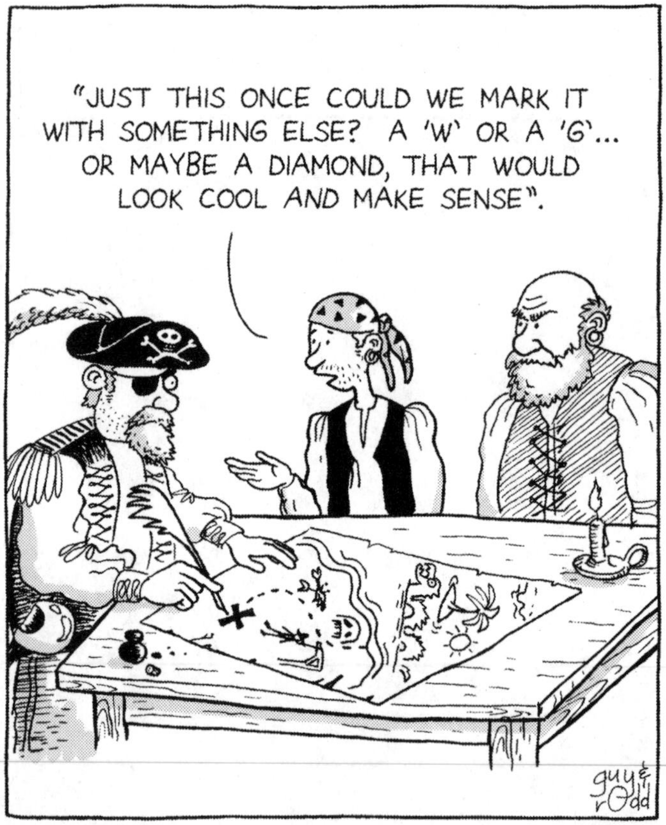
"JUST THIS ONCE COULD WE MARK IT WITH SOMETHING ELSE? A 'W' OR A 'G'... OR MAYBE A DIAMOND, THAT WOULD LOOK COOL AND MAKE SENSE".
guy & rOdd

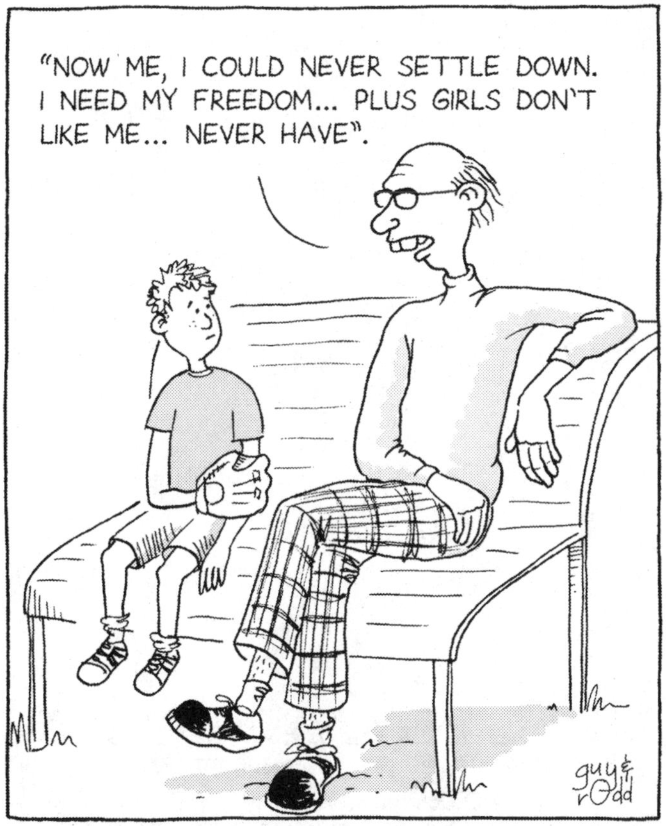
"NOW ME, I COULD NEVER SETTLE DOWN. I NEED MY FREEDOM... PLUS GIRLS DON'T LIKE ME... NEVER HAVE".
guy & rodd

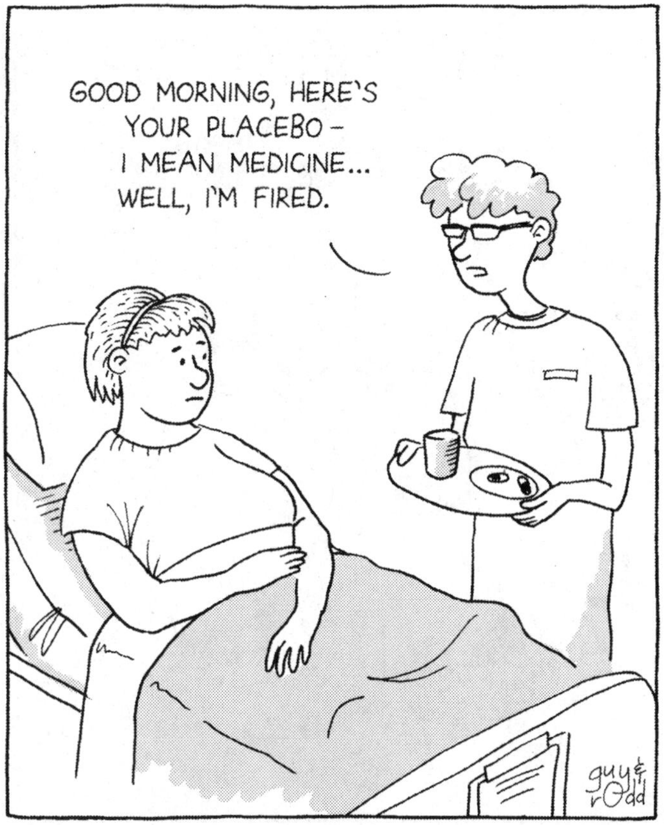
GOOD MORNING, HERE'S YOUR PLACEBO - I MEAN MEDICINE... WELL, I'M FIRED.
guy & rodd

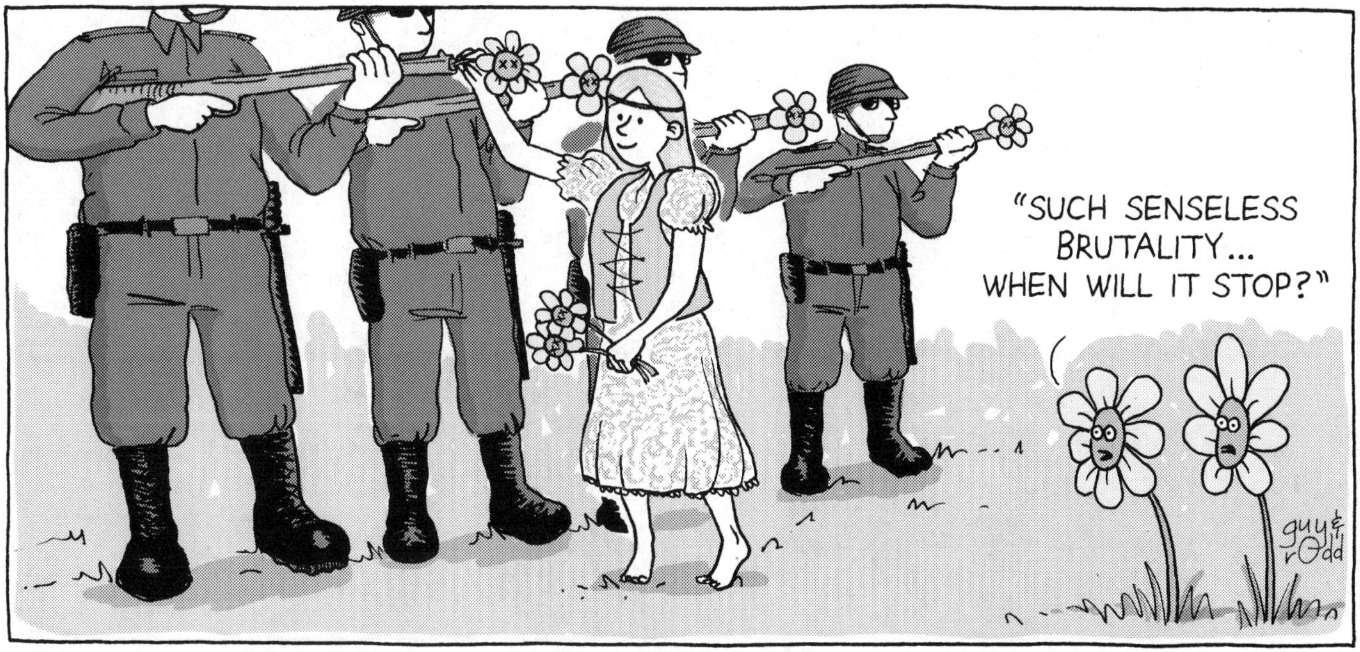
"SUCH SENSELESS BRUTALITY... WHEN WILL IT STOP?"
guy & rodd

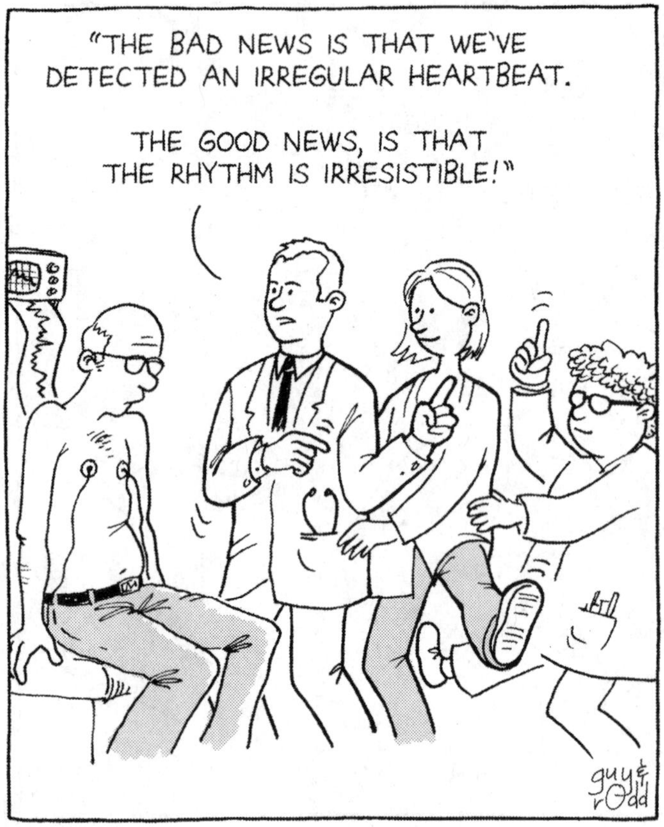
"THE BAD NEWS IS THAT WE'VE DETECTED AN IRREGULAR HEARTBEAT.
THE GOOD NEWS, IS THAT THE RHYTHM IS IRRESISTIBLE!"
guy & rOdd

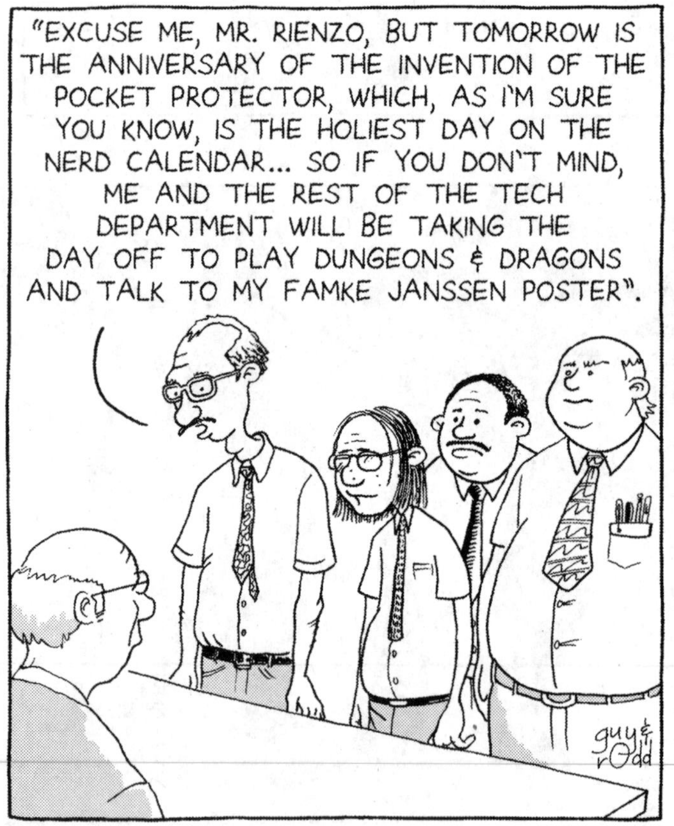
"EXCUSE ME, MR. RIENZO, BUT TOMORROW IS THE ANNIVERSARY OF THE INVENTION OF THE POCKET PROTECTOR, WHICH, AS I'M SURE YOU KNOW, IS THE HOLIEST DAY ON THE NERD CALENDAR... SO IF YOU DON'T MIND, ME AND THE REST OF THE TECH DEPARTMENT WILL BE TAKING THE DAY OFF TO PLAY DUNGEONS & DRAGONS AND TALK TO MY FAMKE JANSSEN POSTER".
guy & rOdd

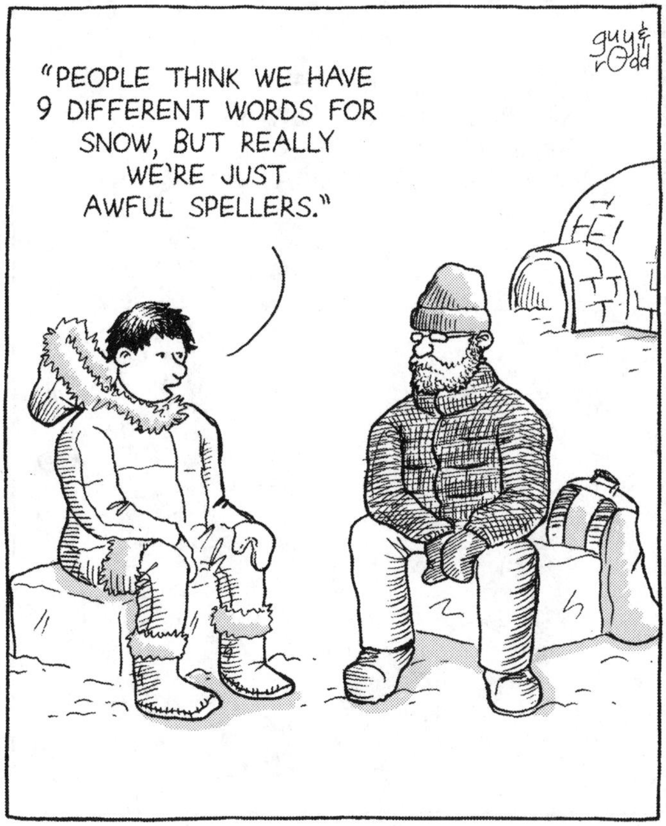
"PEOPLE THINK WE HAVE 9 DIFFERENT WORDS FOR SNOW, BUT REALLY WE'RE JUST AWFUL SPELLERS."
guy & rodd

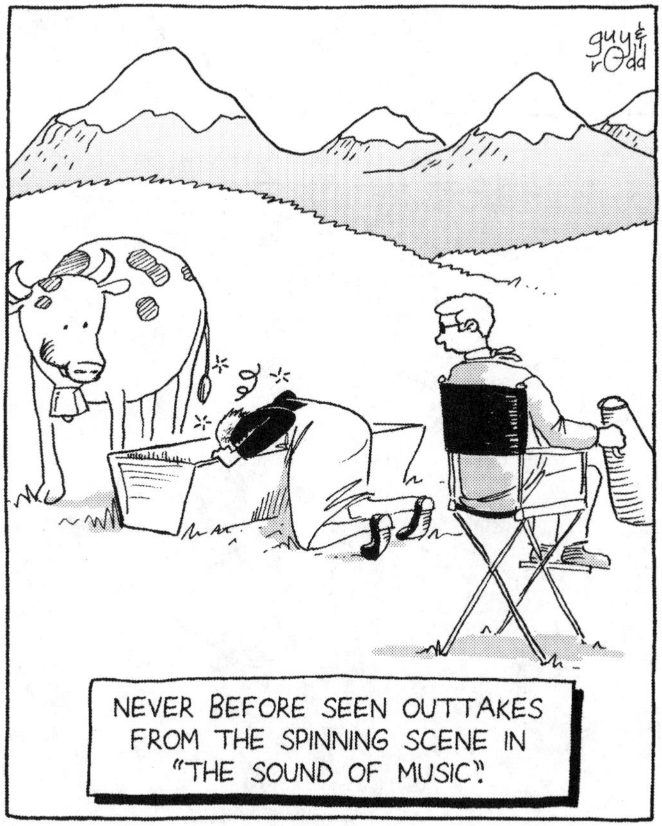
guy & rodd
NEVER BEFORE SEEN OUTTAKES FROM THE SPINNING SCENE IN "THE SOUND OF MUSIC."

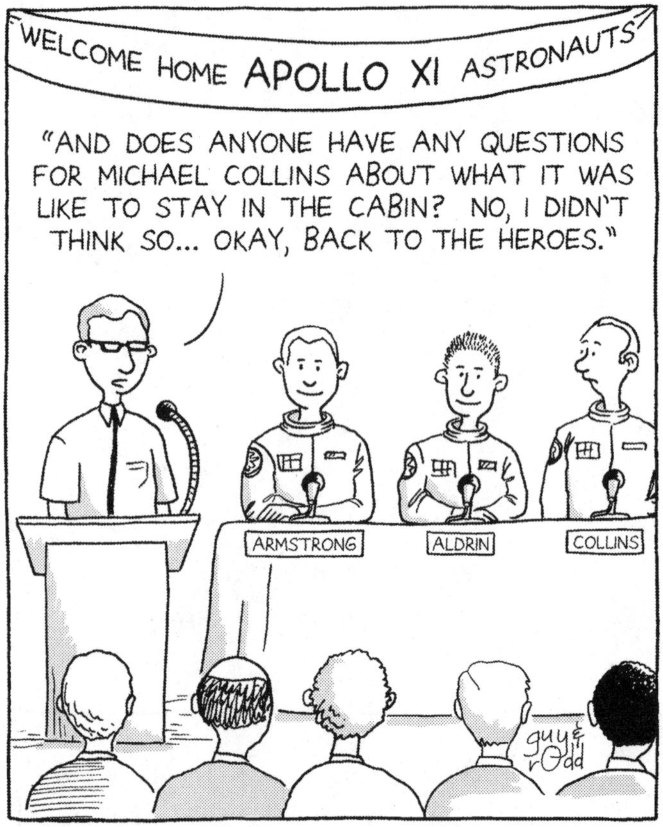
WELCOME HOME APOLLO XI ASTRONAUTS
"AND DOES ANYONE HAVE ANY QUESTIONS FOR MICHAEL COLLINS ABOUT WHAT IT WAS LIKE TO STAY IN THE CABIN? NO, I DIDN'T THINK SO... OKAY, BACK TO THE HEROES."
ARMSTRONG
ALDRIN
COLLINS
guy & rOdd

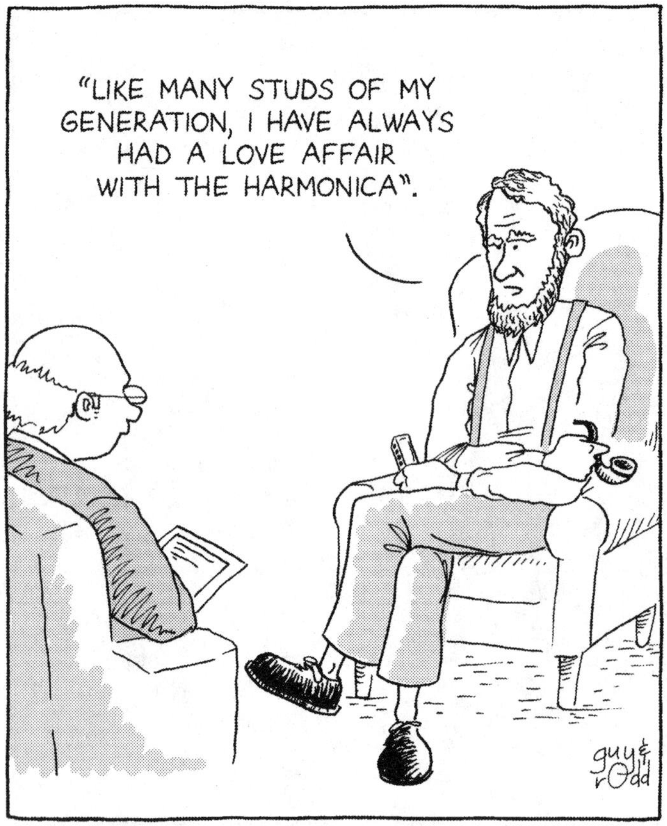
"LIKE MANY STUDS OF MY GENERATION, I HAVE ALWAYS HAD A LOVE AFFAIR WITH THE HARMONICA".
guy & rOdd

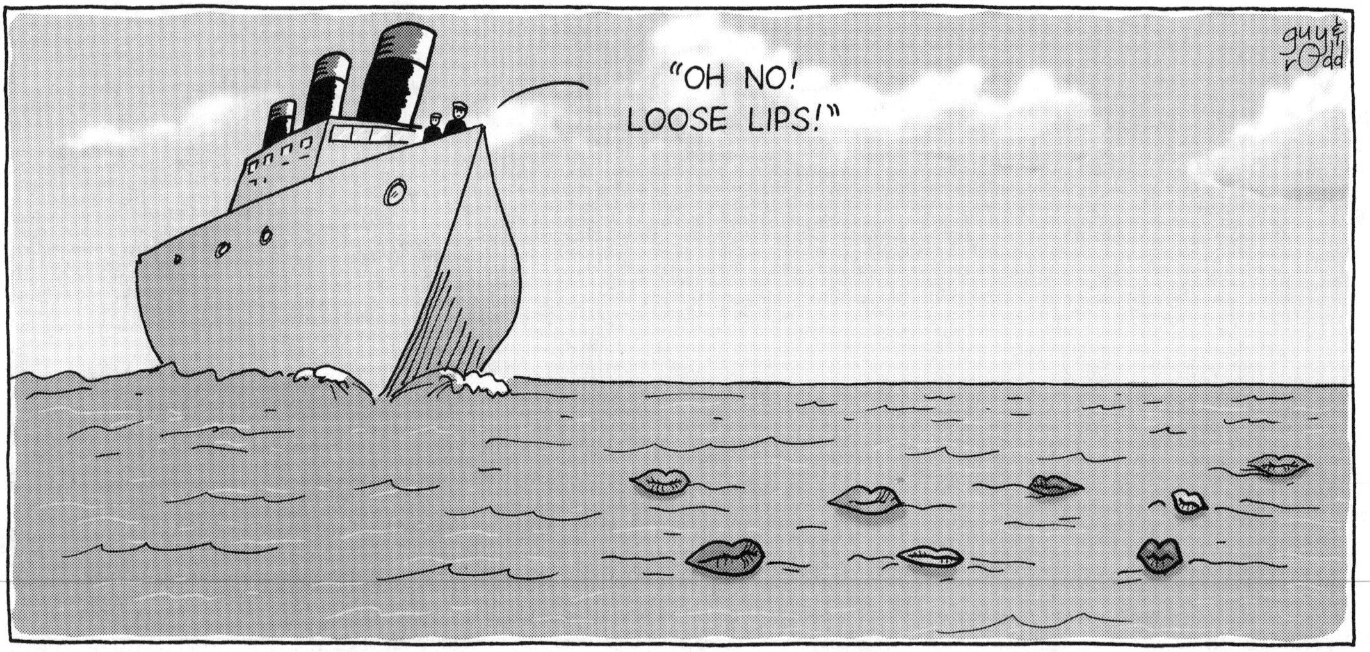
guy & rOdd
"OH NO! LOOSE LIPS!"

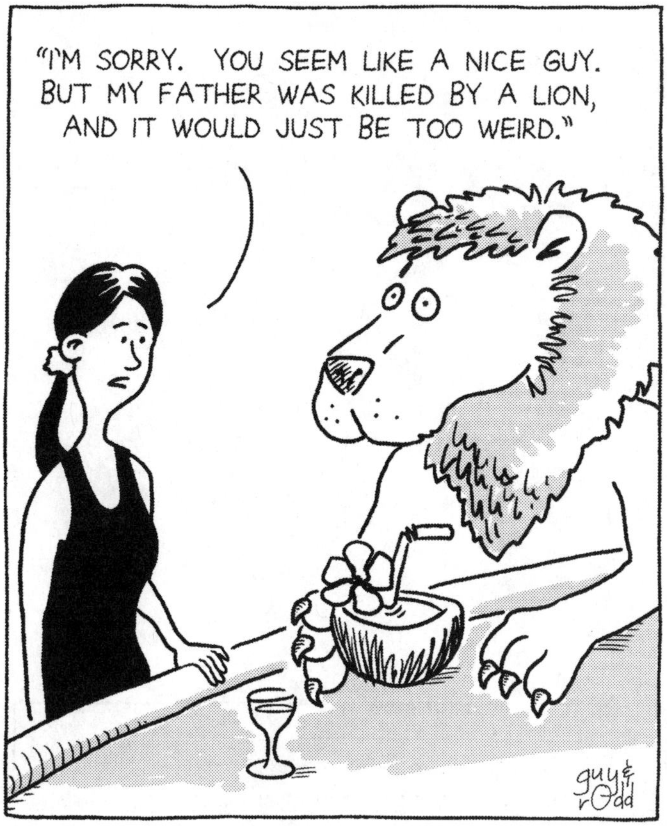
"I'M SORRY. YOU SEEM LIKE A NICE GUY. BUT MY FATHER WAS KILLED BY A LION, AND IT WOULD JUST BE TOO WEIRD."
guy & rOdd

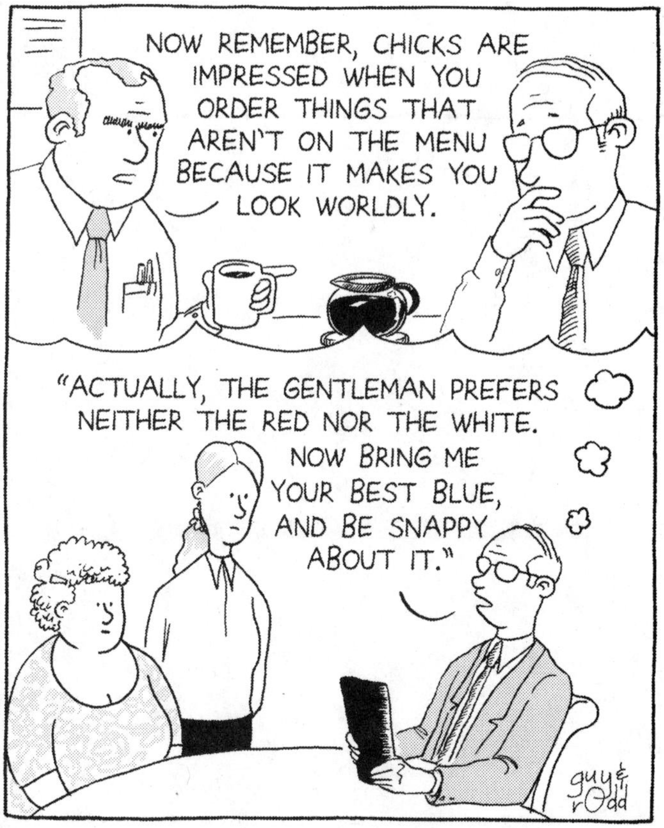
NOW REMEMBER, CHICKS ARE IMPRESSED WHEN YOU ORDER THINGS THAT AREN'T ON THE MENU BECAUSE IT MAKES YOU LOOK WORLDLY.
"ACTUALLY, THE GENTLEMAN PREFERS NEITHER THE RED NOR THE WHITE. NOW BRING ME YOUR BEST BLUE, AND BE SNAPPY ABOUT IT."
guy & rOdd

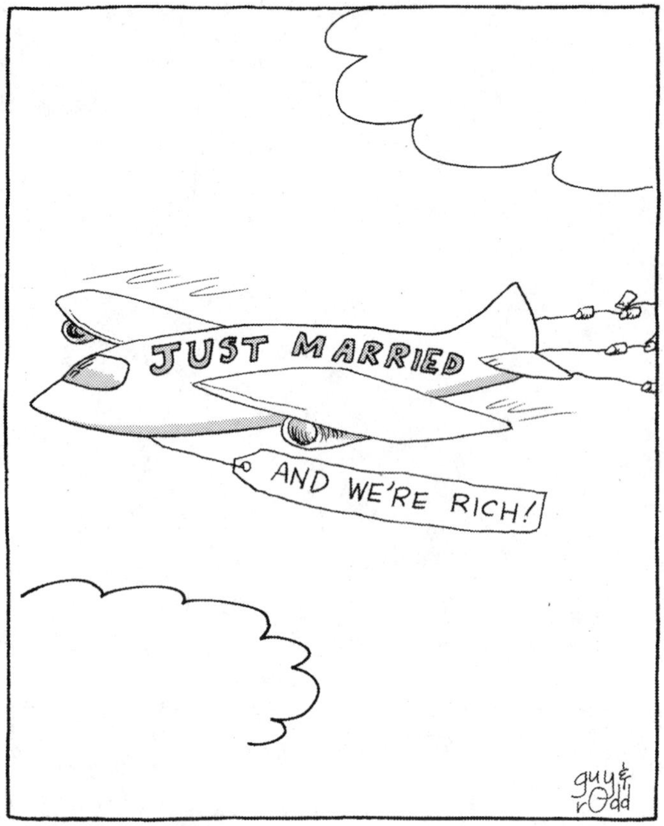
JUST MARRIED
AND WE'RE RICH!
guy & rOdd

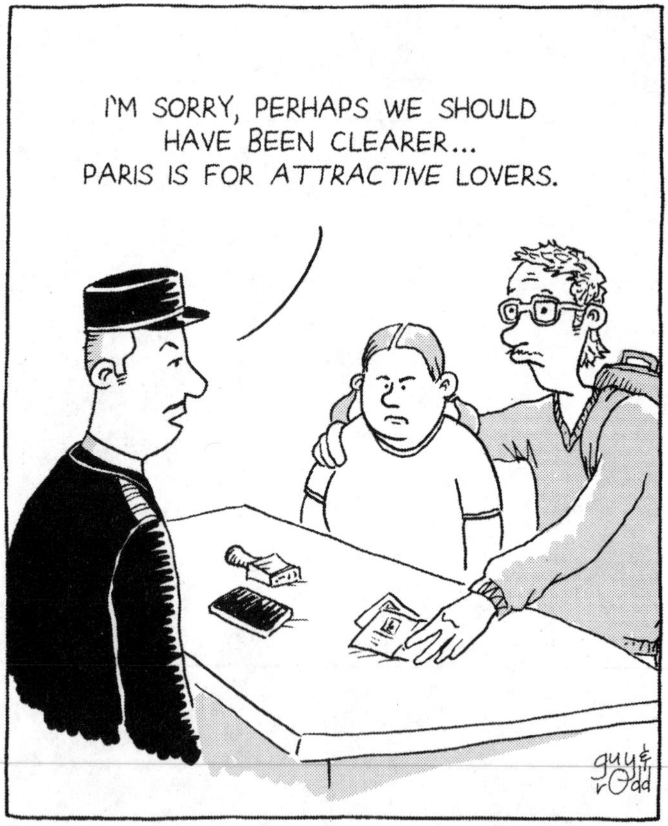
I'M SORRY, PERHAPS WE SHOULD
HAVE BEEN CLEARER...
PARIS IS FOR ATTRACTIVE LOVERS.
guy & rOdd